BASIC PSYCHOLOGICAL THERAPIES: COMPARATIVE EFFECTIVENESS

Psychotherapy Series

Family Therapy
G.H. Zuk, Ph.D.

Brief Therapies
H.H. Barten, M.D.

Children and Their Parents in Brief Therapy
H.H. Barten, M.D. and S. Barten, Ph.D.

Psychotherapy and the Role of the Environment
H.M. Voth, M.D. and M.H. Orth, M.S.W.

Psychodrama: Theory and Therapy
I.A. Greenberg, Ph.D.

The Art of Empathy
K. Bullmer, Ed.D.

Basic Psychological Therapies: Comparative Effectiveness
A.J. Fix, Ph.D. and E.A. Haffke, M.D.

Emotional Flooding (Vol. 1 in New Directions in Psychotherapy Series)
P.T. Olsen, Ph.D.

The Initial Interview in Psychotherapy (Translated by H. Freud Bernays)
H. Argelander, M.D.

The Self-In-Process, Vol. 1: Narcissistic Life Styles
M. Nelson

BASIC PSYCHOLOGICAL THERAPIES: COMPARATIVE EFFECTIVENESS

A. James Fix, Ph.D.
E. A. Haffke, M.D.

HUMAN SCIENCES PRESS
SUBSIDIARY OF BEHAVIORAL PUBLICATIONS INC.
72 FIFTH AVENUE, NEW YORK, N.Y. 10011

Library of Congress Catalog Number 74-19095

ISBN: 0-87705-237-9

Printed in the United States of America
6789   987654321

Library of Congress Cataloging in Publication Data

Fix, A. James.
    Basic psychological therapies.

    (Psychotherapy series)
    Bibliography: p.
    Includes index.
    1. Psychotherapy—Evaluation. I. Haffke,
E. A., joint author. II. Title. [DNLM: 1. Psychotherapy. WM420 F566b]
RC480.5.F53   616.8'914   74-19095
ISBN 0-87705-237-9

To:

Laurelee and Corinne,
the wives to whom the authors, as well as the book,
are dedicated.

Dr. Emmet Kenney,
bigger than life, who provided the stimulus, the
model, and the opportunity to develop those
qualities most worthy of emulation.

Mr. Charles Garetz,
who taught how therapy could be lived.

CONTENTS

7

PREFACE

The psychological therapies that settled out from the deluge of research in psychiatry and other mental health professions have long been fraught with assumptions, speculations, and broad generalizations. Now there seems to be a tacit plea from resident psychiatrists, intern clinical psychologists, nursing students, social work students, medical students, counselors in many areas, undergraduates, parents, and even the clergy, for a summary and analysis of the relevant research associated with the major psychological therapies.

This book responds to that plea. We have attempted to present a clear, concise summary of the objective evidence on the major psychological therapies for professionals, students, and interested laymen. After all, it is for these persons that this book was written.

The reader who wants practical guidelines for his own therapeutic endeavors may find them here. The student who seeks answers to such questions as these: "What evidence is there to support the claim that one therapeutic technique is more beneficial than another?" and "How much evidence is there to support that claim?" may find the answers here. The researcher who hunts for leads into neglected areas of inquiry may find them here; and the administrator and educator who search for ways to revitalize tired programs or to redesign ineffective ones may also find some surprising and possibly revolutionary suggestions in this book.

Through the entire preparation of this book, we have enjoyed the warm support and helpful assistance of both the administration and staff of the Nebraska Psychiatric Institute (NPI). We are especially grateful to Dr. Merrill Eaton, Director of NPI, who provided facilities and encouragement. Special credit goes to Dr. Frank J. Menolascino, who, in his usual energetic style, spent much time shaping thoughts into readable form; and we appreciate the work of Dr. Robert Ellingson, who helped to edit this and other endeavors of the authors.

A host of other persons also contributed to the finished work. We extend our sincere thanks to Mrs. Rosella Thrapp, who daily guarded the authors from the consequences of their mistakes in scheduling and their erratic work habits. We also gratefully acknowledge the work of Mrs. Bea Young and Mrs. Darlene Albright in providing a precise typescript. Finally, the senior author wishes to thank Donald and Patricia Quermback, Francis and Mary Ellen Bongiovonni, Dick and Carol Nelson, Bob and Constance Haase, and Norman and Joan Newhouse, for offering their moral support when he was most in need of it.

A. James Fix
E. A. Haffke
Omaha, Nebraska 1974

Chapter 1

INTRODUCTION[1]

All who drink this remedy recover in a short time, except those whom it does not help, who all die and have no relief from any other medicine. Therefore it is obvious that it fails only in incurable cases. [2]

Today, we have little difficulty in exposing the shaky basis of such a conclusion, but in Galen's day (the second century A.D.) the conclusion was unopposed. Today we recognize that logic such as Galen's is faulty. Galen assumed that the medicine was effective, and implied that without it, patients would not recover.

[1]This chapter was written with the editorial assistance of Joe P. Ercoloni, Department of Biocommunications, University of Nebraska College of Medicine.
[2]Galen. Quoted by H. J. Eysenck: The effects of psychotherapy. In H. J. Eysenck (Ed.), *Handbook of abnormal psychology.* New York: Basic Books, 1960, p. 697.

Broadly speaking, the psychological therapies suffer from the same ill-conceived logic. So-called "effective" psychological treatments litter the field of psychiatry, yet critical investigations show that these treatments are far from effective. Are we then to conclude that we are dealing with incurable cases? Not necessarily! But we do need to reassess those techniques and strategies that are used to alter the self-defeating and sometimes self-destructive behavior of psychiatric patients. That is exactly what we intend to do in this volume.

Though we will discuss some of the contemporary philosophical issues that surround the use of these techniques, our central focus will be to examine, evaluate, and unify the knowledge gained from research in the fields of psychotherapy, operant and classical conditioning therapies, and modeling techniques. Our approach will be: (1) to present research relevant to each technique, (2) to give a critical assessment of each technique, and (3) to unite the best elements of psychotherapy and behavior modification into a single effective therapeutic approach.

Every therapeutic approach is founded on certain assumptions or principles. It is on this framework of principles that we will build our analysis.

PRINCIPLES OF PSYCHOTHERAPY

All psychotherapeutic endeavors rest on two basic assumptions: first, that one human being can reduce the emotional sufferings of another human being by talking with him; and second, that a person must learn special techniques of verbal interviewing if he intends to be a good therapist. Accordingly, the therapist's level of effectiveness usually reflects how well he has mastered these techniques.

After reviewing the evidence on current attitudes to these principles, we find that the first has in fact gained some degree of support, while the second has met with mixed reactions. If we are to uphold its reputation as an underlying principle that guides the delivery of psychotherapeutic services, this second postulate will need some restructuring. How it should be restructured depends on the goals one wants to achieve. Our goal is to derive valid principles upon which to base therapeutic programs that will yield positive results under objective analysis.

The number of the available psychotherapeutic techniques seems to be limited only by human ingenuity: they are countless. Unfortunately, so are the theoretical justifications offered to support these techniques. For most of them, the evidence that supports their effectiveness is at best meager, and at worst nonexistent. Only a few have been adequately evaluated.

Principles of Behavior Modification

Currently, all techniques derived from learning theory that are used to modify the behavior of living organisms rest on two basic assumptions. They are, first, that social behavior is learned, and second, that behavior is regulated by its reinforcers. In other words, behavior that is rewarded or praised will be maintained or will increase in frequency, while behavior that is unrewarded or punished will decrease in frequency.

Here we will not only examine the various treatment methods based on behavior modification, we will also analyze the problems and shortcomings of each.

Principles of Modeling

The basic principles of modeling are two: first, that observation of another person's successful behavior raises the probability that the observer will imitate that behavior; and second, that when a therapist repeatedly demonstrates the desired patterns of behavior for his patient, and when he successfully guides his patient through imitations of those behaviors, he increases the probability that his patient will adopt those same patterns of conduct.

Research findings have shown modeling to be highly effective. Unfortunately (for many patients), modeling has been largely overlooked as an effective therapeutic tool. We can only guess why. Perhaps the oversight occurred because modeling therapies have long been thrown in under the general heading of behavior modification. To rectify this injustice, and to draw more attention to the modeling therapies, we will investigate them separately from other behavior modification techniques.

In the following chapters, we will present, examine, and expand upon the specific approaches listed above. In addition, we will critically evaluate the various psychological therapies in the light of the research evidence. Such evidence, we feel, is the sole criterion on which to base a clinical practice. Consequently, our efforts are directed toward examining the effectiveness, limits, and side effects of various therapeutic approaches.

UNITING PSYCHOTHERAPY AND BEHAVIOR MODIFICATION

The fields of psychotherapy and of behavior modification are believed by many to be opposing camps that have little in common. Psychotherapists tend to label behaviorists as cold, unfeeling scientists who misapply to human beings concepts that are more appropriate to the rat in the laboratory. On the other hand, behaviorists often view classical psychotherapists as soft-thinking but well-meaning individuals, who muddle along with their inefficient strategies in a hopeless search for the "unconscious," "self-esteem," "congruence," or whatever. This dichotomous view was dramatically illustrated in a letter we received from a candidate who was applying for a position as a psychologist at our facility. He stated that he was somewhat undecided whether to seek work in a clinic that specialized in behavior modification or in classical psychotherapy. He wanted to "do a great deal of behavior modification; but," he added regretfully, "I like to talk to people, too."

Talking to people and helping them to modify their own behavior are, we think, essentially the same activity. This theme is woven throughout this book. Admittedly, the idea is not original; Dollard and Miller tried to fuse learning theory and psychoanalysis in 1950, and in 1962, Krasner theorized that effective psychotherapy was essentially effective operant conditioning.[3]

If you browse through the psychotherapy and behaviorist journals, you will find that an increasing number of articles are pointing to the similarities in the two approaches. Some writers (including Rosenthal, 1967; Orne, 1962; and Efran and Marcia, 1967) contend that the same processes underlie all forms of psychotherapy and behavior modification. Lazarus, in his 1971 study, foresees a reconcilation between psychotherapists and behavioralists, and further calls for an end to the artificial dichotomy:

> The tendency to establish competing factions between insight and action therapy is like proclaiming that penicillin is better (or worse) than vitamins. Behavior therapy and insight oriented therapy often have different aims, goals and purposes. Increased awareness of personal understanding through self-exploration is a viable goal in and of itself. . . . Of course, most cases call for increased self-understanding and specific behavior change. [p. 349]

The treatment approach that we advocate includes these seemingly divergent therapies. We maintain that in combination, these approaches are both synergistic and

[3]All references are to be found in a reference list at the end of the book (p. 223).

efficacious. Taken individually, psychotherapy, behavior modification, and modeling do seem to be helpful to certain patients. But their success has been limited, and the distressing fact remains that current forms of psychiatric hospital treatment generally do not reduce the number of relapses, nor do they increase the probability of post-treatment employment. This has most recently been documented by Anthony *et al.* (1972). It is clear from Anthony's work that in the future, treatment professionals, regardless of their philosophical leanings, will undoubtedly be called upon to provide more evidence of effectiveness than they have provided thus far.

The techniques assessed in this volume do not involve medication or surgical intervention (although they can well be used in conjunction with these treatments). Thus, the term "psychological therapy" refers to any form of treatment the results of which are attributable to psychological rather than somatic intervention. (Regretfully, we leave unanswered the untapped but vitally important questions that surround the interactions between somatic and psychological treatments.)

Psychology is overflowing with journals and textbooks that present research data in the fields of psychotherapy and behavior modification. We have combined into one volume what we consider to be a relevant cross-section of this research.

The book is not intended to be a "how to" prescription. It is designed instead to illuminate "overlooked" areas of research that underlie the delivery of most approaches to psychological treatment. We trust that this information will serve you well in evaluating the various psychotherapeutic orientations.

Part I

PSYCHOTHERAPY

Chapter 2

THE EFFECTIVENESS OF PSYCHOTHERAPY

I remember being on the Committee on Therapeutics of the American Psychiatric Association in the early '50's when we were working on a protocol for a very major research project on the effects of frontal lobotomy vs. intensive psychoanalytically-oriented psychotherapy in schizophrenia. . . . Both treatments were claimed to produce permanent cures. [1]

DEFINITIONS

During the development of psychiatry, the term "psychotherapy" has had several definitions. When Freud origi-

[1] H. J. Lyman. Review of the history of psychopharmacological medication. Annual Meeting of the Section of Psychiatry of the American Medical Association, San Francisco. Recorded by *Audio Digest, Psychiatry,* 1972, *1* (3), August 7, 1972.

nated the talking therapy, our definition of psychotherapy would have been simply "psychoanalysis," or "the method of exploration of the human mind as developed by Sigmund Freud and practiced by him and his followers." But the term later came to require further specification, such as "traditional psychoanalytic psychotherapy," "Adlerian psychotherapy," or "client-centered psychotherapy," depending on the orientation of the practitioner. Eventually the field amassed so many theories and approaches (for example, that of Harper, 1959) that psychotherapy might have been best defined as "any regularly scheduled mode of talking between a patient or client and a licensed mental health practitioner." In this chapter we will use the definition supplied by the two tenets of psychotherapy presented in the introduction. Psychotherapy, then, is here used to refer to any procedure delivered by a licensed mental health professional that (1) relies on "talking" as the major component; and (2) is based on any technique directly taught or assimilated through training at a medical or other professional school. This definition holds only through this present chapter. In the following chapter, we will refine our definition to reflect the implications of the evaluative research on all forms of talking therapies.

Is Psychotherapy Effective?

The student of psychotherapy needs first to have an answer to the most basic and fundamental question of all: Is psychotherapy effective? More precisely stated, the question becomes: Does psychotherapy provide people with more benefits than they would receive without it? Before the 1950s there had been only a few attempts to answer this in scientific fashion. These appeared in rather scattered studies, and most of them never found their way into the mainstream of psychiatric or psychological literature. H. J.

Eysenck was the first investigator to pull these diverse efforts together, and to interpret the results on a broad scale for the entire professional community. In a now classic paper, Eysenck (1952) organized the findings of nineteen studies that had reported personality change in "neurotic" patients over time, under various forms of treatment. He found that the following percentages of patients showed improvement:

Of all patients who received psychoanalysis, 44 per cent improved.

Of patients treated by psychoanalysis (discounting those who stopped treatment before their therapists felt they should), 66 per cent improved.

Of patients treated "eclectically" (that is, by methods other than psychoanalysis), 64 per cent improved.

Of "patients treated only custodially or by general practitioners," 72 per cent improved.

Until Eysenck added the "control group," that is, those neurotic patients who received only custodial or nonpsychiatric treatment, the practitioner could rest easy, content in the impression that he was helping two-thirds of his patients. What a rude shock, however, to discover that over two-thirds of similar patients showed improvement without the "benefits" of psychotherapy! Eysenck (1952) puts it thus:

> In general, certain conclusions are possible from these data. They fail to prove that psychotherapy, Freudian or otherwise, facilitates the recovery of neurotic patients. They show that roughly two thirds of a group of neurotic patients will recover or improve to a marked extent within about two years of the onset of their illness, whether they are treated by means of psychotherapy or not. This figure appears to be remarkably stable from one investigation to another, regardless of type of patient treated, standard of recovery employed, or method of therapy used. From the point of view of the psychotherapist, they can hardly be called very favorable to his claims. [p. 322]

As could be predicted, Eysenck has come in for unprecedented attack and criticism in the professional journals and from the lecture rostrums of the training institutions.

> Sanford (1953) immediately concluded: ' . . . the only sensible course with respect to such a challenge is to ignore it.' For many practitioners, the whole notion of questioning the efficiency of the therapeutic process 'seemed . . . blasphemous, as if we were attempting a statistical test of the efficacy of prayer . . .' (Tenber and Powers, 1953). Others were more critically systematic in their emotion-laden observations, calling attention to the many uncontrolled variables in Eysenck's actuarial study and concluding in effect that there were no data on the basis of which to evaluate the therapeutic effects of psychotherapy (De Charms, Levy, and Wertheimer, 1954; Luborsky, 1954; Rosenzweig, 1954). [Berenson & Carkhuff, 1967, p. 32]

Let us focus carefully on the conclusion that Eysenck drew from his data, and clearly distinguish this from a similar conclusion that Eysenck did not feel was justified by the evidence at hand. Eysenck did not conclude that psychotherapy was ineffective; he did conclude that there was at that time no evidence that psychotherapy was effective. Before we are accused of hairsplitting, let us note why we feel, as Eysenck did, that this is a crucial distinction. In the light of Eysenck's conclusion, the issue of psychotherapeutic efficacy is still an open one, to be resolved by better experimental evidence. If we who practice psychotherapy and who are most responsible for its promotion to the public as legitimate medical practice still maintain that it does provide beneficial results, it is then up to us to prove that these benefits occur. We must not drown out objections to psychotherapeutic practice by clever arguments or logical discourse. The first shot has been fired; it was a statistical shot, stemming from a far-from-perfect experimental design. If therapists wish to persist in promoting and disseminating their "curative techniques," it seems to us that they should provide empirical evidence to support their claims of efficacy for these techniques. Such evidence is needed to justify our transactions with those who come to us for help. Eysenck's challenging study and conclusions deserve to be answered by solid, objective evidence that psychotherapy does in fact provide the patient with some form of relief from the symptoms of emotional disorder, and that this relief would not have been gained without psychotherapy. This is not an unusual or unfair request. This very stipulation is made for all forms of chemotherapy or other medical intervention in any physical or emotional disorder. In fact, it is the presence of supportive empirical evidence behind the therapeutic claims in any field that distinguishes the legitimate practitioner from the charlatan.

The possibility that Eysenck's data may be biased does not alter in the least the need for scientific evidence to show the value of psychotherapy. When we are presented with flawed data, there are only two actions that we can take to rectify the conclusions that flow from these data. The least convincing of the two is to take the same data, show the bias involved, and reanalyze the data under specified, unbiased rules. This method allows us to determine whether the data at hand actually permit a different deduction from the one originally presented. Only Bergin (1971) has done this in a systematic fashion. He has shown that Eysenck's data, originally categorized at certain points on the basis of "subjective biases," can be realigned according to "subjective biases" that differ from those of Eysenck. Bergin attempted this and produced data that tend to indicate that psychotherapy has "some therapeutic effect," although this is "not dramatic." Eysenck's data, therefore, could be interpreted in more than one way—clearly not good scientific methodology.

The second method of dealing with possibly flawed data is to conduct a *better* study that will yield less distorted evidence on the efficacy of psychotherapy. The basic point that we will develop in the following paragraphs is that, in the more than 20 years since Eysenck's initial challenge, no one has reported a better study that opposed Eysenck's conclusion! This is not to state that better studies have not been conducted. As we will show, many studies have been made over the last two decades that have been substantially superior in scientific design to Eysenck's inaugural contribution. Also, we are not stating that all researchers agree with our evaluation of the evidence. With only one exception, however (Meltzoff and Kornreich, 1970), the most recent reviewers of the literature (for example, Bergin, 1971; Carkhuff and Berenson, 1967; Luborsky, 1971; Truax and Carkhuff, 1967; Truax and Mitchell, 1971; and Levitt, 1971) agree that no convincing evidence has been produced to cause us to abandon Eysenck's original position on the overall average effects of psychotherapy.

A study similar to Eysenck's was conducted by Levitt in 1957. Where Eysenck had been concerned with the effects of psychotherapy on adults, Levitt focused his interests on the effects on children. He was able to find in the literature 18 studies of the outcome of psychotherapy with children. None of these, however, utilized control groups for comparison, in order to reach a reasonable conclusion as to whether it was, in fact, more beneficial to receive therapy than to receive no therapy. Levitt found that of the total 3,399 cases covered (all classified as neurotic), 67.05 per cent were rated as having shown some improvement at close of treatment. Since no directly comparable control data were included in these studies, Levitt used the results of two research projects that contained information on waiting-list children. (These were children who had been placed on child guidance clinic waiting lists, but whose parents had broken the clinic relationship before treatment was obtained.) The authors of the two investigations that examined this group judged the amount of change in these "control" subjects. They reported that 72.5 per cent of these untreated children could be listed as improved.

Of the children who had received treatment, 78 per cent were estimated as improved, in follow-up studies that ranged in time from 6 months to 27 years after treatment. More children were improved when evaluated some time after treatment than when they were assessed immediately after therapy; this suggested to Levitt that time is a factor in improvement, regardless of whether psychotherapy has been administered or not. To substantiate this conclusion further, Levitt arranged the studies on the basis of follow-up interval. He found a nearly perfect relationship between the follow-up interval and the percentage of improvement; that is, the shortest intervals between treatment and follow-up study yielded the lowest improvement rates. "The results," he concluded, "do not support the hypothesis that recovery from neurotic disorder is facilitated by psychotherapy" (Levitt, 1957, p. 195). More recently, he noted: "After 60 years, the intervention hypothesis is not yet conclusively demonstrated. Evaluation research fails to show unequivocally that child psychotherapy is effective" (Levitt, 1971, p. 474).

The data in Levitt's 1971 study encompass 9,359 child cases and yield the following conclusions: two-thirds of neurotic and psychotic patients show improvement at the close of treatment, while 55 per cent of "acting-out" children can be so classified, and 80 per cent of all these patients are found to be improved in follow-up evaluations conducted some months later.

It is interesting, then, to note that Eysenck's work has been replicated, this time with children, and that we are still looking for clear proof that therapists, on average, help to reduce the symptoms of emotional illness. We need not belabor the point much further. The reader who is interested in becoming more familiar with the studies along this line will find them listed in the references. Just one final review article needs to be mentioned in relation to the general question of whether psychotherapy is effective.

Luborsky, et al. (1971) considered 166 studies of the outcome of adult psychotherapy. The approach taken by this team of researchers was somewhat more sophisticated than those of previous reviews. Not merely searching for average improvement statistics, the investigators arranged the reviewed studies in a manner designed to reveal information about the factors or variables that were most associated with a patient's improvement following therapy. They found three major sets of variables in patients, therapists, and mechanisms. In other words, Luborsky and his coworkers were able to specify those characteristics of the patient, his therapist, and the mechanics of therapy that affect the patient's chances for improvement. In the following paragraphs we will summarize these variables.

Patient Variables

The characteristics of the patient that the Luborsky team found predicted improvement best were the following, with no attempt made to assess the relative importance of the variables:

1. the patient's initial level of psychological health
2. the adequacy of the patient's personality functioning
3. absence of schizoid trends in the patient
4. his motivation for change
5. his level of intelligence
6. his level of anxiety (The higher the anxiety level, the better the chances for improvement, possibly because the uncomfortable presence of anxiety increases motivation for help.)
7. his educational and social assets.

Before we advance to the second and third sets of variables that affect the outcome of treatment, let us analyze the patient variables and interpret their meaning for the practicing therapist. In essence, this set of variables tells us that if we have a patient who is not particularly disturbed to begin with, is intelligent, articulate, highly motivated to change, and has a number of social contacts and sources of emotional support to fall back upon, the treatment will have a high probability of ending in "success." That is, the patient will improve. We cannot necessarily conclude, however, that the treatment is responsible for the improvement. A more reasonable assumption would be that a patient who possesses these advantages is precisely the one who would recover anyway. Such a patient is also probably the one least in need of positive intervention, not only from a psychodynamic point of view, but also in terms of statistical probabilities. It is a fairly well documented fact that emotional illness is both most serious and most prevalent in the lower intellectual and socioeconomic groups of our society (Hollingshead and Redlick, 1958; Srole *et al.*, 1962). Yet Luborsky's findings suggest that our treatments produce improvement only in those members of our society who are least uncomfortable, and who also possess higher intelligence and supportive assets.

Treatment Variables

Here it was found that only the *number of* sessions were related to patient improvement. No particular technique or type of treatment was found to be superior to any other in this respect. This is of such significance that we will look more carefully at the supporting evidence and the implications of this conclusion later in this chapter.

The reader should note that to find that the number of therapy sessions is related to patient improvement does not necessarily demonstrate that the sessions themselves are responsible for the change. Since an increased number of sessions invariably requires an increase also in the passage of time, this may simply be another verification of Levitt's contention that time itself is the curative agent.

In brief, the research of Luborsky *et al.* (1971) strongly suggests that if we treat a patient who is not very sick, and if we treat him for a long time, he will get better. Parenthetically, while we view these conclusions as bearing ill for the more grand pronouncements on the utility of psychotherapy, the same general conclusions might apply to many other areas of medicine as well. For almost any disorder, the practitioner's potential for effecting cures or inducing improvement is greater when the disorder is less serious, when the patient brings more positive factors with him for cooperating in the treatment program, and often, when the physician can maintain longer contact with the patient.

Therapist Variables

In this final category, the Luborsky team found that the following characteristics of the therapist helped the prognostications for his patient's improvement:

1. his number of years of experience as a therapist
2. the similarity of the therapist to his patient
3. his ability to communicate empathy
4. certain attitude and interest patterns.

Here we finally get our first inkling that contact with a therapist *might* have some beneficial effects—if he is the right type of therapist. If he has a number of years of experience, if he can communicate empathic concern, and if he has certain personality characteristics, he may be helpful to his patient. Again, this is an important point, which we intend to cover later in depth.

The preceding studies are the best examples of what we term the first line of research on psychotherapy. This genre of study sought simply to determine whether persons treated by psychotherapy improved more than equally disturbed but untreated individuals. The answer is this: there is still no evidence that psychotherapy, as normally practiced, is on average effective in relieving emotional disorders.

TECHNIQUES DON'T COUNT

What we term the second line of research on psychotherapy sought to determine which psychotherapeutic *technique* was most effective. This was a natural question, since several approaches to psychotherapy had been proposed: those of Freud, Adler, Jung, Rogers, and others. The most important goal, particularly for a novice who was attempting to choose among the various approaches, was to find out which of these therapies was most beneficial to the patients receiving it. Seeman (1949) undertook the first crude attempts to make such an assessment. He interviewed clients who had received vocational counseling from directive and nondirective counselors. In evaluating the reactions of the clients, he found that the two techniques did not produce identifiable differences. Differences in reactions were found, however, between clients who received similar counseling, but from different counselors. The only tenable conclusion from these unexpected results was that the differences in client reaction must be due to something other than therapeutic method. This "something else" might be some unspecified aspect of the therapist himself, rather than of his technique.

Fiedler (1950a, 1950b, 1951) recorded on audiotapes the treatment sessions of therapists who represented the Freudian, Adlerian and Rogerian orientations. The taped sessions were then rated by other therapists in terms of how closely they approached the "ideal" therapeutic relationship. Fiedler discovered that nationally prominent therapists, regardless of their orientations, were consistently seen to approach such an ideal more closely than nonexpert therapists. There was more similarity between the experts of different orientations than between experts and nonexperts within the *same* theoretical framework. Again it was the therapist, not the technique, that made the therapy "work."

If our techniques (that is, our methods of engaging in psychotherapy) were responsible for the development of a good therapeutic relationship, Fiedler's results would have shown marked differences between the ratings of the various approaches. All that was really found, however, was that therapists recognized as outstanding in their fields were better able than less experienced therapists to establish a positive therapeutic relationship. It was assumed (and future inquiries lent support to this assumption) that the development of an "adequate" or "ideal" relationship would yield positive therapeutic results.

On the basis of these early studies alone, we get a hint of a premise that has received impressive subsequent confirmation: positive results in psychotherapy are not demonstrably due to the techniques applied, nor to the theory used, but to something inherent in the relationship between the therapist and the patient. A further point that we expect to verify in this and the coming chapters is one first suggested by Fiedler in 1950: "The therapeutic relationship . . . is but a variation of good interpersonal relationships in general" (1950a, p. 245).

WHAT REALLY HELPS PATIENTS?

The third line of research in psychotherapy has been much less concerned with evaluating the overall general effectiveness of psychotherapy. Most recent studies have

aimed at dissecting the therapeutic process in an attempt
to uncover what it is that actually helps persons, whether
or not they receive formal treatment. The impetus toward
a more careful assessment of the functioning of treated and
control subjects came largely by accident. Since the effectiveness of psychotherapy had not been demonstrated in
initial tests, most researchers during the 1950s moved to
other areas. Similarly, most clinicians preferred to ignore
the previously noted research evidence, and entrenched
themselves in the faith that psychotherapy was an esoteric
and deeply internal experience, which could never be
quantified or affected by research in any way at all.

This stalemate was serendipitously altered by the statistical data of a study by Barron and Leary (1955). Essentially, this study was yet another research report that
reached the same dreary conclusion: the outcome of psychotherapy (this time as measured by Minnesota Multi-
phasic Personality Inventory [MMPI] scores) was no better
than the average improvement shown by neurotics without
treatment. Cartwright (1956), while studying Barron and
Leary's statistics, noted that although the scores of both the
treated and untreated groups showed, on average, about
the same amount of change over the course of the study,
the results for the treated group showed a much wider
range of variation; that is to say, the treated group showed
more extreme changes in both directions—greater positive
and negative changes. This led Cartwright and Vogel
(1960) on a course of study unique in the field at that time;
they suggested that therapy does have "some impact not
found in its absence" (p. 121), and that the nature and
direction of this impact could be assessed by more precise
observation. By giving psychological tests at specified intervals, and using the subjects as their own controls (by
incorporating a period of "no treatment"), these researchers verified that patients showed a greater amount of
change (not necessarily improvement!) during a period of

therapy than during an equal period without treatment. The quality of the change, however, was related to at least one variable: the experience of the therapist. Patients who received treatment from experienced therapists tended to show improvement. Those who were exposed to inexperienced therapists fared much less well: so much less well, in fact, that Cartwright and Vogel concluded that inexperienced therapists "may actually be effective in decreasing the health [of the patient]" (p. 127).

An extremely simplified representation of what we are discussing here may help to illustrate the concept of variability of outcome more clearly. Figure 1 illustrates that when the percentage of improvement, the total change scores, or any other *average* measure of outcome is used, no differences will be found between the treated and untreated groups. When the variability of change is taken into account, however, it becomes clear that psychotherapy is doing something. It is promoting change. In those cases that show improvement, their improvement is often much greater than it is without psychotherapy. But, in contrast to the predictions of most of our theories, the change due to psychotherapy is also often negative. When deterioration takes place, it is often more serious under psychotherapy than when treatment is not given.

It appears that these results are due to certain characteristics of the therapist. The positive effects of some therapists are cancelled out by the negative effects of others. If the psychotherapeutic professionals are to take credit for the improvements they promote, they must also stand accountable for the destructive influences they bring to bear. Particularly embarrassing for us as mental health practitioners is the implication that many of us are in fact breaking one of the first rules for physicians, *primum non nocere* (first of all, do no damage). As Truax and Mitchell (1971) bluntly stated, "The implications for the practitioner are relatively straightforward. . . . Two out of three of his col-

FIGURE I

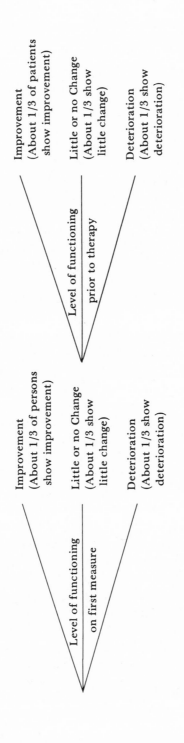

NO TREATMENT
(Control)

TREATMENT

Improvement
(About 1/3 of persons
show improvement)

Little or no Change
(About 1/3 show
little change)

Deterioration
(About 1/3 show
deterioration)

Level of functioning
on first measure

Improvement
(About 1/3 of patients
show improvement)

Little or no Change
(About 1/3 show
little change)

Deterioration
(About 1/3 show
deterioration)

Level of functioning
prior to therapy

Level of functioning
after passage of time

Level of functioning
following therapy

leagues, he can be quite certain, are ineffective or harmful" (p. 340).

Almost as a resounding confirmation of this, Lieberman, Yalom, and Miles (1973) found just how destructive psychological therapy can be when they examined the "casualty rate" of encounter groups. Counting as casualties only those participants who completed the course of encounter sessions, and showed "serious psychological harm six to eight months after the group ended and ... the difficulties could reasonably be attributed to the group experience," the researchers found that there was a casualty rate of nine per cent. This in itself constitutes an alarming negative side effect of encounter groups. It suggests that one person will be rather seriously hurt for nearly every group of individuals who engage in encounter sessions. An even more shocking finding than this, however, is that the group leaders were often quite unaware of the damage that was inflicted in their groups! It seems impossible to avoid the conclusion that this study, with the others we have presented in this chapter, suggests that even therapists with high credentials are not always beneficial to their patients, and may sometimes be harmful.

In a research area in which the phenomena under observation are so difficult to measure, it is truly remarkable when many forms of investigation yield results so similar that they almost become redundant. Yet this is exactly what has happened with research into the outcome of psychotherapy. The previously noted study by Lieberman, Yalom, and Miles (1973) on the effects upon people of their experiences in various types of encounter groups is a well-constructed work, capable of yielding the first objective, broad, and definitive statements on the benefits and dangers attendant upon participation in encounter groups. The results, however, should be quite unsurprising to anyone who has closely followed the research into the outcome of psychotherapy over the years. What the work by Lieberman and his colleagues provides is probably the most concise summary and replication available anywhere of the last 20 years of research into the results of psychotherapy. This one study captures in nucleus form the findings that have been painfully elicited from controlled observations over the years.

The authors of this study assigned more than 200 student volunteers from Stanford University to 17 encounter groups. Using the participants' self-evaluations, assessments by their therapists, and the judgments of friends and relatives of the participants, Lieberman and his colleagues were able to make statements of the effects of these groups from several standpoints. The groups represented virtually every major theoretical orientation currently alive in the psychiatric and psychological fields. They were all conducted by highly competent, and in some cases "expert," professionals. The group techniques included psychoanalysis, psychodrama, Rogerian marathon, Gestalt, National Training Laboratories T-groups and encounter groups, Esalen eclectic, Synanon, transactional analysis, eclectic marathon, two leaderless tape-instructional encounter groups, and no group participation at all.

This study can stand as a summary of the findings we have presented to this point. In brief, these researchers made the following findings:

1. The method, technique, or type of group had no bearing upon outcome.

2. Eighty per cent of the subjects showed some specific positive changes, regardless of whether or not they had participated in any group. Group participants showed no more positive changes than did those chosen for nonparticipation. In terms of broad, general change, about a third showed "positive change" (what other studies have traditionally termed improvement), one-third showed no change, and one-third showed "negative changes."

3.   Regardless of the type of therapy that the leaders espoused, or the theoretical school with which they aligned themselves, the specific behavior of the group leader did not differ according to these theoretical lines. There were large differences in the behavior of leaders within the same theoretical school, and striking similarities in the performances of leaders of different orientations.

4.   Technical competence, as rated by the researchers, bore no relation to participant benefit.

5.   The personality of the group leader, rather than his technique, had the most influence on the change elicited in the group members. The most successful leaders were "caring," and gave explanations of the group processes and the experiences that were provided through the group.

Effective versus Ineffective Therapists

"I've found a lot of aides who've really aided me."
"Q.. By being companions?"
"A.. By being people. By understanding."[2]

It appears that it is not the therapy but the therapist who helps patients. Looking back over the studies presented here, we find only the most vague clues on what distinguishes the beneficial therapist from his less potent colleague. Luborsky (1971) mentioned the therapist's "ability to communicate empathy" as one discriminating feature of the effective therapist. Similarly, Lieberman, Yalom, and Miles (1973) described the best therapists as "caring." Yet these terms are too vague to help us to

[2]Schizophrenic patient, quoted by B. M. Braginsky and Dorothea Braginsky. Mental hospitals as resorts. *Psychology Today,* 1973, *6* (March): 100.

differentiate the most beneficial therapists from their less effective peers. Experience tends to aid this differentiation, which suggests that whatever skills the more advanced therapists possess, they have apparently learned or developed over time. This implies in turn that these skills can be taught—possibly in much the same way in which psychotherapy techniques have traditionally been taught.

Further information on the characteristics that differentiate the more from the less beneficial therapists can be found in some earlier work, apparently quite unassociated with the research we have been discussing. In 1954 Whitehorn and Betz had compared successful therapists with therapists who did not produce a high rate of improvement in their schizophrenic patients. Since quantification of interpersonal processes has always been difficult, this and many subsequent studies reported their results in an impressionistic fashion, but they did provide leads for later verification and refinement. The authors found that the successful therapists were best characterized by the "warmth" they showed toward the patient. Less successful therapists related in a rather impersonal manner. Successful therapists were alert to the present feelings and actions of the patient, and responded to each patient in an individual manner. Less successful therapists did not seem to follow the patients' present experiences so well; their "understanding" was more external. These therapists also focused more on the pathology, or "sick" aspects, of their patients.

Another series of studies by Truax and his colleagues clarified the picture further. When summarizing their work, Truax and Carkhuff (1964) portrayed the effective and ineffective therapists in this manner:

> Patients whose therapists offered a high level of unconditional positive warmth, self-congruence or genuineness, and accurate empathic understanding, showed significant posi-

tive personality and behavioral change on a wide variety of indices, and . . . patients whose therapists offered relatively low levels of these conditions during therapy exhibited significant deterioration in personality and behavioral functioning. [pp. 130–131]

The choice of words to describe the therapist were clearly derived from the system of client-centered therapy developed by Carl Rogers (1951); yet the authors in no way suggest that the Rogerian system is thus the prime approach to be used in psychotherapy. The authors' conclusion that we have quoted here has served as a stimulus for a substantial amount of research up to the present. In the research that stemmed from these findings, both Truax and Carkhuff have produced major advances in our ability to describe and differentiate the more and the less effective therapist. The first task of these researchers was to better quantify or operationalize those qualities or activities that characterize beneficial and nonbeneficial therapists. By doing this, the imprecise meanings that mere words such as "effective" and "ineffective" carry could be redefined with more precision, and in a manner that would yield a higher degree of agreement among observers. The second task was closely aligned with this. The data at hand literally screamed for a predictive measuring instrument. What was clearly needed was a scale or other tool by which the probable level of effectiveness of any given individual who wanted to engage in the practice of psychotherapy could be quickly assessed.

As we will show, both of these goals have recently been met, at least to a modest degree. The tools developed to meet them do require substantial further verification, and will need a great deal of refinement; in particular, the measures must be made more objective. At this time, we view the work of Charles B. Truax, Robert R. Carkhuff, and their associates as of dynamic importance in pointing the way to the effective delivery of psychotherapy and the training of therapists, or "helpers," for years to come.

In their 1967 volumes, Truax and Carkhuff reported that they had measured and validated the therapist qualities of accurate empathy, genuineness, and nonpossessive warmth. Carkhuff (1967, 1969) later changed and refined this scale, developing a measure capable of quantifying a wider range of those "facilitative factors" that were, in his survey of the contemporary research literature, consistently found to be most related to patient change. In several subsequent studies, the Carkhuff scale has shown the ability not only to identify therapists who are currently producing various levels of patient change (Carkhuff, 1967b), but also to predict therapist performance during treatment sessions. The importance of this work cannot be emphasized enough: these studies are the first within the mental health field to show clearly the relationship between what a therapist does and the resultant change in his patient!

In the next chapter, we will examine Carkhuff's system at length, in order to draw guidelines for the practice of effective psychotherapy. At this point, however, we would stress the major significance of the development of a scale to rate and predict the therapist's effectiveness. This can be better appreciated if we compare the utility of such a scale with an analogous psychological product that has achieved widely recognized usefulness, the intelligence scale. Before Binet constructed his first device for the measurement of intelligence, one might have questioned the need for such an instrument. After all, everyone had a pretty good concept of intelligence; people recognized that some persons were brighter or duller than others, that there were intellectual giants and pygmies. The value of an intelligence test, it was found, lay in the predictions that could be made from the scores. As summarized by Herrnstein (1971) the predictions we can make from an estimate of intelligence are truly amazing; they range from probable school success at any grade level to ultimate income level, socioeconomic standing, and even life expectancy. Of course, it has often been pointed out that I.Q. scores have been widely misused and that the entire concept of intelligence tends to be generally misunderstood (for example, see McClelland, 1973). The tests, it has been repeatedly charged (for example, by Garcia, 1972, and Mercer, 1972), are prone to cultural bias. These comments are entirely valid; nevertheless, the intelligence scale, which requires only an insignificant portion of one's life, remains probably the most useful and important assessment tool developed through psychological research.

Just as people have always been able to make gross estimates of intellectual ability, most of us recognize in an intuitive and imprecise manner that certain therapists gain more productive relationships with their patients than do others. A concise, objective measure of this ability could lead to accurate predictions of probable therapeutic outcome, and such a measure could also bring about great changes in the procedures for selecting potential therapists. In addition, it could be useful in assessing the areas of weakness shown by any practitioner, so that specific corrective efforts could be prescribed.

SUMMARY

Research on the outcome of psychotherapy has failed to show that any given technique or system is superior to any other technique or system. On average, psychotherapy has not been shown to produce benefits above the improvements found when no therapy is given. Psychotherapy, therefore, has not been shown to "cure" or "heal." Recent research, however, has indicated that certain therapists do help patients, while others may produce a negative effect;

the patients are worse off than if they had never been treated by these practitioners at all. Two researchers in particular, Charles Truax and Robert Carkhuff, have developed scales capable of differentiating the more from the less effective therapists. The following chapter will present the therapeutic skills that these researchers have isolated in their scales. Since the Truax (1971) and Carkhuff (1967) scales tap virtually the same factors, the Carkhuff scale will receive the bulk of our attention. This is mainly due to the added clinical information that this scale is capable of yielding.

Chapter 3

COMPONENTS OF EFFECTIVE PSYCHOTHERAPY

*Normally, I'm a fairly even-tempered guy . . . but I be-
come frustrated and even irascible at times when I see out-
moded theories . . . perpetuated and . . . new findings go un-
recognized.* [1]

FACTORS IN FACILITATIVE COMMUNICATION

After examining the flow of research on the processes
and outcome of psychotherapy procedures, it becomes
clear that currently there is no "one way" to administer
psychotherapy. Also, there is only slender evidence upon
which to choose among the numerous theories and techniques advocated by various writers. Since very few of these
practices have been empirically evaluated, we prefer to
maintain the definition of psychotherapy that we presented

[1]George Edward Schauf. Quoted by Bruce Jackson. Lose weight without counting calories. *Science Digest,* 1972, *72* (July): 68

in the Introduction—*"a facilitative communication relationship"*—and to present psychotherapeutic procedures and our critical analysis from this standpoint. Our definition of psychotherapy derives from the research that we examined in Chapter 2. In brief, this research has never shown any technique of psychotherapy to be in itself more "therapeutic" than any other technique, nor more therapeutic even, indeed, than control conditions in which the patients do not receive psychotherapy. It has shown, however, that while therapy techniques in themselves may not be effective, some therapists are effective. Apparently it is the way in which a therapist *communicates* with his patients that determines his effectiveness.

As we noted in Chapter 2, Truax and Carkhuff have labelled and defined some factors that distinguish the most effective therapists from those who are least effective. Carkhuff (1967) has refined some of the factors originally isolated by Truax, and has designed a scale to quantify and predict the level of effectiveness at which a prospective therapist will characteristically function. He refers to the factors collectively as components of "facilitative communication."[2]

In the following paragraphs we shall present each of the Carkhuff factors, and shall illustrate them with an explanation and illustration of their nature.

[2]Truax (1971) continues to supply data which indicate that his scales for the measurement of "accurate empathy," "genuineness," and "nonpossessive warmth" are eminently useful in predicting patient change on a wide variety of measures. It is still difficult to assess the relative values of the Truax and the Carkhuff scales, since no studies have compared the two. We have chosen to focus more closely on the Carkhuff scale because we feel that the broader scope of this instrument can elicit greater knowledge and produce more extensive investigation of specific therapist activities. In addition, we suspect that the two scales probably measure much the same things, even though the labels are slightly different ("respect" versus "nonpossessive warmth," for instance).

Empathy

This word is widely utilized in the counseling professions, but much of its meaning has been eroded in the mental health fields, since it has become too closely tied to particular theoretical approaches to psychotherapy. In defining empathy, the term "sympathy" is often used for contrast. Sympathy deals with one emotion, sorrow, and conveys the idea that one person feels sorry for another. Empathy, on the other hand, covers all the emotions, and actually involves the observer in the feelings or experiences of the observed person. A person who communicates empathy shows, in some manner, that he knows how it feels to experience the feelings that another individual is expressing.

While much of the communication of empathy does come through verbal channels, a great deal is also expressed nonverbally, through facial expression, posture, and other behaviors.[3] Similarly, empathy is often communicated by indirect expressions, which show the patient that the therapist is closely following the feelings that he is experiencing. This might be conveyed through a simple smile, a frown, or a mild grimace. Verbally, empathic statements deal with the emotion that is being felt or discussed by the patient, although these statements need not always directly label the emotion. If we want to determine whether we are communicating more than a minimal level of empathy, one guide is to note whether the patient responds to

[3]Much facilitative communication in psychotherapy is brought about through nonverbal means. The Carkhuff Communication Scale (Carkhuff, 1969) is usually scored only according to the verbal responses written or spoken by the respondent. Carkhuff (1969) does contend, however, that the best measurement of these factors comes from *in vivo* or videotape scorings of all dimensions of communication. A more thorough analysis of verbal versus behavioral communication of empathy and warmth is presented in Chapter 4.

our communications with remarks like, "Yeah, that's exactly what I mean!" or "Yes, I was so unhappy with myself for even letting the thought cross my mind," or, "Yes, I'm frustrated and hurt right now," and so on. Below is a hypothetical example in which a therapist communicates a high level of empathy to his adolescent patient:

Patient: That's when Dad said, "Come here, Stupid."

Therapist: Ouch!

Patient: I didn't mind. I just shrugged my shoulders and walked away.

Therapist: "If that's all my help means to you, you can do the job yourself!"

Patient: Yeah; getting angry is one thing, but calling a guy a name is somethin' else.

Therapist: Especially from a guy's own Dad.

Patient: Yeah [voice quivering]. I don't want nothin' to do with him no more.

Therapist: "I don't want to be hurt like that again."

Patient: [long pause] And then I get angry and skip school and get in trouble.

Many inexperienced therapists are under the impression that to show empathy means to talk about feelings. Note in this example, however, that the therapist only once mentioned a specific emotion (hurt). He did not resort to the often clumsy method of pointing out and naming all the emotions that occurred. Yet the content of the interchange is clearly emotional. The following is the same dialogue as it might have been handled by a therapist who thinks that to display empathy means to label every emotion he spots:

Patient: That's when Dad said "Come here, Stupid."

Therapist: Bet it made you angry.

Patient: No, I just shrugged my shoulders and walked away.

Therapist: But you were mad at him for calling you a name.

Patient: No, I just don't want nothin' to do with him no more.

Therapist: Oh, I see! You were hurt by what he said. It made you feel bad and you got angry. I'll bet that's why you skip school too. Huh?

Patient: [Silence].

Therapist: Now you're angry at me.

Below we present the same example again. This time the interaction is between the patient and a nondirective therapist who makes a common misinterpretation of Rogers' (1951) therapeutic approach. This therapist's impression is that he should reflect back to the patient the words or the general content of each of the patient's statements. (The more correct interpretation of Rogers' writing is that the therapist should reflect the patient's emotional tone and deeper feelings.) The technique based on the misinterpretation is much easier; and partly for this reason, it is often more popular than the actual method Rogers advocates. The technique based on the misinterpretation does not demand of the therapist that he become involved as a full human being. It brings therapy down to an almost mechanical exercise—a much more comfortable approach for many therapists.

Patient: That's when Dad said "Come here, Stupid."

Therapist: Your father called you stupid.

Patient: Uh . . . yes, but I just shrugged my shoulders and walked away.

Therapist: You just shrugged and walked off, as if you didn't care at all.

Patient: Yeah, and I don't. I don't want nothin' to do with him any more.

Therapist: You don't want to have anything more to do with your father because he called you stupid.

Patient: No.

This type of therapist in pure form is fortunately somewhat rare, but this example is meant to illustrate the nonproductive and deteriorating interactions that take place when too heavy a reliance is placed on a "technique" or a programmed approach. Note that this method shed no new light on the patient's self-exploration. No new area of self-discovery or experience was offered to the patient, because the therapist added nothing that the patient had not already expressed. The whole realm of feeling went untapped.

Far more common (particularly in training institutions, in which inexperienced therapists from non-psychiatric backgrounds are often present) is the therapist who tries to "reason" with his patients. The following example illustrates the type of difficulty this therapist meets as he attempts to handle with cool logic problems that are deeply emotional in nature.

Patient: That's when Dad said "Come here, Stupid."

Therapist: So what did you do?

Patient: I didn't mind. I just shrugged my shoulders and walked away.

Therapist: Well, don't you think a better way of handling it would have been to tell him how you felt?

Patient: Yeah, and get myself slugged? No way.

Therapist: So now how are you and your Dad going to be able to live together again?

Patient: I don't want nothin' to do with him no more.

Therapist: But don't you think that it would be better if you two could work something out?

Patient: Nothin' to work out. I'm not gonna see him no more.

Therapist: Just because he called you stupid? What about the rest of your life—and school?

Patient: I don't care. I don't need school anyway.

Once again it is apparent that facilitative empathy *opens* discussion and exploration, while the nonfacilitative communication shown here *closes* it.

These examples demonstrate in a simplified manner how only the therapist with a high level of empathic functioning helps the patient to make progress toward a full consideration and confrontation of the conflicts and pressures in his life. It is also only the empathic therapist who avoids constructing a wall between himself and the patient. This therapist builds his credibility with the patient, making himself seen as a person who is ready to understand and to help. He realizes that the patient's problems in living have a large emotional component, as well as a realistic component. He speaks to the emotions, or as Ginott (1972) is fond of saying, "to the heart." Both the cold, logical approach and the application of a "technique" of psychotherapy damage communication; they break communication, rather than encouraging it. They move the parties away from each other, to such a point that they continue their contacts in the roles of antagonists, rather than as coworkers toward a common goal. While a patient's behavior is often quite illogical, irrational, or self-destructive, it is an *emotional* choice that has made it so. He has not in most cases made a logical choice to behave in the way he does, and he will resent and resist "logical" solutions to his problems. It is as if he were saying, "Understand me first. Look at things through my eyes. Feel what I feel. Only when you have shown me this will I consider your suggestions."

Many novices, in an attempt to raise their empathy levels, and to "discuss feelings," use the query, "How do you feel about that, George?" or "How did that make you feel?" No matter that tears may be streaming down the patient's face; the question still comes. The empathic therapist, on the other hand, does not need to ask. He communicates—by facial expression, tone of voice, and words—a recognition and an acceptance of the patient's feeling, or at least of how he, the therapist, might feel if he were in the patient's situation. The question, "How do you feel?" shows a low level of empathy. At best, it is an awkward probe into a sensitive area for the patient; if it were not sensitive, the patient could express his feelings directly. At worst, since it fails to disclose anything of the therapist's real self, it can be experienced by the patient as little more than a voyeuristic assault.

Empathy is often thought to be relevant only to the negative emotions (feelings of anger, pain, despair, and so on). But to function empathically, the therapist must be able to recognize and share the full range of emotions, the euphoric as well as the unhappy. When the patient expresses delight, joy, or pride, the empathic therapist conveys his understanding of these feelings. "Wow, you're really flying high today!" "I'm happy for you!" "It was a tough job, but you stuck with it." Here is an example from Carkhuff (1967, pp. 32–33):

Client: I can't wait to get out of school. I just want to get out and get started and be on my way. I know I'm going to make it one of these days!

Therapist: Hey, you sound like you're really going somewhere!

Client: Yup, I'm gonna make it big—I just know it! I just have that feeling!

Therapist: Wow—Sky's the limit, huh?

Client: The future looks so darn bright, I just want to be out of school and—and—get into what I want to be doing. I'm so happy, I can't wait for the semester to be over!

Therapist: Boy, I can remember the feeling—its a wonderful feeling. Maybe we can spell out the possibilities and any other things that maybe we can fruitfully consider here.

Client: O.K.—As soon as I get out of school, I'm going to go into fashion designing and—um—the only thing is I have several different possibilities and—um—in different areas, and I don't really know which one I'm going to take.

Respect

The second factor that underlies therapeutic effectiveness, according to Carkhuff, is respect. The individual is probably extremely rare who would state that he does not treat his patients, clients, students, or other people with respect. Asking people if they treat others with respect is probably very like asking them if they have a sense of humor. A probably fictitious story has it that a psychologist once asked a random sample of the United States population if they possessed a "better than average sense of humor," and 97 per cent replied affirmatively! We would probably receive a similar response were we to ask therapists, "Do you treat patients with better than average respect?" or "Do you communicate to your patients that you clearly respect them?" Yet when observers rate therapists on the degree of respect that they communicate to their patients, they consistently agree that some therapists are far more adept than others in this regard.

This factor may not be strongly independent from the others, since Carkhuff (1967) and Pierce (1967) have found indications that the rating of the therapist's level of respect depends upon his communication of warmth and understanding. But even then, we are warned that "respect is not always communicated in warm, modulated tones of voice; it may be communicated, for example, in anger" (Carkhuff, 1967, p. 28). This does not mean that all angry expressions are expressions of respect, but that properly expressed anger can convey to the patient that he is important. He is a force to be reckoned with. His behavior is not to be ignored; it does have an emotional impact on others.

Genuineness

The next factor to be considered is termed genuineness. Some people prefer to label this "emotional honesty." The effective therapist is attuned to his own feelings, and communicates openly in a spontaneous, unguarded manner. There is, however, an important restriction on this factor. In attempting to be genuine, the therapist must not be hostile, belligerent, or abusive. This would seem to be rather obvious; antagonistic patterns of interaction are directly antithetical to the factors of empathy and respect. Nevertheless, some therapists, who are quite well attuned to their inner feelings, seem to respond to patients primarily with irascibility and pique—all of which they justify by claiming that they are merely being "genuine." In a case where the only genuine feelings toward the patient are negative, it is our belief that the therapist would be well advised to ask another therapist to take over the case.

Genuineness, or emotional honesty, must be differentiated from factual honesty. In being emotionally honest, the therapist does not hide, distort or deny his actual emotional experience in relation to the patient. The therapist can be entirely emotionally honest in relating all his present feelings, but still not divulge all the factual data that may be requested. A recently hired female high school teacher in her mid-twenties, pretty and unmarried, rushed into our office one afternoon complaining, "These kids are about to drive me right up the wall! The three boys are ganging up on me. They want me to tell them whether or not I'm a virgin!" When we laughingly told her that we advocate the "honest" approach, she exclaimed frantically, "But you don't expect me to be honest about *that,* do you?"

The answer is no; we don't expect her to be factually

honest in all cases. In this situation the deck was stacked against her, since whatever factual answer she might have given would have been interpreted negatively, given our present cultural standards. The female is expected to profess chastity before marriage. Yet her attractiveness may be brought into question, and she is sometimes thought prudish if she reaches a certain age without having experienced sexual intimacy with a male. Although we did not advocate factual honesty in this situation, we did urge emotional honesty. This was particularly important, since the behavior of her students was having a marked emotional effect upon her. Emotionally honest responses that do not divulge the data, but still communicate respect, might be: "I get very embarrassed when you dart a question like that at me. I don't feel I know you well enough yet to discuss my private life, especially in public like this;" or "I feel embarrassed when you ask me this. I also become quite irked when I am asked very personal questions without any respect for my needs for privacy. Let's talk about sex when I have calmed down and feel more comfortable—also, when we have more privacy, and can discuss these things with less public display"; or "These questions embarrass me, and I won't discuss them while I have these feelings. But I do understand your desire to know more about sex, and we can talk about these things at a more appropriate time"; or "These questions embarrass me deeply, because to me sexual topics are deeply personal and private things. I also wonder if my actions have encouraged such blunt talk about sex. I'd feel badly if I have done this in any way, because my relationship with you will never include sexual advances."

Concreteness

Concreteness is a factor that is best explained in terms of its direct opposite, abstractness. Abstract communications on the part of the therapist are theoretical, remote, or vague. Concrete statements are concise and explicit, and are delivered in terms that the patient will readily understand. Concrete communication involves speaking to the patient in modes that he can grasp clearly. For example, the therapist's responses can incorporate some of the patient's own language usages. Concrete communication does not, however, require him to adopt the patient's unique or subcultural jargon, which may be foreign to the therapist's normal personality or life-style.

Of the qualities that Carkhuff presents, this and the next to be discussed may, we feel, actually be lowered rather than enhanced in the therapist by the common modes of professional training. The individual who seeks advanced degrees in the mental health professions is generally verbal and intelligent, and is rewarded throughout his training for his capacity to conceptualize human problems and express them in the abstract. But if he communicates on a pedantic level in therapy, he is being less than effective. Some aspects of professional academic training may in fact be responsible for the abstract nature of the communications transmitted by young professionals to their clients. An example was given by a psychology trainee at our institution, who urged a group of adolescents in therapy: "O.K., now let's get some consensual validation here."

Here are two caricature examples of extremes in abstract and concrete communication. Here is the abstract therapist:

Patient: Damn! My mother makes me so mad! I know I should love her, but some of the things she does just drive me up the wall!

Therapist: Ah, yes! I see; you have an unresolved emotional fixation stemming from the phallic stage of development with residual conflictual feelings of love and hate . . .

And here is the concrete therapist:

Patient: Damn! My mother makes me so mad! I know I should love her, but some of the things she does just drive me up the wall!

Therapist: Boy! Mothers sure can be a pip!

David Viscott, in *The Making of a Psychiatrist* (1972), gives a very similar example:

> Stanley would describe Mrs. Sacks' outburst at me as "a failure of the anxiety-binding defenses to operate effectively with a resultant displacement of the unresolved hostility from Dr. Jagers to Dr. Viscott as part of the process of decathecting" . . . anyone else . . . would say that Mrs. Sacks was hurt and upset that her old therapist had left and was angry at her new doctor for trying to take his place. . . . [If] you always think about patients in the language of jargon rather than feelings, you make it more difficult to think of them as human and to identify with them. [pp. 24–25]

Self-Disclosure

This is the second facilitative quality that appears to be actually reduced in therapists by most current professional programs (Fix and Haffke, 1972). The self-disclosing therapist does not impose a unilateral demand that the client shall lay bare his very soul to the therapist's critical scrutiny. He understands that it is an uncomfortable and difficult task to express one's deep inner feelings. He also knows that many of the feelings and conflicts the patient is currently experiencing, he, the therapist, has experienced in some form in his own life. The difference may lie only in the behavior that the patient and therapist use in response to their feelings. To be given this insight into the therapist's personality can be a source of relief to the patient. Such disclosures can also give the patient information on possible methods of handling various situations. The therapist becomes a colleague and an accessible companion, who partly leads the way, because he has "been there" too. He can guide the patient over the road that he has already travelled. The patient learns several valuable things that have often been neglected in traditional therapy: that he is not significantly different from other human beings, even very successful human beings such as the therapist; that his emotions are not unique and disgraceful; and that he can truly share his feelings with a person who can understand. As with genuineness, here again the most important factor is an honest communication of emotional experiences. This is because virtually every therapist will have experienced feelings very similar to those of the patient, even though he may never have undergone similar life circumstances. Simply as a result of our shared humanity, at some time in our lives we have all experienced rage, sexual urges, fear, euphoria, hopelessness, and deep depression. The therapist may be different from the patient not in having these feelings, but in his way of conducting himself when he does experience them. His disclosures on his personal experiences in dealing with feelings can be useful to the patient if they are given in the context of warmth, acceptance, and respect.

The only restriction that Carkhuff places upon self-disclosure is that it should be used less with lower-functioning patients than with patients who are themselves able to communicate at a higher level. As the patient improves, then, increasing self-disclosure by the therapist may be indicated.

Fix and Haffke (1976) found that there were almost no self-disclosures at all in the Carkhuff Scale responses of a group of psychiatry residents. This may reflect the emphasis on astute diagnostic acumen that is conveyed to the physician in training. In generating a diagnosis, he provides a "sick" role for the patient. The therapist may feel that to divulge that he has had many of the feelings that the patient expresses could be very threatening to his professional image. Such considerations do not imply that training programs should reduce their teaching of diagnostic skills. These considerations rather indicate a special orientation that the physician brings with him into training that may initially interfere with his ability to communicate in the most therapeutic manner.

Confrontation

The term "confrontation" has a hard and distasteful connotation in our culture. Confrontations are usually negative experiences, things to be avoided. Carkhuff finds, however, that confrontation can have a somewhat different meaning. Therapeutic confrontations should focus on discrepancies in three areas: (1) between the patient's statements about himself and the therapist's experience of him, (2) between he patient's statements about his behavior and his real actions, and (3) between the patient's ideal image of himself and his actual experience of himself.

In this definition, we can see that confrontation can be expressed in a positive as well as a negative manner. ("Mary, I hear you saying you feel ugly and are afraid that no one could really like you. I know I find you very attractive. I like you a great deal, and I think part of my feelings have come from what I consider your warm good looks, especially when you have that infectious smile. I'm wondering what has happened to make you feel so alone right now.") The therapist can point to strengths in the patient, and note actions of the patient that are incongruent with his negative appraisal of himself. He can also serve as a mirror to the patient, reflecting the patient's actions and communication, and yet remain supportive and understanding.

Naturally this factor has more restraints placed on it than any other. High levels of confrontation cannot be given until the relationship is secure. Early contacts with the patient cannot contain many confrontations. Those that are given can best be presented in an inquiring fashion: "You often refer to yourself as dumb, but you also say that you must be pretty bright to pass that tough algebra course. How do you really see yourself?" In a trusting relationship, however, the two parties can say virtually anything to each other. Therefore, as the relationship develops and grows, the role of confrontation can also grow.

SUMMARY

Before we progress further with an analysis of the most recent research, let us pause here and summarize the conclusions we can make about psychotherapy at this point.

1. Psychotherapy, or the "talking treatment," does produce change.

2. Some aspects of psychotherapy produce positive, healthy change, but other aspects produce negative, detrimental, destructive change.

3. The components of psychotherapy that are related to patient change are basic, nonesoteric elements of communication.

4. It promotes patient improvement to transmit high levels of empathy and respect, while relating to him in a concrete and genuine fashion, and maintaining high levels of self-disclosure and confrontation; but low levels of these factors will produce deterioration in the patient.

We can finally state that the underlying hypothesis which we earlier attributed to Freud, that a human being can help another human being by talking with him, has at last been substantiated. The means by which help takes place, however, is very different from the means that Freud proposed. We might even suggest that one of the reasons why the traditional techniques of psychoanalysis have produced so little empirical success (Luborsky and Spense,

1971) may be that, in general, traditional psychoanalytic techniques foster communication patterns that are the very antithesis of those factors that make psychotherapy beneficial. The pristine trappings of psychoanalysis, including the couch, the seating of the analyst out of the patient's line of vision, the abstract interpretations by the analyst, and his professional aloofness, are all directly opposed to the mode of functioning that has been shown to be most helpful to the patient. While most practitioners, including those adhering to Freudian principles, no longer maintain these formal standards, other more subtle patterns of professional aloofness may still interfere with the full beneficial impact of psychotherapy. The next chapter will critically explore the research further to provide therapeutic guidelines more specific than those elicited to this point.

Chapter 4

A FURTHER ANALYSIS OF FACILITATIVE COMMUNICATION IN PSYCHOTHERAPY

. . . the best therapists are parents whose kids grew up without problems.

Whenever someone uses a lot of psychological jargon around you it is a sign of two possible dangers: first, they may be afraid of getting close to you and dealing with you as a human being with real feelings or, second, they may be trying to impress you. You don't need a mental health professional like that.[1]

SOME CAVEATS

At this point we need to introduce a few *caveats* in relation to the research that we have presented, and upon which we have based our espousal of the Carkhuff-Truax

---

[1]David S. Viscott. *The making of a psychiatrist.* New York: Arbor House, 1972, pp. 119 & 25.

models of psychotherapy. First, the reader should be informed that the research reported here suffers from one significant flaw: the question of how to measure outcome, or quantify improvement, has never been solved in this field. The studies we have cited have all used different definitions of patient change. Until a universal instrument for the measurement of improvement is adopted, our conclusions will not be unassailable. In a scientific sense, then, none of the studies we survey here constitute "good" or "adequate" investigations. We justify our conclusions more on the consistency of their findings than on the precision or statistical validity of the individual studies involved. If the same phenomenon is repeatedly observed by different researchers, who use different approaches and a variety of measures, the phenomenon is validated to much the same extent as if the data came from a few studies using more precise measurements.

We would like to see the clearest possible testing of the hypotheses related to psychotherapy. Until a measure of therapeutic effects that is satisfactory to all researchers is developed, and until unequivocally appropriate control groups are established and studied, we will be forced to rely on the consistency criterion in evaluating research. There are two choices for those who, like ourselves, request scientific verification of the efficacy of a treatment prior to its public use. The first is that we can accept findings that consistently appear in a large number of studies as the best estimate at the moment, subject to their future refinement. The alternative is to call a moratorium on all psychotherapy, due to the lack of evidence on the efficacy of the treatment. We advocate either choice; we prefer the former.

The second cautionary consideration is that almost all of the research surveyed here has been conducted with patients who voluntarily sought help and were desirous of personal change. We do not have the necessary evidence to conclude that the factors presented by Carkhuff would influence change in involuntary patients such as the delinquent, the sociopathic individual, or any other person pressed into therapy by outside force. For example, most children and adolescents who receive psychiatric attention receive it not because they want to, but because someone else wants them "treated." We suspect that the Carkhuff factors are useful in all interpersonal contacts, and we base our approach to the treatment of hospitalized patients on this belief. But lest we make the kind of dogmatic overgeneralizations that have been so common in the field of psychotherapy, we must recognize that as yet this is merely an assumption.

CURRENT REFINEMENTS

Since Carkhuff's early assessment of the factors that facilitate communication in psychotherapy, most research efforts in the area have attempted to clarify these constructs and measure how they interact with each other. This research is still far from complete. Many of the most important questions remain to be answered. Many suggestive leads have been developed, however. Mullen and Abeles (1971) found that experienced therapists were able to express adequate empathy toward each of their patients, regardless of whether or not they liked the patient personally. Inexperienced therapists were able to express adequate empathy only toward those patients they liked. Further, as earlier research would have predicted, only the level of empathy (not the level of liking) was related to patient improvement. This finding suggests that the ability to communicate empathy may be a skill that therapists can be taught. That is, whether or not the therapist likes his patient, he can perhaps learn to be empathic. Similarly, Moos and MacIntosh (1970) measured the levels of empathy communicated by relatively inexperienced therapists during sessions with their patients. They confirmed that these therapists tend to show higher levels of empathy with some patients than with others. This has since been confirmed by Heck and Davis (1973). For the patient's sake, it seems that the therapist in training ought perhaps to work exclusively with those patients he honestly likes, and with whom he therefore can more easily empathize. As the therapist progresses in his ability to transmit accurate empathy, he can then be progressively assigned to less "likeable" patients.

Moos and MacIntosh also found that their therapists were not able to express an equally high level of empathy in all content areas. Each therapist had his own idiosyncratic pattern of topics with which he dealt most empathically. This finding also holds practical implications for the training of therapists. It is likely, for example, that some therapists in early training might be unable to empathize with a patient troubled by homosexual desires, while others might have difficulty with a patient's rage against his parents. Further research should ultimately help us to pinpoint the "sensitive" areas for each therapist in training, so that we can help him to raise his overall level of empathic functioning.

While we can demonstrate that patients show improvement when exposed to high levels of empathic, genuine communications, and to the other facilitative factors, this knowledge does not automatically help us to show a student precisely how these are communicated, nor to teach him how he can raise his level of therapeutic activity. This is because the Carkhuff and the Truax Scales do not precisely specify the exact behaviors that a therapist must show in order to receive a high rating. For example, the following is part of the guideline given by Carkhuff (1967) in rating empathy:

At level 3 of the *empathic understanding* scale, the verbal or behavioral expressions of the first person (the client, student, or child) are essentially *interchangeable* with those of the second person in that they express essentially the same affect and meaning. Below level 3, the responses of the counselor detract from those of the client. Thus, at level 1, the lowest level of interpersonal functioning, the first person's responses either do not *attend to* or *detract significantly* from the expressions of the second person in that they communicate significantly less of the second person's feelings than the second person has communicated himself. At level 2, while the first person does respond to the expressed feelings of the second person, he does so in such a way that he *subtracts noticeably* from the affective communications of the second person. Above level 3, the first person's responses are additive in nature. Thus, at level 4, the responses of the first person add *noticeably* to the expressions of the second person in such a way as to express feelings a level deeper than the second person was able to express himself. [p. 5]

Truax (1973), meanwhile, supplies very similar broad definitions of his factors (accurate empathy, genuineness, and nonpossessive warmth). He states that "feedback" is the best way to raise the levels of these interpersonal skills, and that feedback is best gained through interaction in a group, in which all the group members attempt to improve themselves in these skills. Obviously, the rater of the Carkhuff or Truax Scales, the member of a "feedback" group, and the practicing clinician who attempts to evaluate his own performance may all fall back on a large element of subjectivity. This is not to discredit the studies done with these instruments. The researchers control for this problem by including more than one rater in the study, and by demanding a high degree of agreement before the start of the study. This, however, does not help us to identify the specific factors that the raters respond to in arriving at agreement in scoring. It also does not clarify for us the nature and the importance of the nonverbal cues between the therapist and his patient.

A major future contribution to the psychotherapy literature will come from those researchers who are able to simplify and standardize the scoring system for the Carkhuff or Truax Scales. Such a scoring system would list the objective, countable behaviors of the therapist that can be shown to have a high relationship to patient improvement. Then an observer could simply count the positive and negative behaviors seen, assign the therapist to a Carkhuff Scale "level," and specify what exactly the therapist must do to improve his performance.

Some initial work has already been reported on this problem. Boyes (1972) asked raters to make overall assessments of the "warmth" communicated by peers in videotaped interviews. These global ratings were then compared with assessments of more specific behaviors to determine which of these behaviors showed the highest correlations with the overall ratings of warmth. By asking the raters to judge the persons in the interviews on audio transcripts only, as well as in the full videotape reproduction, Boyes found that, at least on the dimension of warmth, people tended to be fairly consistent; they transmitted nearly the same degree of warmth through their voices as they did through their physical actions. It was a nonverbal behavior (the amount of smiling), however, that was most highly related to the overall rating of warmth. The expression of positive feelings in any form was the verbal activity that showed the greatest correspondence with ratings of general warmth.

While the communication of warmth seems to be accomplished quite effectively through both verbal and nonverbal channels, it appears that the nonverbal components are most important in the communication of "empathy." Indeed, Haase and Tepper (1972) estimate that the nonverbal messages are twice as important in the communication of empathy as are the verbal responses. The simple act of maintaining eye contact was found to correlate more highly than any other factor with the overall rating of a counselor's level of empathy. The other signal that was found to increase empathy ratings was equally simple: leaning forward toward the client. The verbal components of empathic communication seemed in this study to be more important at the lower end of the empathy scale. If verbal responses were low in empathy, even good eye contact and an attentive posture could not raise the counselor's general empathy rating. Yet even when the verbal message was high in empathy, poor messages from the nonverbal spheres lowered the impact of the overall communication to a nonempathic level. Therapists, then, may need to practise empathic responses to at least a medium level. Once they function verbally at a moderately helpful level, they may be able to increase their effectiveness by mastering simple behavioral skills that will raise the appearance, at least, of concern and understanding.

Some practitioners might feel that it would be dishonest and hypocritical to use behavioral "gimmicks" to "fool" the patient into seeing the therapist as more empathic than he really is. While this contention may ultimately be of critical importance in psychotherapy, we see such an urgent need for effective involvement of *any* type that we are attracted to some of the counterarguments against this point. The first is based on a study by Kurtz and Grummon (1972), which showed that while therapist empathy as rated by judges did indeed relate to patient improvement, a far better predictor of patient change was the patient's own rating of his therapist's empathy. If this be the case, then at least part of our endeavor in psychotherapy ought perhaps to be to develop more ways to "sell" ourselves to our clients as concerned, understanding individuals. The previously mentioned works of Boyes (1972) and of Haase and Tepper (1972) have provided some suggestions on how to begin. Some professionals may feel that these behavioral approaches to warmth and empathy are in fact cold or superficial, in that they focus upon technical methods of developing skills that should stem from the emotions. Yet who can say at this point that the therapist who adopts the behavioral patterns of maintaining good eye contact, listening attentively, smiling, and making positive statements will not actually *become* more concerned, involved, caring, and understanding?

In brief, a major accomplishment of these studies to date has been the demonstration that abstract therapeutic factors such as empathy, genuineness, and so on can be objectified in concrete behavioral terms. With more research in this area, the ultimate goal of improving the practice and teaching of psychotherapy may come into reach in the near future. In addition, the identification of potentially talented therapists may be significantly enhanced. We may eventually reach a point at which we can state with precision "what good therapists do," rather than simply labeling, as we do today, those qualities that good therapists possess.

THE "A–B" VARIABLE

It is hoped that by objectifying the scoring system of Carkhuff-type scales, and by specifying more precisely the actions that differentiate the effective therapist from his ineffective or destructive colleague many of the theoretical and scientific arguments that have befallen the work of certain pioneers in research on the effective therapist can be overcome. Whitehorn and Betz (1954, 1957, 1960; Betz and Whitehorn, 1956) first differentiated two types of clinical practitioners, whom they labeled "A" and "B" therapists. The work of these researchers was outstanding, and far ahead of the times when it was conducted. The investigators studied the seven psychiatric residents, who, out of a total of 35, had the best improvement rates in their schizophrenic patients. They labeled these "A" therapists. The seven therapists who had the lowest improvement rates they labeled "B" therapists. Distinctions between these people were sought on as many variables as possible; this culminated in the use of an interest scale having little theoretical relationship with clinical behavior.

The Strong Vocational Interest Test compares a person's interest patterns with patterns of people who have been successful in a number of vocational fields. Somehow, it was found that A therapists scored higher on the Lawyer and CPA (Certified Public Accountant) scales of the Strong test, while B therapists scored higher on the Printer and Mathematics-Science Teacher scales (Whitehorn and Betz, 1960). Even though the authors were able to some extent to predict patient improvement in validation studies, this method left a number of questions to be answered. In terms of training therapists, what should they be trained to do? Should they change their personality "types"? Or raise their scores on the Lawyer and CPA scales of the Strong Vocational Interest Blank? Or should B types simply be screened out of the psychotherapy professions?

A more fruitful approach would perhaps have been to attempt to nail down those behaviors that differentiated A from B therapists during psychotherapy sessions. Direct predictions of patient change due to particular aspects of intervention could have been made, and the effects of training upon the therapist's behavior and effectiveness could have been assessed.

Unfortunately for the A-B researchers, a number of major changes have been made in the treatment of psychiatric patients since Whitehorn and Betz first introduced their material. The major change, of course, has been the introduction of effective chemotherapies, to the extent that psychotherapy is no longer the treatment of first choice for schizophrenia. The results of current studies of the A-B variable are quite mixed (Razin, 1971; Chartier, 1971;

Bowden, Endicott, and Spitzer, 1972; Berzins *et al.,* 1971, 1972). In his review of the A–B literature, Chartier (1971) points out that in recent years improvement rates with schizophrenics have everywhere jumped above the 70 per cent mark, or to a level scarcely achieved previously by the best A therapists. This is clearly due to the "chemical revolution" in psychiatry. Such remarkable results may have pushed to the background the importance of the therapist's characteristics (and perhaps even of psychotherapy?) in the treatment of these patients. Other studies are keeping the A–B variable alive, and have found some suggestive evidence that A therapists, as originally stated, are more effective with schizophrenic patients, while B therapists seem to be somewhat more effective with neurotic patients (McNair, Callahan, and Lorr, 1962; Segal, 1970; Berzins, Ross, and Friedman, 1972).

As might be guessed, we tend to view the Carkhuff and Truax systems as similar to the A–B analysis, but notably advanced from that approach. The Carkhuff measure in particular lends itself to better, more precise teaching of specific therapeutic skills. In addition, it enables one to predict the outcome of therapy at various levels of functioning, rather than being limited in predictive efficiency to two extremes on one dimension. If one looks at the vaguely defined therapeutic "styles" that Whitehorn and Betz saw in their A and B therapists, there is a surprising similarity between these authors' descriptions and the characteristics that Carkhuff and his followers later found in their most effective therapists. In general, the A therapists seemed to understand their patients better, to have a better interpersonal relationship with them, and to gain their confidence more successfully. In addition, here is a summary by Razin (1971) of how they functioned during the therapy sessions: "A's were actively, personally involved. They were characterized by initiative in sympathetic inquiry, honest disagreement, challenging of the self-depreciation in patients, setting of realistic limits on patients' behavior; while B's adopted passive, interpretive and/or instructional, or practical care patterns" (p. 2).

If the Carkhuff approach has some similarity with the A–B dimension, why are A therapists not *always* more effective? Why are there some indications that B therapists are more effective with neurotic patients? A partial answer may be seen in the work of Seidman (1971), who found that A therapists were better able to communicate respect and empathy for patients who tended to "turn against" themselves. B therapists did less well with this type of patient, but were able to raise their respect and empathy scores with patients who tended to avoid others but who wished to be more outgoing. Seidman's findings are only suggestive, given the serious clinical shortcomings of his study. It was not conducted either with actual patients or with actual therapists. The subjects were college students, who responded to videotape recordings of the enactments of other students who were seeking counseling.

If one can apply these findings to the "real" psychotherapy situation, the implication may be that Whitehorn and Betz saw hazily what Truax, Carkhuff, and their followers were later to document with greater precision: the helpful effects of facilitative communication in psychotherapy. What Whitehorn and Betz did not observe was that therapists, except for the most skillful, tend to perform at different levels of effectiveness, according to the different personality characteristics of the various patients with whom they deal. The Moos and MacIntosh (1970) findings were most convincing in this regard; they demonstrated that therapists show varying levels of empathy, depending upon the patient and the subject matter being discussed. Clearly each professional involved in the training and practice of psychotherapy should be aware of the possibility that with certain patients and with certain topics, he may function less therapeutically than he does normally.

An Hypothesis: Confrontation Is the Crucial Fulcrum Factor

The early studies based on Carkhuff's work have made no distinctions between the various facilitative conditions. We can expect that future studies, however, will ferret out the subtle interactions between the communication factors. We can also expect that future research will refine the statements we can now make on how therapists' communication skills are affected by the personality of the patient and the topic being discussed. Such studies must be made, since they are needed to explain certain of the findings that are at variance to the main stream. For example, Garfield and Bergin (1971) failed to find that empathy and positive regard related to the outcome of therapy. This, however, may be because the authors did not note what degree of confrontation was taking place in these sessions; and the interaction between empathy and confrontation is possibly of critical importance in the outcome of therapeutic intervention.

We hypothesize that confrontation is the critical factor —the fulcrum—in all prolonged psychotherapeutic interactions. As yet we have no solid evidence to support this supposition, but it should be fairly easy to test it. The reasoning behind the hypothesis is simple. We are merely predicting that confrontation will be found to be somewhat more powerfully related to therapeutic outcome than some of the other factors. In the context of an empathic, respectful relationship, confrontation may be an extraordinarily powerful factor for positive therapeutic results. On the other hand, confrontation without the supportive communication patterns is probably quite destructive. These assumptions can be stated in another way, more consistent with our comments on the findings of Garfield and Bergin (1971). From this perspective, the hypothesis expects that high levels of empathy, respect, and the other factors will be found to be only minimally related to outcome when little confrontation is used. We postulate further that high levels of confrontation, if not accompanied by similar levels of the other factors, will be found to be associated with patient deterioration.

What kind of situation do we have when the therapist functions at a low level of confrontation, but at a high level of the other factors? This is often seen in a treatment program in which the staff is concerned, caring, and dedicated, and the patients are strong manipulators. The manipulations often go unchecked, because members of the staff are fearful of jeopardizing their "understanding relationship" with the patients. Some community-based projects established to deal with troubled teenagers have run into this problem. People who want to help adolescents are often kind, loving individuals who can, and do, function effectively as "good guys" with the young counselees with whom they work. Many of these volunteers are young, most are inexperienced in the counseling of adolescents, and all are very idealistic. While youth and idealism may be significant therapeutic assets, many of the people who volunteer to work with adolescents in this manner also find it very difficult to confront them directly on their manipulative or self-defeating behaviors. These helpful people are often modestly facilitative in terms of most of the therapeutic factors of communication. Yet the more disturbed a youth is, the more necessary it would seem that he should be exposed to a person who sets firm behavioral limits, and provides clear guidelines for interpersonal interaction.

One of the most difficult problems that we constantly meet in medical students and psychiatry residents beginning training on our adolescent hospital ward is that of teaching them to say "no" to our young patients. Sophistication in confronting the young person with his manipulative or destructive behavior can come later; the first crisis usually occurs when the patient asks a student for a privilege or special dispensation that his behavior clearly has not merited. Since he is afraid of losing his budding relationship with the patient, the student often capitulates. This is often true, whether the patient requests permission to take an unaccompanied walk shortly after he has brought contraband onto the ward, to attend a motion picture although he has missed school during the day, or simply to stay up past the established bedtime.

The opposite communication pattern—high in confrontation, but low in the other communication variables—is not uncommon, both in psychiatric hospitals and in the world at large. We believe this is a particularly common pattern with parents of emotionally or behaviorally disturbed children and adolescents. In fact, one of the basic hypothesis in a study by Fix and Niewoehner (1972) is that this mode of communication on the part of parents may actually contribute to the development of some of the psychiatric disorders of young persons. Parents quite often function very high on the confrontation scale ("I told you not to run in the house! That was my best lamp. You never listen! You never do anything anybody wants you to. You're lazy and rude; I don't know what you'll ever amount to!" and so on).

These, of course, are high-confrontation communications; and at the same time they are very low on empathy and respect. Adults very often confront young persons, and therapists sometimes confront patients, but in doing so they also quite often attack more than the behavior. They attack the core of the personality, the basic worth of the human being. Whenever the person as a whole is attacked, rather than just his deviant behavior, a destructive message is transmitted to the individual.

These considerations are presented to illustrate why we label confrontation as the fulcrum component of the facilitative factors. We point, of course, to the need for caution in making this logical jump without substantive research. In summary, we reiterate our hypothesis that confrontation is the fulcrum factor: without high confrontation, high levels of the other facilitative factors are only minimally constructive, while high confrontation in combination with low levels of the other facilitative factors is destructive.

The nature of confrontation in the hands of high and low-functioning therapists has been examined by Mitchell and Hall (1971). The better therapists used more of what the authors called "experiential confrontations." That is, these therapists more often called attention to discrepancies between the patient's experience of himself and the therapist's experience of the patient. Here is a possible example of this type of confrontation: "You feel that expressing yourself to your father would come across as weak and silly; yet you are expressing yourself to me, and I don't react to your statements as being either weak or silly." A second form of experiential confrontation could involve pointing out any discrepancy between the patient's description of himself and his inner experience of himself: "You like to see yourself as a tough, nonemotional guy, but I hear you saying, too, that there are a lot of times when you're really uneasy and unsure of yourself." A third type involves discrepancies between the patient's and the therapist's experience of the *therapist:* "You see me as passing judgment on you at this point. I see myself as being concerned and feeling close to you, even when it involves talking about things that are uncomfortable for us."

High-functioning therapists also utilized more "strength confrontations"; that is, they pointed to the patient's strengths and constructive resources. The poorer therapists, on the other hand, gave more confrontations that pointed out the patient's weaknesses. That the latter type of confrontations were more common than the former should probably be no great surprise to us, considering the orientations of many therapy training programs. Much of the training in the helping professions focuses on the ability of the student to recognize and point out pathological modes of interaction.

In this particular study, "strength confrontations" were rare, but when they did occur, they were given only by the better therapists. The authors found these confrontations to be rare; we hope this was because they restricted themselves to the assessment of only the initial therapy sessions for each patient. We would expect that as therapy progressed, and as the high-functioning therapists became more familiar with their patients and more aware of their unique abilities and resources, that this type of confrontation would increase. "During the time I've known you, I've seen you make some tremendously difficult decisions; and I've seen you stand alone on a principle, sometimes against the entire group of people here. I know you have the strength to do this. Right now, even when you are saying that group pressure is too strong for you, I feel that you are reaching back for the strength that you have demonstrated you possess."

In an attempt to measure and define the relationships between the various facilitative factors of psychotherapy, Friel, Berenson, and Mitchell (1971) produced a fascinating study of the dynamic process that takes place in therapy conducted by a high-functioning therapist. This process is in sharp contrast to the awkward, out-of-step interaction that transpires between a patient and a low-functioning therapist. Their research method was to apply the statistical technique of factor analysis to the facilitative dimensions. Forty-five therapists were monitored during the first-session contacts with their patients. Factor analysis was used to elicit a picture of the interactions of the communication variables. The researchers wanted to find out which of the dimensions tend to be seen together at any given time. They found that, in fact, the amount of confrontation used by the therapist does correspond to the amount of the other facilitative characteristics he displays. That is, not only were the better therapists more warm and empathic, they also confronted the patient more often than low-functioning therapists. The authors also found that the more the high-level therapist confronted the patient, the more the patient explored himself. The more the low-functioning therapist confronted the patient, however, the less the patient engaged in self-exploration. Here we see partial support for the fulcrum theory of confrontation: while confrontation and the other conditions tend to go together in persons who are working as therapists, confrontation has some specific effects of its own. In the hands of more empathic, understanding, and open therapists, confrontation is therapeutic, in the sense that it increases the patient's self-exploration. But in the hands of other therapists, confrontation in this regard is counter-therapeutic. We will consider how closely "self-exploration" and patient "improvement" are tied together in a later section of this chapter.

CONFRONTATION AND BEHAVIOR MODIFICATION

If we see confrontation as incorporating behavioral guidelines and giving directionality to the patient's activities, this aspect of traditional psychotherapy then becomes very similar to (though less precise than) the field of traditional behavioral modification. We tend to believe that behavior modification approaches derive at least a portion of their benefits from the establishment of a core of positive psychotherapeutic communication patterns. Our hypothesis is that high-functioning psychotherapy facilitates well designed behavior modification programs. This could be tested by giving careful behavior modification training to low- and high-functioning therapists (for example, psychiatric aides), who would then administer identical behavior modification programs. Behavior change in the patients, measured during the hospital stay and at discharge, could then be used to compare the effectiveness of the two programs. We would predict that not only would the low-functioning therapists run into more difficulties in carrying out the program, but that such "treatment" by these poor therapists would actually be destructive to the patient. We would predict that more deviant behavior would appear upon follow-up in patients treated by these therapists than in those who had worked with high-functioning therapists.

IMMEDIACY, "PASTIMING," AND THE REST OF THE GANG

Friel, Berenson, and Mitchell (1971) also found that high-functioning therapists focused doggedly on the immediate relationship with the patient and the patient's current feelings and behavior. We emphasize this point because it is quite difficult for many therapists, and particularly so for most patients, to become involved in the immediate relationship. It is much easier for both parties to talk about problems that exist somewhere "out there." Drugs, or parents, school, or any of a number of situations or people may be defined as "the problem." The therapist who looks exclusively at the difficulties that exist outside of the therapy situation fails to place highest priority on those aspects of the individual that he can observe directly—those responses and characteristic coping styles of the patient that occur right in the very presence of the therapist himself.[2]

Friel and his colleagues describe the low-functioning therapist as simply "interacting" with the patient, but not really attending to him on an emotional level or becoming deeply involved in the immediate relationship. Although this study measured only the events that occurred in the

[2]This point has also been pointed out in an article on group therapy by Garetz and Fix (1972).

first therapy session, the authors tie their results to those of the larger body of research that we have discussed on the effectiveness of psychotherapy. From this standpoint, the authors make the following prognostic statement:

> The implications for outcome are questionable for the clients of low-functioning therapists, who seemed to be involved in a relationship that is focusing on something other than the client or his problems at the moment; and are hopeful for the client of high-functioning therapist, who seems to be involved in a relationship that focuses on the client, and his problems in the moment with support . . . direction . . . and client involvement (i.e., self exploration). [p. 293]

It has long been an axiom of all forms of psychotherapy that it is important for a patient to talk about himself during the treatment sessions. This may seem to be too obvious a proposition to subject to empirical study, but when we find that much of the research on the outcome psychotherapy yields no evidence at all of effectiveness; perhaps the most obvious and basic principles need to be subjected to deep screening. Or perhaps the belief that somehow it is helpful for a person to talk about himself has never been sufficiently specified in measurable hypothesis form to encourage anyone to ask the simple scientific question, "Do patients who talk about themselves a great deal in therapy show more improvement than patients who do not refer to themselves as often?" It was not until quite recently that this question was put to the test. In a very carefully balanced study, Truax and Wittmer (1971b) counted the number of nonpersonal references that patients made during therapy sessions. Patients for this study were matched on all factors that might reasonably be expected to influence outcome, including the chronicity and severity of their disturbances. The authors found, indeed, that patients who spent more time discussing themselves and the important other persons in their lives showed greater improvement and shorter hospitalization than those who spent less time in such references and those who received no treatment.

This study merits attention, but not because the results are particularly surprising. They are not; in fact, the results are rather pedestrian and unstimulating, as research articles go. They are important simply because they urge the therapist to realize that chitchat, "pastiming," and other interactions that are sometimes allowed to absorb time in therapy sessions are demonstrably not useful in promoting patient improvement. All therapists should note the conclusions drawn by the authors:

> The findings of this study support the apparent necessity for a patient to delve into his "personal" self. . . . Our findings indicate that the patient is moved toward his goal of successful therapy more effectively through his ability or willingness to talk about himself and others who have meaning for him. . . . Regardless of the methods used, the results of this study indicate that patient personal reference responses should be reinforced by the therapist to shape the patient's verbal activity toward self-disclosure and self-exploration. [p. 302]

One of the problems that arises from the patient's need for self-examination in therapy is that it is often very painful for him to talk about himself or his relationship with others around him. Both in group meetings and individual sessions, the patient will often try to engage the therapist in chitchat, or he may withdraw into a tense silence. The favorite topic of the chitchat pattern is to discuss any other person who is not present: "Say, whatever happened to old Joe Plattle?" The easiest route (and the most tempting) for a therapist to take is to respond good-naturedly, and to become engaged in these exchanges. Or, if prolonged silence occurs, some inexperienced therapists will themselves launch the chitchat boat: "Hmm, well—it ought to be nice for baseball this weekend; right, Mike?"

The therapist who is most empathically attuned to his patient may share the insecure therapist's hesitancy in these situations. He recognizes the discomfort that his patient feels as he keeps moving the patient toward self- and interpersonal exploration. The insecure therapist recognizes *his own* discomfort, and is more content to let an hour elapse in pleasant superficialities. Yet, as virtually every theory of psychotherapy has contended, and as the findings of Truax and Wittmer (1971b) will attest, self- and interpersonal exploration is essential to successful treatment. Therefore, it is the therapist's duty to keep the patient moving toward self- and interpersonal exploration, despite the patient's temporary discomfort. If the therapist at the same time has high levels of the facilitative factors, the discomfort should be slight and short-lived. The therapist will be helpful in reducing the patient's anxiety. He will express his own discomfort when he experiences it. He will communicate his understanding and acceptance of the patient's anxiety, shame, or guilt. Indeed, the experienced therapist's ability to avoid "pastiming" and to guide the patient into self-exploratory areas may be one of the reasons why the research we reviewed in the previous chapter found that experienced therapists were in general more effective than novices. As he gains more experience and confidence, a therapist may become increasingly adept at focusing his involvement upon those areas of discussion that yield the most therapeutic "pay-off."

This is not the only way in which the therapist must often risk his patients' complacency. The same researchers, Truax and Wittmer (1971a), found that "the more the therapist focused on the anxiety source, the greater was the improvement in social effectiveness" (p. 299). In other words, the therapist is again called upon to move into the most painful areas of his patient's experience. He must focus upon those things that are most associated with the patient's anxiety, and which, probably, therefore, cause both the patient and the therapist the most discomfort to discuss.

Again the tendency of the therapist is often to avoid discussing the source of anxiety. The results reported by Truax and Wittmer (1971a) do not show whether high- or low-functioning therapists are most prone to such avoidance. We would suppose that focusing on the anxiety source is somewhat difficult for both types of therapist: for those who are most attuned to their patient's discomforts, as well as for those who are reacting to their own discomfort. The results indicate, however, that it is not helpful to avoid the anxiety source. Again the therapist is called upon to be the strong member of the therapeutic union. He must encourage exploration of the areas in which his patients may often be most resistant.

Here is a typical example of the type of exchange that we have observed between an adolescent patient and her inexperienced therapist.

Patient: Things are goin' pretty smooth now, but this morning in math class I thought I was going to blow it. I got so nervous I just wanted to scream, or run out, or something.

Therapist: In math class. How are things going in your other classes?

Patient: Oh, real good; Miss Beeves—I really like her in English. She treats me nice. But that gym teacher. She expects too much of me—she really does!

Therapist: So overall things are going pretty good?

Patient: Yeah, pretty much.

Therapist: Good, I'm glad things are working out for you.

The therapist here missed two chances to discuss conflict situations. Math class had been a special problem that day for the patient, and apparently she had difficulty in dealing with her physical education teacher as well. The therapist's crucial mistake here was not that he lost the opportunity to discuss these areas. The opportunity still remained, and the therapist could use it at any time in the future. His critical mistake came in not discussing the issues at the moment that the patient gave indications that she was prepared to deal with them.

We have also seen the following example, and several like it, in group sessions with adolescents.

Therapist: You folks look tired and content—like you've had a busy day.

Female Patient: Yeah we've done a lot of things, but old Meantemper here keeps yellin' at people.

Male Patient: I do not! You keep buggin' me!

Therapist: Well, uh. . . . How'd it go at bowling this afternoon?

The more effective therapist will not be afraid to focus on the critical issues in a patient's life. He will meet the unpleasant emotions directly as they arise, just as he does with the pleasant feelings and actions.

In confronting the source of anxiety directly, the therapist does not necessarily have to cause the patient to experience discomfort that is either prolonged or severe. There are two reasons for this. First, a truly empathic and high functioning therapist will not be a threatening adversary for the patient; he will be an understanding and sensitive guide, whom the patient can trust and turn toward for support. Indeed, Truax and Wittmer's (1971a) results support this view; they found that focusing on the source of anxiety combined additively with accurate empathy in promoting patient improvement. Those therapists who both expressed accurate empathy and focused on the anxiety sources produced the most positive outcome in their patients. The poorest outcome was found in cases where both accurate empathy and focus on anxiety were low.

There is a second reason why confronting the source of anxiety need not produce serious pain in the patient: sometimes the patient himself wants to focus on the source of anxiety, and to eradicate the pain that the tension causes him. This is most frequent with clinically normal outpatients who seek to overcome simple specific fears. Wolpe's (1958) procedures were developed, and are probably most effective, for such specific fears. Sometimes such specific fears may be encountered among a group of more generally disturbed psychiatric patients. Often "school phobias" can be treated as simple specific fears of school, and can be reduced in a number of ways. It is probably rare, however, that the disturbed patient willingly initiates discussion of his fears. Often the patient's background has taught him repeatedly that any admission of fears will be interpreted as weakness. In some segments of our society, fears are taboo. To admit them sets a person apart as a strange individual who has unique infirmities. The therapist, then, must be aware that many patients are hesitant in admitting such feelings. He must clearly communicate his understanding and concern, yet steadfastly move in the direction that research tells him is most related to a satisfactory therapeutic outcome.

GROUP PSYCHOTHERAPY

Up to this point we have focused primarily on the factors related to patient improvement in the traditional one-to-one therapist-patient relationship. We can legitimately ask a number of questions about the effectiveness of the facilitative factors in group treatment as well. Unfortunately, however, we will receive very few answers at this point in time. To date, very few studies have been reported on the effective factors in group psychotherapy.

The only study of which we are currently aware (there most certainly will be many forthcoming) that clearly relates the facilitative communication conditions to patient outcome in group psychotherapy is that of Truax, Wittmer, and Wargo (1971). Using several personality scales as the measure of patient change, the authors found that therapeutic change in schizophrenic patients was directly related to the levels of the therapeutic conditions given by their group therapy leaders. Two aspects of this study should receive special attention. First, the experimental procedures provided for a comparison of several levels of the facilitative conditions. This represents a significant advance from the usual research design, which allows comparisons only between the highest- and the lowest-functioning therapists. The different groups showed improvement consistent with the level of facilitative communication shown by the therapist. A second contribution of this study lies in the subjects that were chosen for study. When such a disturbed group responds to the therapeutic communication factors, it is a convincing testimony to the power of these factors. This is particularly impressive, since schizophrenics have been notoriously resistant to non-chemical intervention techniques. As an interesting sidelight, we should note that one of the measures most notably responsive to the facilitative conditions in this study was the "schizophrenia" scale on the MMPI.

Does a therapist's level of functioning influence the ability of his group members to express accurate empathy? Danish (1971) was unable to find such a correlation in a study of T-group (interpersonal sensitivity-training) participants at Michigan State University. He found that none of the following predicted the group members' score on the

Affect Sensitivity Scale, an estimate of empathy: (A) the counselor's accurate empathy, genuineness, and non-possessive warmth; (B) client motivation; and (C) the relationship between the counselor and the group participant. When all these factors were combined, they did lend some amount of predictability to the patient's score, but only a very low degree.

When evaluating this study, we should remember that patient improvement in the usual sense was not at issue. In the first place, the patients were not necessarily "sick" to begin with; they were mainly university-related persons who paid a fee to gain "sensitivity training." Nor is the Affect Sensitivity Scale related in any way that we now know of to "improvement" measures. The results may suggest to us, however, that if it ever becomes one of our goals to help the patient to learn to communicate with others in an empathic way, perhaps we will need to give him specific training in this skill, rather than expecting him to acquire it through osmosis.

A tangential question that comes to mind from this concerns the expectations of outcome for sensitivity groups. If sensitivity training sessions, as they are now conducted, do not improve the members' capacity to experience or to express empathy for another human being, just what are they learning? And how much less are we teaching people in many of our traditional groups, where we often make very little systematic attempt to develop sensitivity skills? Our suggestions here are only tentative. However, if the group therapist who is functioning at a high therapeutic level decides to use sensitivity training techniques, it appears that he should add to his repertoire a specific training period in the skills of communicating accurate empathy. The group members could then practice empathic communication among themselves, on the model provided by the competent therapist.

The marathon is another new and popular innovation

in the group therapy approach. The marathon group consists of eight to eleven people, plus therapist, who engage in group therapy activity, nonstop, for 24–72 hours. Again, there is currently only the most scant evidence of the effectiveness of this approach. One study, by Dies and Hess (1971), however, dissected the operations of a marathon group and found some results that shed a very intriguing light on the application of our therapeutic endeavors. When the authors examined what transpired during marathon groups, as opposed to more traditional group therapies, they found that the marathons were depicted by the discussion of more personal topics, greater interpersonal attraction, and more emotional sharing. If we now relate these findings to the data on facilitative conditions, we can suggest that patients in marathon groups do indeed engage in quite therapeutic activities. As we have indicated, for instance, discussion of personal topics has been shown to contribute to improvement. In addition, we could ask whether increased "discussion of personal topics" in a marathon group is equivalent to what we have been referring to as self-disclosure. If so, perhaps marathon patients are not only working on their own deep, personal feelings and conflicts, but are also acting themselves as good self-disclosing therapists and providing models for similar interaction by the other group members.

Similarly, we could ask if "greater interpersonal attraction" in marathon groups implies greater empathy and/or respect. If so, once again we have evidence that a very therapeutic process is taking place within these groups. Finally, greater emotional sharing could hardly indicate anything other than increased self-disclosure. We could ask if this emotional sharing implies a higher level of empathy and/or genuineness as well. Overall, the interactions that occur in marathon groups appear to be quite compatible with the processes that contribute to effective individual psychotherapy.

Why marathon groups produce these effects is not entirely clear. The most common assumption is that the prolonged activity in the group wears down the sheltering defenses of the participants. They may tend to drop their social facades, and honestly explore their inner experiences. As this happens, people often reveal things about themselves of which they are embarrassed or ashamed. They leave themselves open and vulnerable for attack by the others. However, such attacks are constrained since the other participants, too, are "opening up" about themselves and are likewise as vulnerable, seeking support, not opportunity for attack.

Certainly all these suggestions must be carefully evaluated by future research. Forthcoming studies that emphasize the measurement of changes and improvement in patients will be most crucial. If these proposals are indeed experimentally confirmed, our conclusions will firmly support the speculation of Dies and Hess (1971) that "the marathon may be a superior form of group therapy." It may be superior because it tends to promote those patient behaviors, such as self-exploration and focusing on immediate experience, that have been shown to relate to improvement in psychotherapy. Also, it may help the patients actually to become effective *therapists* for each other. The marathon group may do this by providing a situation that helps to raise the members' levels of empathy, respect, genuineness, and self-disclosure. In fact, the marathon group may promote what we saw as the missing ingredient in sensitivity training, the verifiable improvement of empathic communication between participants.

In spite of these early positive signs in the evaluation of marathon groups, we expect that future research will find several shortcomings in the present procedures. In those instances in which the marathon is thought to be "therapeutic" in and of itself, the practitioners may fail to attach *directionality* to the activities. Here, again, we reiterate one of the major premises of this book: a program of psychotherapy is only effective to the extent that it has, first, a solid basis in facilitative communication, and second, a clear behavioral goal component. With our current lack of follow-up studies on marathon patients, we need to look to future research to determine long-term benefits of these activities. Considering that such groups as now practiced seldom include clear behavioral goals, future evaluations may find them to be only moderately effective in promoting patient improvement. The major theoretical premise of these groups is that the simple experiencing and expressing of emotion leads to the conscious understanding of unconscious material, and that this is beneficial to patient problems (Sager and Kaplan, 1972). This premise does seem to lead to increased therapeutic work by the participants. Possibly an increased emphasis on behavioral goals can make these groups become truly therapeutic vehicles.

Many, if not most, marathon and T-group activities are operated on an outpatient, or private client, basis. The participants, therefore, are at least emotionally stable enough to live and work outside of a psychiatric setting. Whether results such as those we have cited, which are based primarily on comparatively healthy subjects, can be generalized to include more disturbed populations is not certain. The evidence is not yet strong enough for us to advocate that marathon activities be developed in adolescent or child inpatient treatment programs. The problems of the short attention span and low impulse control, both in younger patients and in patients with serious emotional disturbances, would seem to militate against the marathon concept in these cases. Yet the early research does suggest that we should give a thorough hearing to those who would propose that some elements of the marathon approach be incorporated into psychological treatment.

CAN TRAINING HELP?

At this point in our examination of some of the research, it would appear that the novice therapist is in an anomalous situation: he becomes effective only after he has gained much experience. This could be interpreted as meaning that he gains his experience only at the expense of the patients he sees during his professionally formative years. If so, he is actually "practicing" his profession in more than one sense of the word.

If the facilitative conditions are essential to patient improvement, is it possible to train potential therapists in such a way as to raise their initial levels of functioning? As previously noted, this is currently the most critical issue in the field of psychotherapy. If we can find effective ways of training individuals to function at higher levels of therapeutic communication, then the changes needed in the mental health professions can occur within the present professional structure. The psychiatric, psychological, and social work professions will merely need to incorporate potential therapeutic effectiveness into their student-evaluation procedures and measures, and improve their training procedures to raise their initial therapeutic levels. On the other hand, if it is found that specific training in communication skills cannot raise therapists to effective levels of functioning, the implications will be revolutionary. In this situation, only those who have a pre-existing capacity for therapeutic functioning would be accepted for admission to professional training schools. This might mean that such institutions would need to revise their admission criteria completely, and admit many persons who are now seen as academically underqualified.

One early investigation indicates that when we choose those persons who can gain the greatest benefit from training in facilitative communication, we at least will not be forced to discriminate on the basis of sex. Olesker and

Balter (1972) found that males and females were equal in their capacity for empathic feelings, at least as measured on the Affect Sensitivity Scale. Equally important in this study, however, was the finding that individuals tend to show greater empathy toward persons of their own sex than toward persons of the opposite sex. If this finding is broadly applicable, it may suggest that training programs ought to incorporate special training in recognizing and dealing with the particular emotional responses of the opposite sex. Two other alternatives are available, depending on how easily the facilitative conditions can be taught. The first is to accept for training only those persons who show potential for empathic relations with members of both sexes. The second alternative is more drastic: if it is found that people cannot be trained to effective levels of empathy with members of the opposite sex (a rather unlikely probability), then therapists would need to restrict their practice to patients of the same sex. This would, of course, necessitate a drastic change in the male dominance of the therapeutic field.

The finding that therapists' level of empathy changed with differences in patients and over various topics suggested to Moos and MacIntosh (1970) that empathy, rather than being a stable character trait of the therapist, may instead be a modifiable, or teachable, skill. Only a very few researchers have put this to the test. Collingwood (1971) found that although he could improve the communication skills of counselors by providing 10 hours of specific training, the counselors fell back to their pretraining levels within two months. On the other hand, Holder (1969) did not find that such a relapse occurred when he used a 15-hour training program.

Truax (1973) has a nonspecific approach to training and he reports that significant changes appeared in those who underwent such training. His is an approach very similar to group therapy: the task of the members, as well as of the leader, is to practice being warm, genuine, and empathic. Everyone in the group receives periodic formal "feedback" on his performance with respect to the three factors, as well as almost constant informal feedback. Most training techniques aimed at professionals can be quite threatening to the trainees. One protection that Truax's approach gives, at least in theory, is that if all the group participants are striving at all times to raise their levels of warmth, empathy, and genuineness, then the destructive, cold and hurtful communications that occur in many groups will here be kept to a minimum.

MICROCOUNSELING

A new mode of training has been developed by Allen E. Ivey *et al.* (1968). Called "microcounseling," this approach represents an attempt to break down into behavioral units those "skills" that when combined, supposedly constitute the bulk of the communicational activities of a counselor. The following are the skills taught in microcounseling:

ATTENDING BEHAVIOR. This consists of four specific behaviors: eye contact, relaxed posture, "appropriate" gestures, and making comments that derive directly from what the client is saying.

REFLECTION OF FEELING. Here the counselor uses a "feeling" word regarding the client's emotional experience. The microcounseling format assumes that it is more productive to guide the patient's attention to emotional experiences and reactions than to external "facts" and objective information.

PARAPHRASING. As a check on the accuracy of his perception of the content of what the client is saying, the counselor rephrases, in a concise statement, the essence of the client's communication to him.

OPEN INVITATION TO TALK.   The counselor uses open-ended questions, rather than questions that can be answered with one word or phrase.

MINIMAL RESPONSES, IN ENCOURAGEMENT TO TALK.   The emphasis here is on the word minimal. The counselor uses only the most unobstrusive responses to indicate to the client that he is listening, and that he wishes the client to continue. Examples are: "Go on." "Yes." "Tell me more." "Angry?"

SUMMARIZATION.   This combines paraphrasing and the reflection of feeling. It also involves more verbal communication from the counselor than do the other skills. Here the counselor condenses and recapitulates a session or topic, and indicates areas for further exploration.

The microcounseling format is being used at some institutions to train counselors, interviewers, and even patients (Authier and Fix, 1976) in the use of these basic communication skills. If it can be shown that the originators of the microcounseling paradigm have indeed isolated these specific behaviors that differentiate effective (that is, therapeutic) from ineffective counselors, then a major breakthrough has been made in training. Students will no longer be faced with the task of mastering such vague skills as empathy, respect, and so on. Instead, they will only need to practice relatively simple skills. Autheir and Fix (1976) have proposed just this. They suggest that the acquisition of the microcounseling skills can lead to a more rapid mastery of the Truax factors of empathy, genuineness, and warmth, which they believe simply to be "more global skills" of interpersonal communication. The authors have established a group therapy program based on these assumptions, from which they intend to gain more evidence on the relationship between the microcounseling and the facilitative communication systems.

Authier (1972), however, already reports a negative correlation between the use of microcounseling skills and levels of empathy, genuineness, and warmth in a sample of resident psychiatrists. Although he tends to cite problems inherent in the research design and the narrow range of sampled therapists as reasons for his failure to find a positive relationship between the microcounseling and the Truax systems, the fact remains that these have not been shown to be identical, nor as yet even compatible. It does appear that microcounseling is the first major step toward the task of training counselors in precise behavior-specific steps. Perhaps, with a further evaluation of the basic microcounseling skills and their individual relationships with the facilitative communications skills, the work of Ivey *et al.* may ultimately lead to a more precise analysis of the behavioral skills involved in Truax-Carkhuff therapy. An alternative hypothesis, of course, is that training in *any* specific behaviors may have a negative effect on the counselor's learning of facilitative communications skills. The effective therapist may need to be so highly flexible that having to attend to minor behavioral procedures unduly inhibits him.

"PATIENT, TRAIN THYSELF"

Carkhuff (1971) and Vitalo (1971) have looked at training in a slightly different light. Rather than training counselors alone to be more effective communicators, they have urged that *patients* should be trained in the communicative skills. They advocate this approach as a new form of therapy. They have named the new form of treatment simply "training as treatment" (Carkhuff, 1971). To quote from Carkhuff:

> A most direct form of training as treatment . . . is to train the
> client himself in the skills which he needs to function effec-
> tively. The culmination of such a program is to train the
> client to develop his own training programs. To say, "Client,
> heal thyself" and to train him in the skills necessary to do so
> is not only the most direct—but it is also the most honest
> and effective—form of treatment known to man. [p. 127]

A program that incorporates the microcounseling
skills with the "training as treatment" orientation is a
"step-group therapy" program reported by Authier and
Fix (1976). In this approach, the goal of the group therapy
sessions is to train the patients in both the microcounseling
skills and the more complex skills of therapeutic communications, as defined by Truax and Carkhuff (1967). A patient
enters initially into a lower-level group, until he has mastered the elementary skills of attentive behavior (eye contact, attentive postural position, and responsive statements
to other group members). He then progresses to higher
groups, in which more complex skills are taught by lecture,
demonstration, practice, and feedback. The highest groups
practice the very complex skills of accurate empathy,
warmth, and genuineness.

Are these training approaches to treatment effective?
Neither Carkhuff (1971) nor Authier and Fix (1973) have
provided evidence of the clinical effectiveness of these
methods. Vitalo (1971), however, does provide some experimental data from which we can draw a few tentative
impressions on what to expect from the future development of this approach. Vitalo did indeed find that patients
could raise their levels of interpersonal functioning. He
accomplished this with a 15-hour training program.
Heightened levels of effective communication were demonstrated not only in the training sessions themselves, but
also on tape-recorded excerpts of the patients' interpersonal communications on the hospital ward. This increase
of facilitiative communication, however, was not found to

lessen the individuals' internal conflicts as measured by the MMPI. Also, the patients' level of anxiety actually increased as a result of this program. To make things more difficult for the advocates of training, Carkhuff and Griffin (1971) found, in training counselors, that the individuals who functioned at the highest level at the beginning of training were the ones who demonstrated the most gain from training—a "rich get richer" phenomenon.

To summarize, up to this point the jury is still divided on the question of the usefulness of training in the facilitative dimensions of communication. It appears that we can train people to function at higher levels (at least in quite circumscribed situations). On the other hand, as with most human skills, training seems to be most effective for those persons who have the highest preexisting capacities. Also, there is reason to inquire further into the durability of the training that we might give. We still need to know whether the results of training programs, with periodic "refresher" courses, are worth the expense. Might it not still be simpler and less costly to seek out the already high-functioning individuals in our society and give them public status as psychotherapists or counselors? Our society currently attempts to reward its intellectually (or at least academically) most advanced citizens. Perhaps we should consider all the available means of rewarding our most truly advanced therapeutic human beings as well.

As to the use of "training as treatment" with clinic and hospital patients, it still has to be demonstrated that this produces measurable improvement in the patient. It seems reasonable to assume that a person who can communicate to his peers and superiors a higher level of empathy, emotional honesty, and spontaneity will experience less personal emotional disturbance and display less behavioral deviance. Nevertheless, we still do not have evidence that this is true. Also, the evidence indicates that the lowest-functioning individuals tend to gain the least from training.

If this is true, such training might be found to be too difficult, costly, and nonproductive to be useful for the most
disturbed types of patient.

Teaching "Systems" of Psychotherapy

In the training of psychiatrists, clinical psychologists,
and other professionals who deliver counseling services or
psychotherapeutic treatment, academic instruction often
precedes practical application. Traditionally, a theory of
personality functioning or of the causes and mechanisms of
emotional distress is presented, and a technique of therapeutic intervention is described and studied.

On the basis of the studies reviewed in Chapter 2, we
would urge a change in these training systems. The studies
discussed in that chapter indicated that early in their ca-
reers, professionals tended to be at best ineffective, and
often destructive. This was found despite the undisputed
expertise of these novice therapists in the academic, theoretical, and technical aspects of their particular modes of
psychotherapy. It appeared from these studies that as therapists gain more experience, they tend to modify somewhat
their dogmatic adherence to prescribed techniques, and at
the same time, they become more effective therapists. It is
almost as if the formal approaches to treatment stand in the
way of effective therapy.

Our suggestion is that all professional candidates
should be trained in the facilitative communications skills
first, and should receive more technical training only when
they have reached a prescribed level of competence in
these abilities. It appears that it may be quite dangerous to
arm a poor communicator with many theoretical concepts
which he then often uses in a defensive, rigid manner, to
the detriment of the patient.

Yet today, this seems to be precisely what is advocated

by a number of the disciples of the new and popular "therapies." Below are three examples of some of the lower therapeutic responses that have been made by novice therapists who have gained some level of training in Berne's (1961, 1964) basic transactional analysis concepts:

Patient	I've been so upset by my husband's walking
(with	out. I've got a big test at school the day after
much	tomorrow, but I'm not getting any studying
agitation):	done. I keep thinking about our fight, and—
	and—I just can't keep my mind on it.
Therapist:	You can't? You mean you *won't.*
Patient:	Oh, go to hell!

Patient:	Wow. This is the first place I've been able to be open with people. I feel I can trust you all here. With so many other people, I feel so uncomfortable—I try to have them think I'm feeling good, and I just deflect personal questions.
Therapist:	You play games with them.

Patient:	I feel so uncomfortable with you! You come on so superior, as if you're perfect and I'm nothing.
Therapist:	That's the way you choose to perceive it.

The one thing all these responses have in common is that they convey exceedingly low empathy, and little respect for the patient.

Perhaps the more experienced therapist, or the one specifically trained to think in terms of facilitative communication skills, will be able to use the theoretical concepts and the techniques more effectively because of his practical training. We wonder if a reversal of the current theoretical, academic emphasis in training programs could make a significant impact on the quality of the professionals that enter the field.

Summary

While all the methodological problems that beset research in psychotherapy have by no means been solved, the consistency of findings from a number of areas of examination point to facilitative communication as the effective component of all forms of psychotherapy. We have suggested that confrontation may be the critical factor within the facilitative communication skills. It is critical because it gives the patient behavioral guidance. At the same time, confrontation is dangerous; if not used in a warm, empathic context, it is probably destructive to the patient.

Several guidelines can be given to the therapist who wishes to use his facilitative communications skills in the most efficient manner. The therapist must focus on the present feelings of the patient; he must avoid peripheral discussions, and he must focus his attention on those issues that cause the patient the most anxiety.

Less research has been conducted on the results of group psychotherapy, but here, too, the information we have is consistent with a facilitative communications approach. Several methods have been developed to raise the level of functioning on the facilitative communications dimension. While these methods hold promise for raising the effectiveness of therapists, and patients as well, objective evaluations of the results in this regard have so far been mixed.

Part II

OPERANT AND CLASSICAL CONDITIONING THERAPIES

Chapter 5

BEHAVIORAL APPROACHES: OPERANT AND CLASSICIAL CONDITIONING TECHNIQUES

In my animal experiments I dealt with each subject as an individual. During the course of the experiment the conditions were changed continuously in pace with the subject's performance. I learned the fine grain of my organisms's behavior, and as an experimenter I responded to the details of it. Rarely was an animal too deviant to work with. I always looked for the factor responsible for each animal's uniqueness and tried to take it into account. Each pigeon differed in how much grain was necessary for reinforcement to maintain an adequate amount of behavior. The height of the key or lever had to be adjusted for the size of the animal and the transition from one schedule of reinforcement to another was always a unique affair, carefully adjusted to the animal's current performance, even though the general form of the final performance was common to all the animals. [1]

[1]C. B. Ferster. *The transition from the animal laboratory to the clinic.* New York: Paper read at the September meeting of the 1966 American Psychological Association.

"Operant" versus "Classical" Conditioning Approaches

The possible approaches to the changes in human behavior are virtually unlimited when the principles of learning are systematically applied. The student who is being introduced to the behavior modification approaches should be aware, however, that the specific techniques stem from two bodies of research, rather than one, into the principles of how animals and humans learn. This is because scientists for years have held that we learn things through two different basic processes. These elementary processes are both referred to as conditioning (the simplest, most basic mode of learning). One process is identified by Pavlov (1927), and is called classical conditioning. The learning-theory approaches that aim at changing emotions, feelings, impulses, or desires are based on the classical conditioning model. Techniques that aim primarily at changing the overt behavior, and do not incorporate systematic methods of changing underlying feelings, are generally known as the operant conditioning approaches. These stem mainly from the work of B. F. Skinner (1928), who developed the term "operant conditioning" and quantified many of the variables that influence this type of learning.

For many years operant conditioning was thought to be the appropriate method for changing skeletal muscular responses, while the only appropriate means of changing the functioning of the autonomic bodily activities (those processes usually thought to be outside of conscious control, such as digestion, circulation, etc.) was a classical conditioning approach. Therefore Pavlov elicited salivary secretions with various stimuli, and Lowenback and Gantt (1940) used a bell to condition balance reactions of the inner ear. This dichotomy was shattered by Miller's (1969) initial demonstrations that the procedures of operant conditioning were able to produce dramatic autonomic changes. This was one of the hallmark studies in the foundation of the broadening fields of biofeedback and autonomic control. Despite our current inability to maintain a clear distinction between the two forms of conditioning, we note the difference here, because in clinical applications the operant programs are still aimed at overt, countable behaviors, while the classical conditioning methods are applied when the therapist needs a technique with which to attack pervasive emotional reactions.

Classical conditioning has been referred to as "stimulus learning," since in the Pavlovian experiments and later research efforts, the experimental animal that received conditioning did not learn a new response. The animal instead learned only to produce an already existing response in the presence of a new stimulus. Thus Pavlov's dogs, which had habitually salivated at the sight of food, learned to salivate at the sound of a metronome. The dog gave no new response, just the old response in the presence of new signals. Operant conditioning, on the other hand, is sometimes referred to as "response learning," because within this framework the recipient is taught a new response. Thus, among the many behaviors that have been taught through operant procedures, pigeons learn to peck discs of light to obtain food, rats learn to turn a wheel to leave a compartment, and human infants learn to smile in order to gain adult approval.

RULES OF OPERANT PROCEDURES

Five simple rules serve as the basis of any efficient plan aimed at the operant alteration of a patient's life style. These rules will form the basis of any system of behavioral change; regardless of how complex it becomes or how well it incorporates the best aspects of effective psychotherapy and modeling.

Specify

This is the most difficult rule for most novices in behavior modification to apply. If we wish to supply the patient with a behavior, such as going to school, we must state it precisely. If we are to help to eliminate a behavior, such as hitting people, not only must we specify this negative behavior, but we must also specify an alternate, positive behavior. This positive behavior (perhaps stating his feelings, or saying, "I'm angry because . . .") should provide the patient with something he can do at those times when he would ordinarily be engaging in the negative (hitting) behavior.

At first it may seem easy to specify the behaviors that the patient will contract to change. But in actual practices this is an exasperatingly difficult task. All too often it is an attitude or a feeling that the patient, or the people who bring him to us, want to change: "He just doesn't seem to care about anything!" "His self-esteem is very low." "He thinks he is inferior to everyone else." "I'm pretty lonely and unhappy." "My parents and I don't get along." "We just can't communicate with each other." These are common complaints, but they are exceedingly difficult to break down into behavioral terms. Yet if we do not have clear, precise behavioral criteria to work with, we have no way to document accurately the changes or benefits that the patient derives from his contact with us. Nor can we, as the staff of a psychiatric treatment program, be certain that we are consistently working together. We have no way to verify that everyone involved in the patient's care is rewarding the same behavior in the patient.

In behavior modification programs, then, to specify means to make specific and countable descriptions of both the positive and the negative behaviors. We must also specify *consequences,* both good and bad, that will be contingent upon the denoted behaviors. The consequences must be such that they can easily and consistently be given when-ever the behavior is observed. All specified behaviors and consequences should be mutually agreed upon by the psychiatrist and the patient.

Start Small

If we were training dogs to jump hurdles three feet high, we would begin with hurdles only a few inches high. If we are dealing with a school phobic, our first expectation of him may only be that he should approach to within perhaps two city blocks of a school, and then return home. We do not expect perfect behavior or the early achievement of behavioral goals from our patients. We try to give the patient a clear program of simple steps that will lead to the final goals. Ideally, the initial behaviors in this program should be those that the patient already shows spontaneously, so that these can earn early rewards. To "start small" eliminates a number of the chances for failure, and thus makes adherence to the next rule much easier.

Rely Primarily on Positive Reinforcers: Use Negative Reinforcers as Seldom as Possible

When parents (and very often, treatment planners) hope to elicit new activities from the children under their care, their first question is often, "How do I respond if they don't cooperate?" Usually this question means, "What punishment should I impose when he does not do what I expect of him?" While it is important that we know how to respond when the expected performance is not forthcoming, the more important question, and the first one that should be asked, is "What can this person gain by behaving in the planned manner?" Our purpose is to help the person to gain some reward for trying to deal with his world in a new way. At first the reward may be artificial, such as praise for the school phobic who only approaches a school, or a monetary payment to a chronic shoplifter each day that he does not steal. These artificial reinforcers will be phased out, however, as the person nears his goal and begins to experience an increasing number of the "natural" reinforcers that seem to maintain most people's behaviors in our society.

Parents, in particular, often find the concept of payment for good behavior to be repugnant: "Pay him for doing his duty?" "Pay him for doing what *I expect* of him? That's bribery!" But the question need not be a moral or philosophical one. The answers are seen more clearly when the question becomes a pragmatic issue. Does the provision of special rewards for specified behaviors most effectively induce the desired behaviors to occur? Or do alternate methods, such as nagging, threatening, and punishing yield the most successful results?[2] Sallows (1971) has gone a long way toward answering this in his review. He points out that in every study in which a positive reinforcement program was discontinued, and replaced by a "reinstatement of nagging, threatening, yelling, etc., there was an immediate decline in good behavior" (p. 61).

[2]Of course, it is possible to argue rather successfully on a philosophical basis as well. To the parent who complains that he feels he is engaging in bribery when he offers tangible rewards to his child for certain activities, we can summon many of the arguments presented by O'Leary *et al.* (1972), who maintain that the concept of bribery is not applicable here. As these authors point out, bribery usually connotes dishonest influence, or an attempt to urge the bribe-taker to engage in immoral behavior. In this sense, payments made by parents could seldom be considered as bribes. Also, "parents who balk at giving concrete rewards to their children for schoolwork on the grounds that such a procedure is bribery do not regard their paychecks as bribery. Teachers who feel uneasy about trinkets or candy as incentives for achievement regard merit raises in salary for themselves as legitimate. Similarly, teachers who feel that the use of trinkets or candy as reinforcers is ill-advised freely use stars for the same purpose" (p. 1).

At present we know of no better way to induce desired behavior than to arrange for that behavior to meet positive consequences. The available evidence clearly indicates that providing positive consequences for desired behavior is more effective than its opposite, attempting to eliminate undesirable behavior through the application of negative consequences (Clarke, Montgomery, and Viney, 1971; McConaghy, 1972). Clarke, Montgomery, and Viney, who have written an excellent concise review of the research on the effects of punishment, come to the following conclusions on punishment:

It is most likely to produce avoidance of the punishment agent as a first response, and thus to remove the agent as in information-giving source.

It is not effective in suppressing many responses, unless there is a "concurrently available" response that can be rewarded as soon as it occurs.

It often has negative side effects, including social aggression and emotional responses that may disrupt efficient cognitive functioning.

The authors contend that:

> The use of punishment procedures *alone* in an attempt to modify behavior cannot be supported on either theoretical or empirical grounds.[3] It is suggested that behavior modification be carried out wherever possible, (a) by endeavouring to identify and remove the incentive, or motivation for disapproved responses in the expectation that removal of incentive will result in extinction of the responses and, (b) by using reward and modeling techniques that are known to result in reliably predictable, but slower, changes without the unwanted side effects that occur with punishment procedures. [p. 13]

[3]Aversion therapies, which are essentially uniform punishment (sometimes self-punishment) systems, have yielded predominantly negative results, as we note elsewhere in this volume.

Slowly Increase Expectations

As the patient begins to receive the early rewards programmed for him, he is expected to make more gains in order to continue receiving the rewards. He should be informed at the very outset of this increased expectation.

Reassurance

The therapist should reassure the patient from the outset that the program will not move ahead faster than the patient is able to go. Often the patient is fearful of failure; and afraid that people will expect too much of him. The therapist's openness and daily patience may help to sooth these fears. One method of increasing the patient's confidence is to let him set the goals for his behavior each day.

INCORPORATING SOCIAL REINFORCEMENT

Since the orientation we present in this book emphasizes the social interaction aspects of all forms of therapy, one of the most critical questions is how social reinforcers should be incorporated in a systematic fashion into a behavior modification program, and geared to produce the most positive impact. At this point there are no clear and precise answers. What is clear is that social reinforcement must be used to make a behavioral program effective. It has not yet been fully demonstrated precisely how this should be done. A series of studies must be made to evaluate all the potential effects of interaction between tangible and social reinforcers, as well as the *methods* of delivering social rewards such as praise, attention, and so on.

An initial step toward the uncovering of these interaction effects was made in a very elementary investigation by Brown (1971). Although he was working with children,

Brown used a response traditionally reserved for rats (bar-pressing) to measure the effectiveness of his reinforcers. As we would expect, he found that a combination of tangible (candy) and social rewards (in this case, the words "good" and "fine" in reward for a response) produced more response than did either type of reward when used alone. In addition, however, he found that consistent tangible rewards coupled with *intermittent* social rewards were most productive of bar-pressing behavior, and were more effective than the opposite (consistent social reward with intermittent tangible reinforcement). The extinction rates were also very interesting in this study. Tangible rewards were found to be not nearly as effective as the social reinforcers in maintaining the behavior. It was the group who had received only tangible reinforcement that stopped responding most rapidly after the termination of the reward. Not only did the children in this group lessen their rate of response, they actually fell to a level below their original unrewarded base line! The other groups, in contrast, showed slower extinction rates.

Any impulse we might feel to establish a program that is based heavily upon social reinforcement and ignores or under-emphasizes tangible reward systems, however, will be held in check if we note some problems discussed by Sallows (1971). In his review of research on behavior modification in "conduct problem" adolescents, Sallows notes that seventeen studies give evidence that predelinquent or delinquent adolescents and school dropouts apparently are not responsive to social reinforcements provided by adults. Here they differ from most other adolescents, who do respond in a positive manner to the social reactions of adults toward them. Therefore, while we make a strong plea to all those involved in designing and carrying out behavior modification programs that they should emphasize and systematize the disbursement of social reinforcement, we at the same time believe that they should maintain a strong system of *tangible* rewards for those youths who respond best to this. Our task is to pair the social reinforcers with tangible rewards; the goal here is to raise the level of effectiveness of social reinforcements, so that the patient will respond more readily to these both within and outside the behavioral program.

If social reinforcers are to be used effectively, we need to involve in the administration of behavior modification programs people who are able not only to dispense social rewards at appropriate times, but also to enhance the effectiveness of these rewards through their *manner* of delivering them. In a study of a simple response task, with second-graders as subjects, Warren and Cairns (1972) found that the most effective social reinforcers were responses from adults that gave clear information relative to the task. We might assume from this that social rewards are most useful when they are not personally judgmental ("That's a good boy, Johnny!" "You're such an angel!"), but instead are more relevant to the task ("I saw you were being provoked, but you didn't call names or hit anyone. Good job." "You are sitting attentively at your desk, just like you are all ready to do the schoolwork this morning. Your pencils will need to be sharp.")

Even more important in the delivery of social reinforcement will be the personal qualities of the individuals who are working with the patients. It is here that we feel the fields of psychotherapy, behavior modification, and behavior modeling (see Chapter 6) unite in a complementary relationship. We expect that the essential factors in effective social reinforcement will be found to be very similar to those factors of communication that have been shown to provide effective psychotherapy. Whether in a psychotherapy session or in the delivery of social reinforcement in a behavioral modification program, people are communicating with each other. We see no reason to believe that what constitutes effective communication in one instance will not be found effective in another.

AN ILLUSTRATIVE CASE: LANCE G.

Lance was a tall 14-year-old boy, quiet, unassuming, nervous, and uncertain. During the previous year he had developed a difficulty at school that had led his parents to bring him in for treatment. Each day Lance would enter the classroom, and he was able to remain there for about 15 minutes. At the end of this time he became dizzy and nauseous. His hands perspired and his pulse rate increased. On most occasions Lance would jump up and bolt out of the door, usually to go into the lavatory and gag. This whole routine was extremely upsetting to the teachers and school administrators, and after several weeks of this, Lance was told not to return to school until he had received psychiatric help.

Lance was placed in a class in the adolescent unit of a psychiatric hospital, but was given a special program for his problem. The psychologist on the case talked to Lance at length about the difficulties he had in school, and then asked whether Lance felt that he could survive satisfactorily in the classroom for five minutes. Lance responded affirmatively, stating that his symptoms seemed quite controllable until about 15 minutes had passed. Lance's teacher in the hospital classroom was very helpful, and developed a daily lesson for Lance that could be completed in just five minutes. Lance was to do his assignment, have it signed by the teacher, then bring it into the psychologist's office for examination. After this Lance was excused from school for the rest of the day. He was allowed to engage in any activity that he desired during the day. He could visit the adult patients or the staff. He could play ping-pong, watch television, read, or even go shopping on occasion (if he was accompanied by a staff member).

In Lance's eyes, the trip to the psychologist's office each day was probably just a ritual that made official his status as having completed his lesson for that day. From the psychologist's standpoint, the more important purpose was

to administer strong social rewards during this contact with
Lance. The psychologist constructed a large graph, which
he taped to the wall, and each day, with obvious great
pleasure and much commotion, he plotted on the graph the
amount of time that Lance had spent in the classroom.

When Lance's daily performance had been adequately
charted, the psychologist asked Lance what his target
would be next day; this often lowered Lance's overenthusiastic objectives.

Lance attended school for 10 minutes on the second
day, 15 minutes on the third day, 20 minutes on the fourth
day, 30 minutes on the fifth day, and 40 minutes on the
sixth day. When he had reached the 40-minute mark, he
stated that the last few minutes of that period had required
a very great effort, and that he had again begun to feel some
aspects of his symptoms. Yet he was still optimistic, and did
not want to lose the progress that he had shown. He therefore remained at the 40-minute level for three successive
days, until he decided that he could once again increase his
target.

As Lance became more confident, his progress ac-
celerated. At the end of one month he was attending a full
schedule of classes every day. He was observed on this full
schedule for another week, and then discharged. Six-
month and one-year follow-ups have shown that Lance is
maintaining his successful school attendance. His grades
are above average, which is considered quite good in view
of his Wechsler I.Q. upon initial intake (108). Discussion
with Lance's teachers indicate that he has shown normal
adjustment, and no evidence of the previous symptoms has
been found.

In addition, neither Lance nor his parents report any
new symptoms. In fact, Lance reports feeling happier and
more self-confident, both at school and at home.

It might seem that the psychologist would find it difficult to show enthusiasm for a boy who is attending school

for only 15 minutes a day. In absolute terms this is probably correct, since the psychologist in this case admitted that he was not particularly pleased with the behavior of an adolescent who attended school for such a brief time. He was able to show genuine enthusiasm and excitement, however, over the *improvement* that this boy was showing. Fifteen minutes in a classroom was an improvement of 300% over Lance's original accomplishment of five minutes per day. When improvement, rather than absolute performance, is the basis, praise or recognition comes easily and with genuine feeling.

CLASSICAL CONDITIONING TECHNIQUES: SYSTEMATIC DESENSITIZATION

We will analyze the theoretical underpinnings of the classical conditioning approaches in Chapter 7. Here we will briefly describe the major techniques. The first is systematic desensitization (as presented by Wolpe, 1958).

Systematic desensitization has mainly been applied to persons who suffer from unrealistic fears, but it has also been used to counter many uncomfortable emotions. The technique is designed to teach (or condition) an emotional response that is incompatible with the person's usual (but unwanted) emotional response. Since "relaxation" is thought to be incompatible with most disagreeable emotions, such as fear or anger, it is this response that the patient typically learns.

In the case of a very fearful patient, for example, the therapist first takes very careful notes with the patient, attempting to pinpoint and specify as precisely as possible the things that cause him anxiety. The therapist wants to know all about the features of the feared situations that seem to be most distressful to the patient. The therapist then organizes the patient's impressions of the feared ob-

ject or situation into a *fear hierarchy,* from the most innocuous to the most frightening scene that the person can
imagine. Therapy ultimately consists of getting the patient
to imagine the scenes individually, while in a relaxed state;
he moves on to a more stressful scene only after a less
stressful image no longer causes him any anxiety.

Relaxation is typically induced thus: the patient re-
clines on a couch or lounge chair, while the therapist in a
monotonous voice chants instructions to "relax . . . just
relax . . . let your whole body relax . . . more . . . and more.
. . . Feel the tension drain from your muscles as they relax
. . . relax." Various muscle groups of the body are tensed,
then relaxed. The assumption is that as he feels the tension
leave these muscles, the patient will learn to recognize the
sensation of relaxation more readily, and he will be better
able to react with this set of responses, rather than with
tension responses, in situations that he formerly found
stressful.

Implosive Therapy: "This Is Going to Hurt Me Worse than You"

Implosive therapy, or "flooding" as it is now generally
called, illustrates the current inability of solid theory to
keep up with expanding behavioral technology. The treatment has gained its current title because it involves a flooding of the individual with anxiety (Stampfl and Lewis,
1967), so that the anxiety "extinguishes" (that is, stops
occurring in the presence of a previously feared object or
situation). This rationale, you will note, is just the opposite
of the rationale behind systematic desensitization, which
has as its purpose the induction of a state of relaxation that
is incompatible with a high level of anxiety. Initially, the
existence of two distinctly opposed techniques that ostensibly stem from the same body of research might seem em-

barrassing to the learning theory on which these techniques are found. The similarities between flooding and systematic desensitization are greater, however, than one might realize at first glance. Both, for example, use visualization as the nuclear procedural strategy. Also, both "start small" in terms of the degree of anxiety, and progress to increasingly stronger doses.

In flooding, the therapist maintains an ongoing account of the scenes that the patient is to visualize. He begins by describing a common scene in the individual's life, and then slowly introduces minor elements of the feared object or situation. Ultimately, in a crescendo of descriptive imagery, the therapist bombards the patient with the most total immersion in the phobic situation that his ingenuity can devise. In desensitization, of course, the pattern of imagining the phobic object is similar in one important respect: the order of presentation proceeds from an innocuous beginning to an intense finale. The major difference is that in desensitization, the patient is exposed to a more intense visualization of the feared entity when he expresses a readiness to accept such exposure without his normal anxiety, while in flooding, the aim is to proceed beyond the point at which the patient is comfortable.

In flooding, the patient is deluged with the most overwhelming imaginary contact possible with his feared objects. The underlying theory is that if the patient undergoes this anxiety without the possibility of escape, but also without suffering actual harm, the anxiety will be extinguished. The individual is supposedly incapable of maintaining intense anxiety over a lengthy period of time; therefore the anxiety must eventually decrease. An analogy might be made with the dogs studied by Solomon and Wynne (1953; see Chapter 7). Once these animals had been conditioned to fear a bell, they never learned that the bell could no longer hurt them—so long as escape was possible. Extinction of the fear never occurred when the animal was able to leave the fear-producing situation. Theoretically, fear would necessarily diminish if the dog were shut in with the harmless bell. Baum (1966, 1969a, 1969b) did just this with rats; he prevented their avoidance of a stimulus they had learned to fear. He showed that prevention of the response does lead the animal to stop responding with avoidance when it again gains the opportunity to do so. Such extinction of the response is more effective the longer response prevention is administered; and the lighter the original trauma that caused the avoidance response. Since it is impractical to enclose humans in fear-provoking situations, and since humans have a capacity that animals lack (that is, the ability to visualize) the implosive technique offers the closest analogue to an enclosure procedure. Implosive therapy uses only the imagination to administer response prevention.

Flooding requires a strong patient, and maybe an even stronger therapist! Many therapists find this form of therapy repugnant. The therapist needs to be capable of creating some of the most horrible fantasies imaginable, and he needs to be a vivid describer of the fearful imagery. Few would describe the therapist's role as fun.

AVERSION THERAPY: "THIS IS GOING TO HURT YOU WORSE THAN ME"

An opposite approach to those based on the rewarding of positive behaviors is seen in those techniques that apply obnoxious or aversive stimuli to the individual each time he engages in a behavior that he and the therapist want to eliminate. The theory behind such treatment holds that if the undesired response is often enough associated, in reality or fantasy, with a negative event, the impulses or stimuli that lead to the undesired behavior will come to elicit fear, nausea, or repugnance. You can recognize the hazy outline of the counterconditioning paradigm in this: If the sight of a seminude male (conditioned stimulus) brings arousal (conditioned response) in the homosexual man, then if a picture of a seminude male is paired with an electric shock (unconditioned stimulus), fear should ultimately replace sexual arousal as the response to the stimulus. Aversion therapy has had major applications in the areas of sexual deviance (see, for example, McConahy, 1972), alcoholism (Wallerstein, 1957), smoking (Carlin and Armstrong, 1968), bedwetting (Mowrer, 1938), and self-damaging behavior in autistic children (Lovaas and Simmons, 1969). The aversive stimuli have included nausea-producing drugs (Wallerstein, 1957), electric shocks (Lazarus, 1965), loud noise (Azrin *et al.*, 1968), and stale cigarette smoke blown into the face (Lichtenstein *et al.*, 1973).

COVERT SENSITIZATION

There is, however, one form of aversion therapy that does not require actual physical abuse of the patient. This is covert sensitization, a technique that is apparently very similar to systematic desensitization in its general theoretical rationale and method of application. Covert sensitization, as developed by Cautela (1966, 1967), includes the same relaxation procedures as are used in systematic desensitization. When he has relaxed thoroughly, the patient visualizes himself as engaged in the undesirable behavior that he seeks to change. As he imagines himself performing such activities as drinking alcohol, smoking, or engaging in a homosexual encounter, the patient is told also to visualize a horrible consequence, such as becoming violently ill, nauseous, and vomiting. The theory is that a connection is thus made in the patient's mind between the undesirable behavior and nausea, which reduces the individual's desire to engage in the "sensitized" behavior.

SUMMARY

Classical conditioning techniques are generally used to change pervasive emotional reactions, while operant conditioning procedures are used to change overt, countable behaviors. While the techniques used to implement the two forms of conditioning are quite distinct, the difference between the underlying conditioning mechanisms themselves may not be as great as was once thought.

There are five rules in the clinical application of an operant conditioning approach:

1. Clearly specify the behavior.
2. Make progress in small steps forward.
3. Rely primarily on positive reinforcers. Use negatives sparingly.
4. Increase expectations slowly.
5. Reassure the patient, and inform him of all the plans.

Social reinforcement needs to be paired with tangible reinforcers, so that the new behavior will be maintained.

Classical conditioning therapies include systematic desensitization, which gradually helps the patient to overcome fears; implosive therapy, in which the patient is flooded with anxiety of the feared situation until that anxiety is extinguished; aversion therapy, in which an aversive stimulus is given each time the patient engages in the behavior he wants to eliminate; and covert sensitization, in which the patient systematically pairs persistent negative events with the undesired behavior in his imagination.

In chapter 7, we will examine the research on the effectiveness of the classical conditioning techniques.

Chapter 6

THE OPERANT TECHNIQUES: SOME SELF–ENGENDERED MYTHS

If the science of human behavior has taught us one thing, it is that rearing, training, and teaching can be imposed on no one. The recipient is a partner, and his uniqueness insures the richness of diversity. [1]

. . . if a therapist acts deliberately to alter the behavior of person A for the sake of person B, he may be placing himself in an ethically indefensible position. [2]

. . . if they use behavior modification procedures in (a penal) institution, the inmate should have the right to decide whether or not he wants them. He should be told exactly what the goals are—as a matter of fact, he should help determine or completely determine the goals and procedures. [3]

[1] Harriet L. Rheingold. To rear a child. *American Psychologist,* 1973, *28:* 42–46 (p. 46).

[2] Harold B. Pepinsky and Naomi M. Meara. Student development and counseling. *Annual Review of Psychology,* 1973, *24.*

[3] Montrose Wolf. "This little girl won't interact with other little girls and she crawls around a lot." A conversation about behavior modification with Montrose M. Wolf by Kenneth Goodall. *Psychology Today,* 1973, 7 (June), pp. 64–72 (p. 72).

Shortcomings of Operant Behavioral Approaches

The rules we have presented for the application of the operant principles to individual patients seem easy to remember and to apply. This may be one of the reasons why the behavioral approaches have gained such a wide acceptance in recent years. When we attempt to apply these rules to specific cases, however, we often find out how difficult it is to "make behavior modification work." For many reasons the rules are often quite difficult to follow, and the effectiveness of the best of programs is not guaranteed. As you read the following discussion of the weaknesses of operant behavioral treatment methods, you may gain a deeper understanding of why we do not advocate the use of operant behavioral approaches to the exclusion of other treatment methods. We see the value of operant behavioral programs as lying in their use as efficient *supplemental* tools, to be used in a joint venture by the therapist and patient in the context of a total program of well-defined therapeutic methods. We do not advocate the use of a behavior modification system as the single basic component of a treatment program.

The Difficulty of Defining Precisely the Target Behavior

Regardless of the extent of the background data available on a patient, it is seldom simple or straightforward to choose the most important behavior to be dealt with and specify it so clearly that all members of the staff can readily recognize it each time it occurs. Usually even the patient and those who know him best are unaware of or vague about the specific acts that they would like to see changed. Only rarely can the patient give a straightforward account of the behaviors that lead to trouble for him. Parents, spouses, or relatives may complain, "I don't know what's wrong with him lately. I know something is bothering him terribly. He doesn't have many friends any more, although he could have—he's very likable when he wants to be. He just doesn't seem to care any more. He's actually very cooperative around the house and he doesn't cause us any trouble, but we hate to see him not enjoying life." These expressions of concern probably refer indirectly to many behaviors that might be dealt with, but we will need to help the patient and his relations to become more specific and to discuss the problems in behavioral terms if we are to engage in a program of behavioral change. Even if the family members do give us the information we are seeking, however, we must still decide which behaviors will be the initial targets for treatment. Should we begin by rewarding the patient each time he smiles? Or each time he is found engaging in social interchanges? Or should we help him to engage in more discourse with his spouse or parents, so that they no longer see him as troubled and uncommunicative? Should we reward him for staying out of his bedroom on the basis that people interpret the act of being "alone in the bedroom" as lonely withdrawal behavior? Should we reward this person for engaging in new or expanded activities or hobbies for which he has special talents? Where should treatment begin, and what should be the goals?

Sometimes we are presented with a case in which the target behavior seems well defined: "This boy is always fighting. The school people have kicked him out for numerous fights, and now they won't take him back." But even then, we can miss the crucial behaviors entirely. Our first impulse, of course, is to impose an operant program on his "hitting" behavior. Any instance of hitting another person will be followed by a specific consequence such as removal from all social contact for a time, while any instance in which the patient when under provocation does not hit a person will gain a reward. Such a program, however, is based on the assumption that the patient *starts* his fights by hitting people. After weeks of observation it might be found that in fact it is the boy's sarcasm or disdainful, taunting remarks that evoke aggression from his peers. So even in what at first appears to be a straightforward target for behavior modification, the key behavior can be missed. In an institutional setting, there is a high risk that the key behavior in this type of problem will be overlooked for a long period of time. In such surroundings the patient is under the watchful eyes of the staff for most of the day, and hence the aggression that usually follows his agitation outside the hospital is likely to be inhibited.

The task is not finished when the therapist has effectively isolated the critical behavior to be handled. He must then attach a specific consequence to the behavior, and he must make certain that every staff member in contact with the patient is fully aware of the conditions that have been established.

THE CRITICAL BEHAVIOR MAY OCCUR ONLY RARELY

The problem of modifying a behavior that occurs infrequently is a substantial one for the operant approaches. Suicidal attempts, running away by children or adolescents, fighting, and precipitously quitting jobs are among the behaviors that, because of their seriousness and high emotional impact in the community, often precipitate requests for psychiatric treatment. Yet each of these behaviors may have been demonstrated only a few times, or even just once, by the individual involved. It is clear that we cannot instigate shaping procedures for such behaviors. We must use reinforcers that can be quickly implemented, and are strong enough to prevent the behavior from recurring at all. Our rules on starting small, increasing expectations, and so on, are somewhat irrelevant in such instances. So once again, even when we have a clear-cut behavioral manifestation to which to apply our techniques, we find that the standard operant procedures should not be used as the sole method of the treatment thrust.

CRITICAL DEVIANT BEHAVIOR IS OFTEN SITUATION-SPECIFIC

Very often the deviant behavior that brings an individual into psychiatric treatment is never seen within the psychiatric setting. It is produced and maintained by the home, school, or neighborhood environment, and is not manifested when the precipitating conditions are removed. In such cases, while operant conditioning may be indicated for the relatives or teachers, operant procedures are unnecessary in the psychiatric setting. When there are no symptoms, we need not aim treatment at symptom relief.

Behavior modification is sometimes used in slightly artificial form in those situations where the home environment cannot be changed. "Controlled provocation" situations are sometimes set up within treatment programs; they are designed to incorporate the critical elements of the outside environment to which the patient responds with deviant behavior. In this contrived situation, regular operant procedures are used to help the patient to relinquish his deviant responses and substitute healthier, more effective actions.

MUCH DEVIANT BEHAVIOR IS SECRETIVE

The individual who shoplifts may have a number of successful thefts before he is caught. His secretive behavior thus gains several positive reinforcements, which may also remove that behavior largely out of the realm of effective attack by operant procedures.

TREATMENT IS SOMETIMES SLOW AND OFTEN EXPENSIVE

Careful adherence to the rules for behavior modification often results in a slow and expensive form of treatment. This is not a criticism of behavior modification programs alone; the research that we have presented indicates that other forms of treatment are likewise expensive, and may be less likely to show positive results. We simply wish to counterbalance the impression often conveyed by behavior modification enthusiasts, that these approaches to psychiatric treatment are quick, easy, and efficient in terms of time and expense.

In reality, if we carefully follow the rules presented here, the demand on staff time and ingenuity is profound. If we "start small" and move forward in slight increments each day, we are not offering any "quick cure." The outcome may be more certain and more easily measured, but it is questionable that these programs will be found to be significantly shorter than other forms of nonmedical treatment systems.

Part of the problem is that by "starting small" in attacking specific behaviors, we cannot always make large general changes in life styles in a short time. Often we must work with small portions of the behavioral pattern of the individual, and move on to more general conduct patterns only when he has progressed to a level at which he can deal with these more complex behavioral tendencies.

This takes time, and for each behavioral program much staff attention and consistency is needed. We find, then, that programs of operant behavior modification can be extremely costly. They also occasionally demand prolonged periods of work to produce the desired changes. Behavior modification is no panacea, and so far as we can tell, it does not require less professional, subprofessional, or patient time than other treatment programs; and, much as is found with other modes of treatment, the patient who initially has the lowest problem level will probably be the one who responds with the greatest or most rapid improvement.

Motivation Is a Factor

As we have pointed out, we do not have total control over the patient's life; hence we must rely on the patient's motivation for change to make the program effective. Motivation is known to be a key factor in the outcome of all therapy (Luborsky, 1971), and behavior modification approaches are probably no exception (Lazarus, 1963; Levin et al., 1968). Granted, we can influence the person's motivation. We can point out to him the consequences that his behaviors are currently eliciting. We can attempt to impress upon him the opportunities he has for a "better life" in the form of postive day-to-day consequences from his activities. Similarly, we can model for him life styles that will effectively meet the needs of our program. Yet we do not have the skills or the technology at this point to induce full utilization of a behavioral program in every case.

Failure to Show Generalization

The evidence is very slim that the patient will carry over his newly learned behavioral skills as he moves from the behavior modification programs into more natural settings. Most of the studies show a definite relapse to the old behavior patterns, or even in some cases deterioration to worse patterns, after the patient's departure from the behavioral program (Sallows, 1971). This again is a critical shortcoming of the operant approaches. While these techniques have shown efficacy in changing behavior within the domains of the programs themselves, it is the patient's behavior in the community, in the home, school, or work setting, that should be the ultimate target of any therapeutic approach.

Parents, relatives, or teachers who will be involved with the patient are often given special training in behavioral contingencies (for example, see Stuart, 1971). The hope behind such training is that it will ensure the transfer of the patient's newly acquired behavior from the treatment program to the community. There have not yet been enough reports to evaluate the effectiveness of these attempts (Sallows, 1971). One study was conducted (Walker and Buckley, 1972); it yielded no evidence that training regular classroom teachers in behavior modification techniques prior to the return of pupils from a special classroom behavior modification program was any better than leaving the teachers untrained. The researchers discovered that the most effective method of dealing with these "problem" children was to establish a very precise and thoroughly structured system of rewards within the new classroom. When and how such children could be weaned from such a behavior modification system remains unclear.

Mental health professionals seldom have strong control over the human patient, but even when more than usual control is available, behavior modification programs have often failed to induce behavioral change that extends beyond the controlled situation (O'Leary and Becker, 1967; Meichenbaum, Bowers, and Ross, 1968; Patterson and Gullion, 1968; Broden *et al.,* 1970; Lapuc and Harmatz, 1970). When behavior modification techniques were initiated to improve behavior in an afternoon classroom, the students showed no improvement in a morning class that did not have a systematic behavior modification program (O'Leary *et al.*, 1969). In rather dramatic fashion, Meichenbaum, Bowers, and Ross (1968) report a similar study in a program for delinquent girls. The investigators found that while the girls responded positively to a token classroom program, their behavior became *worse* in a non-token classroom. The girls virtually extracted control over the program, and in essence told their instructors, "If you don't pay us, we won't shape up" (p. 349).

YET BEHAVIORAL MODIFICATION LIVES IN THE HEARTS OF US ALL

It is a sad commentary, but researchers have convincingly shown that when a clear behavioral program is not in effect for patients, the staff tend to an alarming extent actually to reward "sick" or deviant behavior (Gelfand, Gelfand, and Dobson, 1967; Beuhler, Patterson, and Furniss, 1966). Yet it is ostensibly the goal of the treatment program to eliminate these precise behaviors. Of course, psychiatric treatment programs are not the only places in which negative behaviors are inadvertently rewarded. Parents, too, have been found unwittingly to reward negative behavior in their children in a very similar manner (Wahl *et al.*, 1967; see Table 1).

It is not that the psychiatric staffs and the parents desire to maintain the disturbed behavior. The situation is far more subtle than that. Much deviant behavior almost automatically gains attention: the person who whines or complains in a group will probably gain far more attention than all the more rational members put together. A person who adopts a sad, hurt expression will usually gain more sympathy and emotional support than one who does not advertise his suffering. The individual who casts an image of helpless dependence will elicit more assistance from well-meaning

Table I A Comparison of the Responses of Parents to Children's Behaviors (Wahl, et al., 1971) and Nurses to Patients' Behaviors (Gelfand, et al., 1967)

	Percent of Parents' Reactions that were:		
	Positive	Negative	Neutral
Child's behaviors were deviant (Wahl)	42	19	38

	Percent of Nurses' Reactions that were:		
	Positive	Negative	Neutral
Patient's behaviors were deviant (Gelfand)	26	8	66

	Percent of Parents' Reactions that were:		
	Positive	Negative	Neutral
Child's behaviors were nondeviant (Wahl)	68	3	29

	Percent of Nurses' Reactions that were:		
	Positive	Negative	Neutral
Patient's behaviors were nondeviant (Gelfand)	61	5	34

Nurses, it appears, react to behaviors in about the same manner as do parents of non-clinically-deviant children, except that nurses tend to ignore all behaviors slightly more. Nurses tend to ignore deviant behavior significantly more than do parents. An inspiring finding in terms of behavior modification approaches is that people do seem to be attuned to nondeviant behavior and tend to respond to it positively. The tragedy is that deviant behavior is actually rewarded a significant portion of the time.

people than the individual who does not ask for unnecessary help. Yet, for patients who are striving toward independence, autonomy, and the use of their own good judgment on their own behalf, these spontaneous reactions too often work directly against these goals, reinforcing behavior patterns that are incompatible with skills of interpersonal competence. A contingency program *is* needed to direct staff behavior in ways that will help the patient toward his objectives, rather than hindering him.

The question then becomes, "What is the most effective method of establishing such a contingency program?" The previous chapter provides basic guidelines toward an answer to this question, and for maximum effectiveness, these guidelines must be followed. Still, how are we to cope with the problems that we have just discussed? We believe that a crucial variable has generally been overlooked. This variable probably affects the results of operant treatment programs, and can help to overcome many of the shortcomings of pure operant approaches. The variable is that of facilitative communication, the keystone of the psychotherapy we have discussed in earlier chapters. To understand how human communication probably affects the results of all operant programs, we must look backward over the history of the development of operant therapies, and examine some of the myths that accompanied the emergence of operant conditioning out of the laboratory and into the psychiatrist's office.

THE GROWTH OF BEHAVIOR MODIFICATION MYTHS

In many quarters there is strong mistrust and sometimes open hostility toward the basic concepts of behavior modification (Tharp and Wetzel, 1969). As we will show, this may have arisen from some of the early uses of these techniques, which were, if not outright inhumane, at least somewhat callous to the underlying feelings of the human patients involved. These early applications of behavioral treatment approaches fostered a number of myths to which the behavior modification techniques are often tied in the minds of many persons newly entering the field.

Part of the task of this chapter is to shed a new light on some of the probable roots of these myths. The remaining task is to note how corrections of the early misuses can lead to the use of behavior modification techniques in ways that most readers will accept as humane, ethical, and completely acceptable to the patient himself.

The principles that underlie the behavior modification approaches evolved out of laboratory experiments with animals, and particularly with rats; this is the source of both the greatest strengths and the greatest weaknesses of the orientation. The strengths lie in the fact that for the first time, the foundations of a psychiatric therapeutic technique have evolved not from hunches and guesswork, but from tested and verifiable principles, in which the influence of several factors upon behavior could be measured. The weaknesses seem to lie in the overgeneralization of findings on animals to human clinical activities. With these overgeneralizations came the often justified complaint that human rights and dignity were being abused.

When behavioral control was taken out of the laboratory and into the clinic, the transition was not made smoothly. The first clinical approaches were still essentially animal-oriented. Techniques meant for laboratory animals were applied to human beings; this led to what we call the "bludgeon approach" to behavior modification, which we feel typified many of the programs of the 1950s and early 1960s.

One aspect of the bludgeon approach was the early reliance primarily on material, or tangible, items as rewards or "positive reinforcers" of human behavior. Therefore we see Fuller (1949), in the first published application of Skinner's principles of operant conditioning with a human patient, using a warm sugar-milk solution to reward a vegetating retarded youth for various body movements. Lindsley and Skinner (1954) and Lindsley (1956, 1960) were tied so closely to the animal studies that they provided tangible rewards to evoke bar-pressing responses in psychotic patients and normal persons. The bar-pressing response had been so scientifically productive with rats that it was naturally used to study human behavior. To be sure, these studies were not thought of as therapeutic techniques, but merely as theoretical explorations. They were designed to demonstrate operant conditioning procedures with psychotics and normals. Nevertheless, studies like these set the tone for future applications, in which there was a marked tendency to ignore the essential differences between the lower animals and human beings. To make their patients more desirous of the tangible rewards that they planned to administer, Peters and Jenkins (1954) deprived them of sugar. This move was based on the assumption that the patients would then work harder (in ways defined by the "therapist") for sugar rewards. A subtle (but never stated) underlying assumption of these investigations was that patients were to be shaped in the direction desired by the "therapist," and that proper manipulation of their environment would control their behavior. It is this implication of control that so many critics of behavior modification condemn.

There are other forms of reward than the merely tangible, however, even though laboratory rats are not nearly as responsive to them. Social rewards are an example. While many of the researchers writing during the "bludgeon" period (for example, Bachrach, 1964) hinted that social reinforcers could be used, psychiatrists and psychologists as a group did not generally attempt to use them systematically. The basic reason for this seems to be that the professionals had no way to count, measure, or distribute social rewards in a consistent, programmed manner. They were able to count bits of food, hours in bed, cigarettes, and so on; hence the tangible pay-off systems became the backbone of behavior modification programs. But, as O'Leary *et al.* (1972) have claimed, "programs . . . which utilize tangible reinforcers, are probably one of the most misused therapeutic procedures developed with the behavioral framework" (p. 1).

A second characteristic of the bludgeon approach exists more in the popular conception of behavior modification programs than in actual clinical application. This is the use of negative reinforcement, or punishment. Although laymen sometimes carry a stereotyped vision of the behavioral practitioner as an expert in the use of noxious control mechanisms on patients, in fact the reported application of painful or aversive stimuli is low. "Aversive therapy," as any approach is termed that attempts to eliminate an undesirable behavior through the application of an undesirable consequence, has been used extensively only with enuresis and the sexual perversions (McConaghy, 1972). Also, in the latter case, aversive stimulation has been administered only with the patient's permission (or else it has been self-administered). The early applications of an aversive form of treatment to undesired behaviors were the use of chemical agents to produce nausea in alcoholics (for example, see Wallerstein, 1957) and the more widely used "pad and bell" technique to eliminate bedwetting (Mowrer, 1938). The most notorious aversive stimuli are the electrical techniques, in which a painful electric shock is administered to the patient each time he performs the undesired behavior. We will not present all of the reported applications here, but a representative sample of the behaviors that have been treated through the systematic application of electric shock, as reported in the literature, includes homosexual impulses (McConaghy, 1969); alcoholic drinking (Hsu, 1965; Vogler, Lunde, Johnson, and Martin, 1970; Vogler, Lunde, and Martin, 1971); fire-setting by a deteriorated schizophrenic (Royer, Flynn, and Oscada, 1971); exhibitionism (Evans, 1967); transvestism and fetishism (Marks and Gelder, 1967); hallucinations (Bucher and Faricatore, 1970; Weingaertner, 1971); and psychosomatic cough (Alexander *et al.*, 1971).

Many of the reports on the uses of external aversive stimuli are single-case studies, and do not involve the treatment and evaluation of large groups of patients. This again indicates that such techniques are little used at this time. Despite the low number of applications, however, their notoriety in the public eye sometimes makes these treatments appear more important and more widely used than in fact they are.

At this point in the development of the aversive procedures, we do not advocate their use in the treatment of psychiatric patients. There are two major reasons for this: first, with the exception of the treatment of enuresis, the evidence for the effectiveness of aversive treatment programs is not yet convincing (McConaghy, 1971); and second, these modes of treatment may have disturbing and potentially dangerous side effects, including aggression, hostility, and negativism (Rachman and Teasdale, 1969; Ulrich, Hutchinson, and Azrin, 1965; Rachman, 1965).

Overdependence on material rewards and the extensive use of negative reinforcers are manifestations of our hypothetical "bludgeon approach" to behavior modification. Both, we feel, reflect the roots of these procedures in the animal laboratories, and they both also reflect the lack of proper care in the generalization of findings on behavior control from lower mammals to human beings. Here, then, because of the need to distinguish clearly what type of patient we are dealing with, whether rat or human, we offer an accurate (although somewhat facetious) list of "the known differences between rats and humans." Careful consultation of this list will help the practitioner to avoid the inhumane methods that are believed to be often used in behavioral modification programs with human patients.

KNOWN DIFFERENCES BETWEEN RATS AND HUMANS

Basically, the problems of generalization of behavioral data between species are simple—one cannot generalize, but one must. If the competent do not wish to generalize, the incompetent will fill the field. [4]

1: Total Control

Except in the most highly structured prisons, one human being seldom has control over another's behavior to a fraction of the extent that a scientist has control over the laboratory rat. Today the experimental rodent can live its entire lifetime without ever experiencing any part of the world outside of its own laboratory room. This room may have only artificial light, and the temperature and humidity may be controlled and unchanging from the animal's birth to his death. Precise regulation of food and water intake and of social and sexual contacts can also be maintained. Control over the environments of human beings has seldom approached such absolute dimensions, even in the most tightly closed "disturbed" wards of some early psychiatric hospitals. The concern about "behavioral technicians" who exert strong control over their patients' behavior—or even "mind control," as some critics have feared—applies mainly to penal institutions, which blatantly control the behavior of individuals within their walls. Even prisons, however, have so far shown little effect in changing the individuals' behavior outside their domain. As for prisons exerting mind control, most people would find the suggestion absurd.

Behavioral therapists (and their critics), then, should well recognize their lack of control over most aspects of the patient's life, and the therapists should offer their techniques as tools to be used in behalf of the patient, not against his will. Thus as much as possible of the behavior

[4]H. F. Harlow, J. P. Gluck, and S. J. Suomi. Generalization of behavioral data between nonhuman and human animals. *American Psychologist,* 1972, *27:* 709–716 (p. 716).

modification program will be under the patient's own direct control. Any behavior modification program in psychiatry, as in most other medical treatments, should be administered only with the voluntary consent of the patient, who should know that he can withdraw at any time. Regardless of the manner (including court-ordered commitment) in which a person becomes a psychiatric patient, the responsibility for changed behavior should always be his, and not the psychiatrist's. The psychiatrist's responsibility should be simply to make the process of behavioral change and its ultimate consequences as attractive as possible. A patient's decision to refuse or to withdraw from treatment carries separate consequences from those in the treatment itself. Such a decision may carry rather painful consequences in the outside world; for some persons, these may even include the possibility of jail or expulsion from the family. Yet to expect that we can change behavior against the patient's will, while knowing that we will never have total control of all the critical factors in his environment, is naive and misguided.

2: People Can Talk!

People can not only speak to other people, but they can also understand verbal instructions. The only way to communicate with a rat, on the other hand, is to impose consequences upon that animal's behavior. In many respects we can impose consequences upon our patient's behavior, too, but this is not the *only* way to communicate with him. We can make a contract with him for treatment, and we can make very specific agreements on which behaviors will earn specifiable consequences.

It is remarkable how often this simple piece of knowledge has been overlooked. The earliest applications of the learning principles to patient treatment concentrated on "shaping" the individual's behavior through successive reinforcement, just as had been done with animals (for example, see Hauserman *et al.*, 1972). But what could not be shown with animals was the effect of verbal instructions: "If you press that bar, you will receive a piece of food." The rat is unable to understand this. We *must* shape his bar-pressing behavior by rewarding successive approximations to the goal behavior. People are different. They can be informed of the consequences; and they can, if they so desire, skip many of the intervening steps toward the final goal. For example, Parrino (1971) elegantly demonstrated the importance of instructions in human conditioning. Working with psychiatric inpatients, he attempted to "shape" their behavior toward approaching a feared snake. The shaping was done by rewarding the patients for steps successively nearer to the reptile. Some of the patients, in addition to being rewarded, were given information on what was expected of them and on the rewards available for the expected behavior. This practical information greatly enhanced the performance of the patients who received it; they showed much more approach behavior than did those who were simply rewarded without being given clear information. This is not to say that basic shaping did not work with the latter patients, for it did change their behavior significantly, as compared to that of an untreated control group. The point is simply that without information it was inefficient and, critics might contend, dehumanizing.

The efficiency of an operant shaping procedure, as compared with a similar procedure in which instructions were given, was also assessed in a study by Vogler, Masters, and Morrill (1971). Children were taught a complex skill in mutual cooperation. Some children simply received reinforcement for successive approximations toward the goal behavior. Other children received the same contingent rewards, but they were also given instructions before and during the learning of the task. It probably comes as no large surprise to note that "acquisition was more rapid and time to extinction [i.e., time the children demonstrated the skill when rewards were removed] was greater for the instructed group" (p. 239).

Therapists in all areas are increasing the amount of definitive information they give the patient concerning his treatment. They are finding that this tactic greatly enhances the efficacy of the therapy. Two examples will demonstrate this. Herman and Tramontana (1971) found that reinforcement was only partially effective, and instructions were ineffective, in controlling the disruptive behavior of children in the Federal Government's Head Start Program, a preschool academic training program for low-income children. However, the combination of reinforcement and instructions "reduced the inappropriate behavior to near zero" (p. 113). In a learning task, Spence (1972) found that rewarding correct responses and punishing incorrect answers was no more effective in increasing the number of correct responses from children than was the simple neutral disclosure of their performance. In further analysis of her results, Spence concluded that reinforcement alone was not as effective in changing behavior as was the giving of information about the person's performance.

People do not have to be treated as rats. They do not need to be handled as if they cannot understand our esoteric procedures. They are, after all, the focus of the treatment program. It does not harm "the purity" of a behavior-modificatin system to talk with the patient about the goals of treatment and the steps toward these goals. By providing the patient with pertinent information, we can eliminate many steps along the "shaping" route. Also, by helping the patient in this manner, the therapist actually brings the patient into a relationship with him as a co-therapist. The patient no longer has a treatment administered *to* him. Instead he becomes a co-instructor in his own behavioral learning program, who can now use the treatment for his own improvement.

3: People Want to Change

We assume that all voluntary patients want to make some change in their pattern of living. For this reason they have a vested interest in the success of their treatment. There is no evidence, to our knowledge, that any behavior modification system has yet been devised that has proved effective with humans who did not wish to change their behavior. Only if the therapist has total control over the entire life system of the patient, as he does with rats, can an imposed program be expected to lead to the desired behavioral change. Even then, as we have already pointed out, behavior that has been changed within the control system does not necessarily remain changed outside the controlled environment.

Rats, on the other hand, are notably lax in their desire to change their manner of living. We have never found a rat that showed any great spontaneous impulse to press a bar. Rats seem to be a rather satisfied lot. If their physical needs are met, we see little attempt on their part to change their habits or enroll in self-improvement programs. But since he has total control over the rat's environment, the trainer can impose his will for certain changes of behavior, and can evoke remarkably novel and complex behaviors from the laboratory animal.

In treating homosexuality, Levin *et al.* (1968) admit that the effectiveness of the behavioral methods depends on the patient's level of motivation for change. Hunt and Dyrud (1968) cite several examples of the ways in which alcoholics undermine and abuse treatment programs. Again, as we have seen before, the level of the patient's desire to change his behavior should be considered by the therapist in developing treatment plans. The evidence suggests that motivation for change is as important in the therapeutic outcome of a behavior modification system as it is in all other forms of psychiatric treatment. We must have the patient's cooperation and full support of the program if we are to make behavioral programs effective.

4: Social Reinforcement

In the human learning involved in the development of personality most of the crucial conditions are social.[5]

We have never personally met a rat for whom social reinforcement was an effective reward in guiding behavioral change. We have tried praise, friendship, warm greetings, and individual attention, all to no avail. Our rats have never been influenced toward positive behavioral change by any of these methods. For *people,* however, social factors can function as very powerful reinforcers indeed. In fact, as Hill (1968) points out, social reinforcers seem to be more powerful with humans than is any type of material reinforcer with animals. Social reinforcers are capable of producing more complex behaviors than material reinforcers, and they are apparently highly resistant to extinction (that is, people don't seem to become satiated with social rewards as they do with tangible reinforcers).

COMBINING FACILITATIVE COMMUNICATION AND OPERANT CONDITIONING

Our short list of the known differences between rats and humans points out how remarkably important social interaction is in the operant conditioning programs, even though this factor has been amazingly little recognized by researchers and clinicians alike. These "known differ-

[5]N. E. Miller. Experiments relevant to learning theory and psychopathology. In W. S. Sahakian (Ed.), *Psychopathology Today.* Itasca, Ill.: F. E. Peacock, 1970: 148–166.

ences" indicate the importance of talking to the patient, giving helpful advice on behavioral change, persuasively increasing his motivation, and encouraging him through social rewards. If talking to the patient is important within the behavior modification systems, our knowledge of the most useful ways to talk to patients (which we presented in the chapters on psychotherapy) may well be the cornerstone of therapeutic effectiveness in both psychotherapy and behavior modification!

In the concluding chapter, we will expand the point that facilitative communication probably underlies the effectiveness of all psychological therapies. We are now in a position to recognize how many of the myths, with their attendant suspicion, arose around the operant conditioning approaches. If we arm the clinical practitioner with more effective communication skills, operant procedures need never be described as "bludgeon approaches", and psychotherapeutic skills need never be seen as irrelevant to the proper administration of the behavioral therapies.

SUMMARY

We have discussed the most common problems in the application of the operant conditioning procedures. The major difficulties are the definition of the target behavior, dealing with rare behaviors, dealing with behaviors that are situation-specific or secretive, the fact that behavioral approaches are often as slow and expensive as other forms of treatment, dealing with the unmotivated patient, and getting the new behavior patterns to maintain themselves beyond the treatment setting.

Most of the misapplications of the operant approaches, and many overenthusiastic claims for these modes of intervention, have come from the too rigid application of animal research data to human treatment. We have failed to recognize that we do not have total control over the human patient's environment, that many patients do want to change their behavior, that we can discuss our treatment plans openly with our human patients, and that, for humans, social reinforcement is probably more powerful than any other available reinforcement mechanism. Effective social reinforcement probably has the same essential qualities as effective psychotherapy. A therapist who has high skills in facilitative communication is probably not only the best psychotherapist, but the best behavior modifier as well.

Chapter 7

THE CLASSICAL CONDITIONING METHODS: A HOUSE BUILT ON PLACEBO

Desensitization may be a poor deduction from conditioning, but it is a fine treatment for phobias. [1]

Is NEUROSIS LEARNED?

Many of the treatment techniques that stemmed from learning studies gained a large amount of early impetus from Pavlov's disclosure (1941) that he had produced seriously disturbed and maladaptive behavior in laboratory animals. He referred to his disruption of the normal functioning of his animals as "experimental neurosis," analogous to the neurotic disturbances observed in man. If it could be demonstrated that neurosis could be produced

[1]Perry London. The end of ideology in behavior modification. *American Psychologist,* 1972, *27:* 913–920 (p. 918).

146

through the disruption of the processes of learning, then the theoretical door was open to search for a treatment based upon these same processes. Thus treatment could be aimed directly at the symptoms, from an understanding of their learned origins. There would no longer be a need to deal with instinctual conflicts and unconscious pressures as the underlying factors in neurosis.

Later, Liddell (1964) added another dimension to Pavlov's findings on experimental neurosis. Liddell showed that there were at least two ways to produce an experimental neurosis. The first means of precipitating such disordered behavior was Pavlov's method: expose the animal to a task of discrimination that exceeds its discriminative ability. Thus, Pavlov originally induced the experimental neurosis in a dog by feeding the animal whenever an ellipse was displayed, and not feeding the animal when a circle was shown. At first the dog easily distinguished between the two stimuli, and came to salivate consistently at the sight of the ellipse. But as Pavlov made the ellipse successively closer in appearance to the circle, the animal's capacity to discriminate between the two became strained. When it was no longer capable of consistently making the discrimination, it became agitated, growled, and pulled at its restraints. A previously compliant and gentle dog became a dangerous and disturbed animal, which never regained the composure it had previously exhibited.

Liddell showed that similar neurotic behavior could be induced by exposing the experimental animal to a repeated signal, followed by an unavoidable painful stimulus. In addition to their "psychological symptoms," Liddell's animals developed actual physiological damage as well. As with the Pavlovian type of experimental neurosis, these animals maintained their disorders throughout their lifetimes. No amount of rest or exposure to pleasant living surroundings led to any predictable long-term remission of symptoms. Virtually until death, these animals continued to display postural rigidity, overreaction to innocuous stimuli, and nervous tics.

A very informative demonstration of how both emotional and behavioral responses may be learned in the neurotic disorders was provided by Miller (1949). An apparatus similar to that used by Miller in demonstrating "abnormal" behavior in rats is shown in Figure 1. Miller tells about the behavior of the animals placed in this apparatus:

> If rats are placed in this apparatus with the door between the two compartments open, they wander aimlessly about showing no particular motivation to get to any particular side.
>
> If they are given a number of trials during which they are dropped into the left-hand side of the apparatus and given an electric shock through the grid floor, they rapidly learn to escape by running through the open door to the right side. Even after the shock is turned off they continue to run. Is this the mere automatic persistence of the response of running, or has a drive been conditioned to the left side?
>
> To answer this question the door between the two compartments is closed. The rats cannot escape to the other side. The tension, agitation, urination and defecation indicate strong fear. They perform a variety of motor responses. If switches are set so that one of these responses, that of turning the little wheel above the door, causes it to drop open so that they can escape to the other side, most of the rats eventually will happen to perform this response of turning the wheel and those that do will learn it. We can see that the escape from the fear-producing situation has reinforced the learning of one particular response, turning a wheel. The learning is the same as if the drive had been hunger, instead of fear, and the reward food instead of a sudden reduction in the strength of fear. [Miller, 1966; in Sahakian, 1970, p. 149]

Since Miller originally performed these experiments, a common procedure in studies of the learning of avoidance responses has been to make both compartments equal in

FIGURE 1
APPARATUS SIMILAR TO THAT USED BY MILLER (1949).

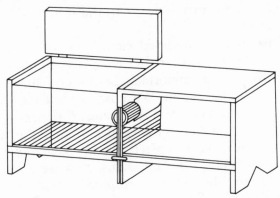

appearance, with grid floor on both sides; a buzzer is added as a signal to the animal that a shock is forthcoming. One side is electrified when the buzzer is sounded, and the other is not; the animal's task is to learn to jump the center hurdle and get to the opposite side, where no shock will be experienced. Once he performs the hurdle-jumping (or avoidance behavior), the sound of the buzzer is also terminated.

The typical initial response in the learning sequence occurs when the buzzer sounds for the first time. At that time the rat's typical reaction is simply to sniff inquisitively at the buzzer. As in Miller's example, the animal shows little concern over the buzzer, since the mild noise is not in itself a noxious stimulus. When the shock then hits, the untrained rat shows all sorts of disordered and frantic behaviors. It often screams, defecates, claws the apparatus, and jumps randomly around the compartment. Eventually, the animal jumps or falls over the center divider into the opposite compartment. When this happens the rat is free of both the shock and the sound of the buzzer. From the frantic, random, disordered behavior that the animal shows in early trials, it eventually develops (after several exposures) a fluid, goal-oriented response to the buzzer. The rat that has thoroughly made the avoidance connection need never again experience the shock. Now, as soon as the rat hears the buzzer, it immediately leaps to the other side of the apparatus.

Because we have observed the training of this animal, we can be sympathetic to its behavior. We do not classify the rat as in any way abnormal. Let us now make some alterations in the situation. We now turn off the electric current to the grid floor, and disconnect the wires, so that the rat will never again receive a shock while in the experimental apparatus. We also place a highly palatable dish of rat food at one end of the apparatus. Now we send out a rat trained to the buzzer response, who for anthropomorphically illustrative purposes we will name "Jake," into the apparatus. With Jake we also send in two of his hungry rat companions (not trained to the buzzer response), and, in a manner typical of hungry rats, the three begin to consume the feast laid out for them. Just at this point the buzzer sounds. Two of the three animals look around for the source of the noise, but Jake in one fluid motion jumps the entire distance over the hurdle into the neighboring compartment. There he sits, hungry, while his companions finish their meal. Anthropomorphizing a step further, we listen to the comments of Jake's two companions:

First rat: Hey, what's with Jake? Sure is jumpy, ain't he? Did you see him fly out of here when that sound went off?

Second rat: Yeah, well you know he's always been the nervous type.

First rat: Boy, he's spooky. He's just as hungry as us, but just over a little noise he's gonna sit over there and not eat. I'm tellin' you, he should do something about those nerves of his.

Second rat: You bet, but let's act like nothin's unusual. We don't want to hurt his feelings. Takes all kinds to make a world, you know.

To his companions, Jake's behavior was abnormal. Jake might even be termed neurotic; he definitely was a "buzzerphobic." There is no question that his behavior was maladaptive; if a buzzer went off when food was available, Jake would not eat. His behavior also shut the door on future learning: so long as Jake fled when he heard the buzzer, he would never learn that *there was, in fact, no further danger*. To outsiders, unaware of Jake's previous experiences, his behavior was inexplicable.

To Dollard and Miller (1950), animals like Jake provided a productive analogy between the behaviors elicited in the laboratory in this manner, and the behaviors shown by human neurotics. All analogies between animal and human behavior, especially in the complex area of human emotional disorders, are tenuous; in this case the similarities between Jake's symptoms and symptoms of neurosis are that both are maladaptive, self-defeating, and based on previously learned experiences that no longer apply. Jake is afraid of buzzers because he has experienced pain that was associated with buzzers. Analogously, we can hypothesize that the tense, seclusive woman who is afraid of potential sexual encounter was severely punished for sexual expressions or curiosity as a child. Her anxiety and withdrawal are unremitting, since members of the opposite sex are virtually everywhere, and thus the threat of sexual stimulus is pervasive. Her behavior sets her apart from the potential support of other persons, and keeps her from ever establishing a close emotional relationship with a male companion. Also, it is based on a set of circumstances that no longer exists; she will not be punished as an adult for sexual conduct that was punished when she was a child.

Earlier we mentioned certain distinctions between the classical and operant forms of conditioning. Miller's demonstration of "abnormal" behavior in the rat shows the two forms of conditioning working together, in the same organism, under the same progression of circumstances.

As in many learning experiments, to Jake the buzzer

was initially a neutral stimulus; perhaps it aroused his curiosity, but it did not evoke any of the "symptoms" Jake was later to display. Eventually, however, the buzzer came to elicit a very dramatic response. Electric shock, on the other hand, certainly evoked several responses. Basic to all of these was the emotional response of fear. Although we label Jake's response as fear, what we could actually have observed were those physical and physiological reactions that we recognize as indicating strong emotion. We observed defecation, squealing, and increased motor activity; and if we had possessed the equipment to measure these, we would have observed a rapidly increased heart rate, elevated skin potential, and changes of blood pressure. We would still see these same responses for a time if we were to sound the buzzer again, after sealing the compartment off so that Jake could not cross the hurdle.

Jake's response of "fear" was originally shown only in reaction to electric shock, but since it is now expressed in response to a buzzer, it satisfies the paradigm for classically conditioned learning. This is illustrated in Figure 2. With Jake, as with Pavlov's dogs, a previously neutral stimulus (the buzzer) has been paired with another stimulus (shock) and now evokes the same response (fear) as did the latter stimulus.

Therefore, until extinction occurs (that is, until Jake has had many experiences in which the buzzer is not followed by shock), he will always be fearful in the presence of buzzers. Some children and adolescents who have been severely hurt in interpersonal relationships may withdraw into solitude or become quiet and shy until their fears also extinguish. But will these fears extinguish? According to clinical experts, human fears, even those of a highly irrational nature, survive for years. Some irrational fears never become extinct at all. Bandura (1969) has documented this, compiling a large list of fears expressed by human patients. In his notation of the length and virulence of these fears

FIGURE 2
TWO OCCURRENCES OF CLASSICAL CONDITIONING

PAVLOV'S   EMOTIONAL CONDITIONING IN
CLASSICAL CONDITIONING   AVOIDANCE LEARNING

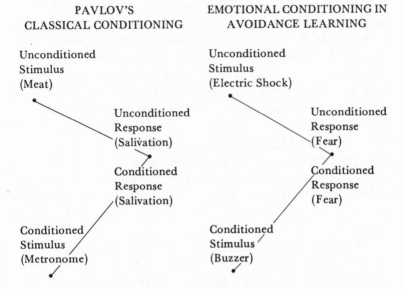

prior to classical conditioning therapy, Bandura demonstrates their longevity, which extended into many years.

Why do irrational fears (that is, fears that exist where there is no real danger) not extinguish readily? The answer is simple: because the person never remains in the fear-producing situation long enough to stop responding with fear. Jake does not linger to find out whether the current has been turned off; when the buzzer sounds, he jumps. A person terrified of snakes does not tour the reptile house of the zoo; and the man who constantly tears newspapers into tiny bits, scattering them to ward off elephants, does not stop this ritual to find out whether elephants in fact appear if he ceases. The proof of the effectiveness of his symptoms is that no elephants appear while he practices these activities.

But surely, sooner or later, the phobic individual must find out that nothing serious happens to him when he receives extended exposure to the feared stimulus. Apparently he does not learn this, if animal research can again shed light on this question. Solomon and Wynne (1953) showed that when an experience is, like Jake's, of traumatic proportions, a "partial irreversibility" of the response sets in, and the individual never again finds out under normal circumstances that no painful stimulus is now associated with the feared situation. These researchers set up essentially the same apparatus as we have used to illustrate Jake's problem, except that they worked with dogs rather than rats. Once the dogs had learned to jump from one side of the apparatus to the other to avoid an intense electric shock, the experimenters turned off the electric current in order to determine how long it would take for the animals to stop jumping the hurdle in reaction to the signal of the buzzer.

Solomon and Wynne tested the dogs in many trials, presenting the buzzer without shock. The frightened animal repeatedly leapt the barrier to the other side. They observed this for 10 trials, then 25, 50, and 100 trials, and still the dogs jumped. Finally, after 200 trials—with the dogs still jumping—the authors stopped the experiment. They had been searching throughout these trials for some sign that the response was weakening. It never came. The response that these animals had learned had become impervious to extinction! Unless they physically restrained the dogs, the authors would probably never see them learn new responses. The response of jumping at the sound of a buzzer was maintained in spite of its inappropriateness to the reality of the situation. The current theoretical explanation of this is that the behavior is maintained because it is rewarded: relief from fear functions as a reward, and hence the relief-producing response is maintained. The introverted patient who wishes to withdraw from others by isolating himself in his room will not easily come to group meetings. He will avoid the opportunity for new experience. Left to himself, he will miss the opportunity to learn that he will not be seriously hurt in group interaction. He will never learn new social skills that could provide him with much pleasurable interchange over a lifetime.

We have said, then, that part of Jake's "abnormal" behavior was a result of classical conditioning. The fear that was attached to the sound of the buzzer can be seen as a classically conditioned response. The overt behavior, on the other hand (in this case jumping the hurdle), has ostensibly been operantly conditioned. The behavior is maintained because it is rewarded, or reinforced. The reward in this case is the relief that occurs when the behavior is performed. This behavior can change, depending on how effective it is in reducing fear. The fear itself, however, may yet remain, prompting new behaviors that will be seen as abnormal, symptomatic, or bizarre, according to the degree of "irrationality" of the fear. In providing his rats with a wheel to turn or a bar to press to escape the compartment of his box, Miller (1970) makes the following comment:

> If we did not know the special history of these animals, we would find their behavior abnormal. Normal rats merely explore the apparatus, but these have a wheel-turning compulsion. If they are prevented from performing this compulsion, they develop a new symptom, bar-pressing. This bizarre behavior is all perfectly clear once we know the antecedent conditions which have conditioned fear to the left-hand compartment, so that escape into the right-hand one produces a sudden relief that serves as a reward to reinforce further learning. [p. 150]

In brief, then, we have a picture of the way in which a neurosis may develop from a learning standpoint. Essentially, the hypothesized sequence begins when the person experiences severe punishment at some early point in his life. The fear that this produces may then become attached to any of the otherwise neutral stimuli that were connected with the original situation: the physical setting, the people, the clothes that the person was wearing, or even his actions or thoughts at the time of the punishment. In the future, then, any of these things may elicit fear. The person naturally begins to learn ways to avoid the fear-producing stimuli. He may avoid riding in elevators, or he may avoid older men. He may avoid females by adopting one of many possible stylistic responses: he may withdraw from them, stutter in their presence, or actually make himself physically unattractive to them. A frightened individual who is trying to avoid "dirty thoughts" may also adopt any of a number of maladaptive techniques to interrupt his continuous thought-process. He may develop nervous habits such as head-twisting or finger-snapping when tension increases, or he may obsessively wash his hands or become engrossed in counting rituals.

There are two general approaches that we could take to alleviate the neuroses of people thus afflicted. We could remove the symptom itself. We might attempt to do this by rewarding the person for engaging in social interaction rather than withdrawing. In essence, this is what the operant conditioning procedures are devised to do: to take away the symptom. Another way of helping the person would be to attempt to alleviate the underlying anxiety, so that there would be no further need for the symptom. The classical conditioning techniques generally are aimed toward this goal, as are the more traditional approaches of psychotherapy (White, 1964). The treatments based upon classical conditioning theory aim to weaken the emotion, or to detach it from the stimulus that has come to elicit it.

ORIGIN OF THE CLINICAL TECHNIQUES

Procedures that stem generally from the classical conditioning paradigm gained their greatest impetus from the publication of Wolpe's (1958) book, *Psychotherapy by Reciprocal Inhibition*. In that volume Wolpe laid out the procedures he and his colleagues had developed for the administration of a new treatment, which they called systematic desensitization.

In simplified terms, the theory behind the classical conditioning therapies began with the assumption that if, as Miller and others had demonstrated, fear was a classically conditioned response to an objectively neutral stimulus, then it should be possible to eliminate the unrealistic fear through the proper reconditioning procedures. "[R]ecovery from neurosis should be achieved by applying the learning process in a reverse direction: whatever undesirable behavior has been learned may be unlearned" (Wolpe, 1964, p. 10). Since fear is already attached to the stimulus when the patient appears for treatment, possibly the emotion of fear could be eliminated by conditioning the patient to respond to the stimulus with a *different* emotion. In other words, fear could be counterconditioned through a treatment that attaches another emotion or response to the stimulus in place of the fear. This is illustrated in Figure 3.

To accomplish this, Wolpe (1964) formulated the concept of reciprocal inhibition: "If a response antagonistic to anxiety can be made to occur in the presence of anxiety-provoking stimuli so that it is accompanied by a complete or partial suppression of the anxiety responses, the bond between the stimuli and the anxiety responses will be weakened" (p. 10). In more simple terms, he merely postulated that it is difficult to have two contrary emotional or physiological responses at the same time. Relaxation and fear, for example, are antagonistic experiences. Either one or the other predominates at the same time in a given individual; the two cannot exist together. Therefore, if the person is conditioned to experience relaxation in the presence of the feared object, this relaxation will necessarily reduce or eliminate the fear.

FIGURE 3

A. Counterconditioning

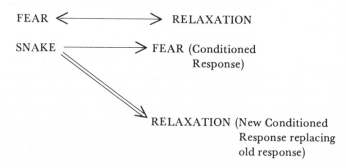

B. Systematic Desensitization

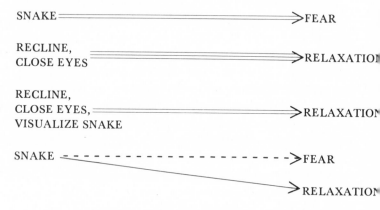

SYSTEMATIC DESENSITIZATION

The research most commonly cited in support of this theory is the famous study in 1920 by Watson and Rayner, whose "Little Albert" was made to show fear of a white rat, then was cured of this fear. The elimination of the fear was effected by bringing the animal successively closer to Little Albert while he was eating. Theoretically, this technique pitted the positive feelings of eating against the response of fear to the rat. Wolpe has also used his own studies of animals (Wolpe, 1948) as the basis for the formulation of his systematic desensitization approach, which he states thus (1964):

> Anxiety reactions had been strongly conditioned to a small confining cage and to other stimuli, and could not be made to extinguish despite repeated exposure to the stimuli. The anxiety response habits could, however, be overcome in piecemeal fashion by counterposing feeding to weak anxiety responses. At first, stimuli distantly similar to the conditioned stimuli were used, until anxiety decreased to zero, and then, step by step, stimuli closer in resemblance to the original conditioned stimuli were introduced, until even the strongest eventually lost its power to evoke anxiety. [p. 10]

Conveniently, Jacobson (1939) had produced evidence which indicated that the response of relaxation was physiologically opposite to that of anxiety. Wolpe used this as a central concept in the development of his techniques to condition his patients systematically to relax in response to fear-producing stimuli. The core procedure of systematic desensitization became the induction of a state of relaxation (specifically, deep muscle relaxation in the patient).

Note that Wolpe has made some large theoretical jumps in adjusting a treatment technique based on sketchy laboratory findings to fit humans who are to be treated in an office setting. No previous research existed to show that a response could be conditioned through imaginary processes. To assume that a response that had been learned *in vivo* could be eradicated by learning a new response through the imagination was a large supposition. There also was no evidence that, on a physiological level, counterconditioning could in fact take place. Jacobson (1939) had shown that several opposite physical processes differentiated the responses of anxiety and relaxation, but it had not been demonstrated that relaxation could be induced by conditioning, or that such conditioning could overcome a previously learned anxiety response. Finally, the case seemed strong only for the contention that some form of counterconditioning could alleviate *specific* fears. To go beyond this, and propose that simple counterconditioning could overcome clinically defined phobias or eliminate other forms of neurosis, would need support from further research.

We mention these theoretical shortcomings of the systematic desensitization method for two reasons. First, we hope the reader will avoid the dogmatic pitfalls that the proponents of many therapies have fallen into over the years. It is important that we should not consider the technique, as it is used today, as an ultimate therapeutic product. We cannot accept all theoretical claims simply because they are delivered by a person who has developed an apparently useful therapeutic tool. All the questions have not yet been answered; we have not yet reached a point at which we can throw away illuminating research. The foundations of the technique are not yet secure. We cannot, therefore, become exclusive practitioners of a technique that will not be modified, streamlined, and improved as time passes. As Eysenck and Beech (1971) have said, "It is abundantly clear that the theory of reciprocal inhibition as formulated by Wolpe is only one of several possible theoretical accounts of desensitization procedures and it could well be that other alternatives will be forthcoming. That is, of course, the hallmark of a developing field and a cause for optimism rather than dismay" (p. 567).

Our second purpose in presenting these weaknesses is to alert the reader to specific areas in which research is opening roads to new ways of applying Wolpe's procedures. These we will present later in this chapter. We have not presented all the theoretical criticisms of systematic desensitization (see, for instance, Breger and McGaugh, 1965, and Locke, 1971), just two that appear at this time to be highly relevant for important modifications of the clinical techniques within the desensitization scheme.

Yet regardless of the theoretical niceties, the important question still is, does it work? In the following paragraphs we will examine the relevant research. A summary answer to the question, "Does systematic desensitization work?" can be given here: for individuals with specific, encapsulated fears, it does; for persons with broader underlying emotional disorders, probably not; and for children and adolescents, no studies have been made from which to draw a conclusion.

In addition to the numerous specific fears (ranging from fear of storms to fear of hyperdermic injections) that have been treated through systematic desensitization, other symptoms and syndromes that have each responded to treatment in at least one reported instance are listed in Table 2.

An overwhelming amount of the research on systematic desensitization has been carried out with adequately functioning college students as subjects. The fears that have been counterconditioned are nondebilitating ones, such as the fear of snakes (Lazovik and Lang, 1960; Lang and Lazovik, 1963), spiders (Rachman, 1965), and public speaking (Paul, 1966). College students are usually fairly well motivated to accept treatment; at least we might guess this from the fact that the participants in these studies were primarily volunteer patients. In clinical work, however, our major concern will not be the relatively healthy adult or adolescent, but rather the patient who differs in many untold ways from the subjects of the laboratory research.

The younger patient in particular presents several special problems for the application of systematic desensitization. The child or adolescent probably has much lower

Table 2   Non-phobic Reaction Treated by
Systematic Desensitization

LSD "Freak-out"	Suinn & Brittain, 1970
Test anxiety	Robinson & Suinn, 1969; Allen, 1971[2]
Falling asleep while driving	Suinn & Richardson, 1970
Obsessive-compulsive states	Walton & Mather, 1964
Insommia	Geer & Katkin, 1966
Recurrent nightmare	Geer & Silverman, 1967
Chronic Alcoholism	Kraft & Al-Issa, 1967a
Frigidity	Kraft & Al-Issa, 1967b; Madsen & Ullman, 1967
Rage reactions	Fix, 1970
Menstrual pain	Mullen, 1971
Speech anxiety	Paul, 1966; Meichenbaum, Gilmore, & Federavicius, 1971
Exhibitionism	Bond & Hutchinson, 1960
Bronchial asthma	Moore, 1965
Anorexia nervosa	Shurer, Rubin, & Roy, 1973

[2] In both of these studies, while nervousness about academic tests decreased subjectively, systematic desensitization alone did not raise academic performance. In fact, examination scores decreased for those students who received desensitization in Allen's study. Only desensitization in combination with counseling helped their final examination scores.

motivation for treatment. Most young inpatients do not seek treatment on their own; they come under outside pressure from parents, courts, or schools. In addition, a disproportionate number of adolescents given psychiatric treatment for deviant behavior or unorthodox means of emotional expression have an I.Q. of below 100, while we can presume that the much-researched college student generally scores in, or close to, the Bright Normal range in intellectual tests. The patient's intelligence, after all, may well be a factor in the effectiveness of this technique. The skills that the patient must bring to bear in systematic desensitization are somewhat similar to those tapped by intelligence tests, although the focus of the former is on more emotional material. Systematic desensitization calls on the patient to specify emotionally charged stimuli, and to visualize emotion-arousing scenes clearly.

Finally, many adolescents who receive psychiatric care very rigidly deny their own contributions to their difficulties. They maintain that they are chronically mistreated (which may be true), and that therefore all their behaviors are justified (which is not necessarily true). An individual who has been relentlessly taught that it is a sign of weakness or guilt to have certain feelings will find it difficult to accept in himself emotions such as fear, anxiety, or perpetual rage. It seems to us that such a person would find it quite difficult to accept and work with a treatment program that asks him to direct his attention to an irrational emotion in himself. Since to him the emotion is justified by an unfair world, he has no motivation to change that emotion.

Systematic desensitization has proved effective in virtually all the studies conducted upon relatively circumscribed fears and phobias in otherwise adequately functioning personalities (Eysenck, 1971). In these relatively healthy groups, the effects of systematic desensitization have been compared with those of other treatments. These other treatments have usually been insight or nondirective psychotherapy, but they have also included "relaxation, graded exposure, flooding, visualizating non-phobic scenes, suggestion and hypnosis . . . drug, placebo, and no treatment or a period on a waiting list" (Marks and Gelder, 1968: p. 79). Systematic desensitization has consistently been found to be either more effective, or just as effective, but more efficient than the other approaches.[3] That is,

[3]An exception to these results was recently reported by Sherman (1972), who found that the hoped-for positive effects of systematic desensitization did not generalize to a "real life" situation in persons treated for fear of the water. Progressive exposure to a swimming situation was effective, however. Additional findings of a similar nature could seriously impair the theory that imagination can produce reduction of fear in a comparable way to *in vivo* contact. One advantage of many of the classical conditioning approaches has been that their procedures, by taking place through private imagery, could avoid the need for environmental manipulation. This has been one of the hypothetical bases of the claimed efficiency.

systematic desensitization produces comparable or superior improvement, but it does so in less time.

Yet even if future research continues to indicate that systematic desensitization is useful in treating single-symptom problems such as we have described, how effective can we expect the therapeutic procedure to be among our clinic and inpatient populations? Here is where the research on systematic desensitization has been most discouraging. Not many studies have been reported in which psychiatric patients were the treatment group. Marks and Gelder (1968) reviewed four partially controlled studies of the results of this technique in psychiatric patients with phobias, and concluded that the counterconditioning technique was not beneficial to patients with a great deal of "free-floating anxiety." Similarly, Cowden and Ford (1962) reported that systematic desensitization failed with phobic schizophrenic patients. The investigators suggested that this may possibly have been due to their patients' inability "to identify the various anxiety-producing stimuli." Cowden and Ford also suggested that the patients' report of anxiety during the visualization procedures may be "frequently discrepant from the actual feeling ... of the subject" (p. 244). Even with a nonhospitalized group of subjects receiving psychiatric treatment, Branham (1976) found that while systematic desensitization helped to cure volunteer, nonpsychiatric patients of minor fears, it was not effective in aiding psychiatric outpatients.

In our evaluation of the research, therefore, we must question the efficacy of systematic desensitization for most psychiatric cases. Although the technique has been highly touted for the treatment of "the distress and disability of neurosis" (Wolpe, 1964: p. 15), we see no evidence that systematic desensitization has any impact on either full neurotic disorders or any of the most common problems seen by practicing psychiatrists. We would agree with Marks, Boulougouris, and Marset (1971) in this statement:

"The value of desensitization is limited clinically in that it is of least benefit to the handicapped anxious phobics who need it most" (p. 373).

In addition, there seem to be at least some instances where desensitization is not as effective even in a normal population as we have been led to expect. The problem of test anxiety provides the most clear example of this. To reduce the anxiety a person experiences while taking an academic examination would seem to be a desirable goal. Yet the ultimate purpose behind an attempt to reduce test anxiety should surely be to free the individual from disruptive emotional interferences, so that his level of performance, as ultimately measured by his academic grades, would be raised. The demonstration of such benefit to grades, however, has been a very elusive goal. Most of the studies on the desensitization of test anxiety have reported that the anxiety has been reduced successfully (see, for example, Suinn, 1968; Mitchell and Ng, 1972; Crighton and Jehn, 1969; and Freeling and Shemberg, 1970), but improved grade-point averages are only sporadically reported. In fact, the psychologists who have conducted the more recent research (such as Allen, 1971; Mitchell and Ng, 1972; and Meichenbaum, 1972) have moved away from simple reliance on desensitization, finding that better results are attained when other forms of treatment are added to the desensitization approach.

With the foregoing in mind, it appears that the use of systematic desensitization has relatively few applications in clinical practice. For the most part we would restrict its use to those cases in which the total personality functioning is relatively intact, but specific, circumscribed fears or anxieties exist. We would further urge full research of the effects of this treatment on children and adolescents in order to determine its precise range of applicability in these groups.

To date, there have been no reports that systematic

desensitization has produced negative side effects. Therefore, we expect this technique to be used occasionally as an
experimental tool for the alleviation of anxiety or other
emotions, in cases of more pervasive emotional disorder.

Whenever systematic desensitization is administered,
regardless of the type of patient, there is more to be considered than just the specific procedures of administration.
We must also pay attention to the degree of faith the patient has in our treatment. We must enhance the patient's
belief in the value of our approach. As we will show, such
enhancement of his belief improves the results of systematic desensitization. While the attempt to increase the patient's faith in this treatment strategy has been known in the
psychological literature as "expectancy manipulation," we
refer to it with a more familiar term widely used in medicine, "the placebo effect." We urge that whenever systematic desensitization is contemplated, the placebo effect be
used to the fullest.

THE PLACEBO EFFECT; OR "YOU MAY FOOL THE MIND, BUT YOU CAN'T FOOL THE BODY"

As we have mentioned, some would contend that the
foundations of systematic desensitization in learning theory are very shaky. Probably the least firm support is the
use by Wolpe (1958, 1964) and Lang (1964) of a physiological theory of the emotions to describe the underlying
effects of the treatment. Wolpe (1964) maintains that unrealistic fear responses "are, as a rule, autonomic reactions
first and foremost" (p. 10). When a subject shows an irrational phobia, systematic desensitization supposedly conditions him to respond with relaxation, an opposed
physiological response, to the fear-evoking stimuli. If this
is true, we should be able to measure the original physiological reaction to the feared stimuli, and to note the physiological changes produced by the therapy.

Only a few attempts have been made to do this. In a doctoral thesis, Fix (1970) was the first to measure physiological responses before and after therapy, although Melamed and Lang (1967) had recorded the physiological processes that occurred within the actual desensitization sessions. In his study, Fix used skin conductance as a physiologic indication of his subjects' reaction to objects (in this case, snakes and spiders) toward which they claimed to feel intense fear or terror. He found that his fearful subjects did indeed react with sharply increased skin conductance as the feared object was moved toward them, and that their physiological reaction was significantly different from that of similar subjects allegedly not afraid of these objects. This latter group, the nonphobic controls, showed no increase at all in skin conductance, even up to the point of nearly direct physical contact with the snake or spider.

If systematic desensitization works in the way that Wolpe contends, after treatment the originally fearful subjects should show behavior, both overt and physiological, that has become more similar to that of the nonphobics. As was expected, the treated phobics become increasingly able to achieve closer proximity to the feared animal. Physiologically, though, the desensitized subjects did not show a change or reduction in the fear response, and they did not become more like nonphobics in this regard. The author concluded that the treatment was "effective on the (overt) behavioral dimension but failed to affect the actual emotional reaction" (Fix, 1970b, p. 82). In his doctoral thesis, he summed up his findings as follows:

> The pattern of increasing arousal in the phobic Ss tends to confirm the observations of a number of other researchers (i.e., Lang & Lazovik, 1963; Lang, et al, 1965; Paul, 1966; Davison, 1968) who noted that their "successfully desensitized subjects still showed signs of trepidation while approaching the object." That systematic desensitization failed to change the pattern of physiological response to the phobic object toward an approximation of the pattern dis-

played by nonphobics provides further evidence from which to question Wolpe's (1961) contention that, "at every stage a stimulus evokes no anxiety when encountered in reality (p. 191)." [Fix, 1970b, pp. 86–87]

In a more thorough study, Rappaport (1972) emerged with dramatically similar findings and conclusions. He found no significant change on two measures of skin conductance activity brought about by systematic desensitization. Also, even though systematic desensitization did produce a reduction of avoidance behavior toward a dead, but "preserved" and "lifelike" tarantula, it reduced avoidance only when the subjects had been presented with an expectancy of therapeutic effects. A group of fearful subjects who received systematic desensitization, but were given no therapeutic expectancy, behaved no differently from subjects who had received no treatment at all.

These studies, in turn, followed the findings of several studies (for example, those of Crowder and Thornton, 1969; Cooke, 1966; Craighead, 1971; and Sue, 1972) that behavioral change could be provided through systematic desensitization even if the treatment was conducted without relaxation. From the other side of the coin, Leitenberg *et al.* (1971) studied systematic desensitization and other treatment strategies, and found that phobic behavior could change even though the heart rate (yet another physiological indication of anxiety) in the phobic situation was not reduced during treatment. These authors suggest politely that "Wolpe's hypothesis may be incorrect" (p. 59). Sue (1972) was more direct in stating that "counterconditioning is no longer an adequate explanation" (p. 157).

If not counterconditioning, then what? It appears that systematic desensitization does help the basically healthy individual to change his overt behavior in relation to the object or situation that he fears, although it does not seem to affect the underlying emotion to any great extent (at least over the short term). Somehow the person does become more able to enter a reptile house, to work in a small animal laboratory, or to give talks in front of large groups, even though physiologically his level of fear during his first post-therapy attempts at these behaviors is the same as it was before therapy!

How can we account for this overt change of behavior? It certainly is not the result of counterconditioning in the Wolpean sense, since this theoretical structure clearly holds that there should be an initial decrease in the physiological response, and this decrease makes possible the change in overt behavior. Something else is helping these people to overcome their phobic behavior patterns. Rappaport's (1972) finding, that only those subjects who had been told to expect a therapeutic effect from desensitization showed behavioral change, gives a strong clue to what this something else might be.

Marcia, Rubin, and Efran (1969) and Efran and Marcia (1967) state that the key element is "expectancy," or as we have labeled it, "placebo." These authors set up a completely artificial "therapy" for college girls suffering from spider phobia, in which virtually every tenet of systematic desensitization was broken. Each girl sat alone in a straight-backed wooden chair, in a darkened room. Periodically, a flash of light briefly illuminated the wall; this was occasionally accompanied by a brief, slightly painful shock. The girls were supposedly viewing slides presented "too fast for the conscious mind to perceive," but allegedly presented at speeds adequate to reach the "unconscious roots" of their fears. The presentations accompanied by shock were ostensibly slides of spiders, while neutral slides such as country scenes were not accompanied by shock. Thus, the girls were assured, the unconscious fear reaction to the spider could be eradicated at its roots via the electrical shock. To increase their expectancy of improvement, a "GSR technician" met with the girls after their sessions, and showed their galvanic skin responses as adapting quite well to the spider stimuli. In actuality, of course, there were no slides in the projector at all: the girls were simply spending 30 minutes of each day in total darkness, watching periodic flashes of light and getting shocked for doing it! But even more amazing than the fact that intelligent, adult human beings were willing to participate in this foolishness was the finding that these girls showed as much overt behavioral improvement, and as much satisfaction with the treatment, as similar girls whom the authors treated with systematic desensitization!

The researchers concluded that the effect of the bogus therapy was due simply to the strong expectancy for improvement that they had administered with this procedure. Later Fix (1970) confirmed the findings of Marcia *et al.*, and further illustrated that electric shock was not necessary. Less noxious stimulation could suffice. Also, the girls presented with expectancy showed physiologically the same responses after treatment as a group of systematically desensitized girls. This demonstration that a procedure which had no more reason for its effectiveness than the subjects' expectation could produce the precise changes created by a more "scientific" process allowed Marcia *et al.* (1969) to suggest that similar placebo effects perhaps acted in systematic desensitization.

> In brief, desensitization, as currently practiced, may teach Ss (directly and indirectly) that they will be different; it may give them opportunities to feel they are changing, to participate in a sensible, structured, "scientific" process. In addition, they are given a chance to think about and rehearse a new reaction to fear-provoking stimuli—expectancy manipulation provides a theoretical rationale for improvement underlying (several) forms of behavior therapy, and perhaps, varieties of insight therapy as well. [p. 386]

In the years since that statement was written, the placebo effect has been found to be actively operative within systematic desensitization itself. We have already mentioned Rappaport's report (1972) that systematic desensitization reduced fears only when it was presented by the researcher as having a potential therapeutic effect. Similarly, Miller (1972) found, from a thorough study of the effects of various forms of information given to the experimental "patient," that systematic desensitization was effective whenever it was presented as an attempt to reduce the subject's fear of a harmless snake. It did not, however, lead to a reduction of fear when it was presented as an investigation of the "imagination." Once again, this demonstrated the powerful influence that expectancy for change exerts on the outcome of treatment by systematic desensitization. Even though the therapeutic technique is always the same, it is what the patient is led to believe about the treatment that appears from these studies to be the actual therapeutic agent, not reciprocal inhibition or counterconditioning. In all fields of medicine, whenever a treatment exists that relies on the patient's belief that it will produce a positive effect, that treatment is called placebo. This is the class to which it currently appears that systematic desensitization belongs.

While several studies (Davison, 1968; Perkins, 1966; Zeisset, 1966) have looked for, and failed to find, a placebo effect when only some portions of the systematic desensitization procedures were administered (such as relaxation without visualization, visualization without relaxation, visualization of only neutral scenes, and so on); expectancy in these studies was not manipulated to the strong degree that it was by Marcia and his colleagues.

To us, there is a moral in all of this. We do not present these studies to diminish Wolpe's contribution, but to help to ensure that when Wolpe's procedures are administered, they will be given in a manner that assures maximum impact. Since there is a good deal of suggestive evidence that the effects of systematic desensitization may be based on, or enhanced by, placebo factors, we urge those who choose this technique to use these placebo factors to the greatest extent possible. When introducing systematic desensitization to the patient, do not say, "I have a technique that I think will help you." Say instead, "We have a treatment that's just the thing for your situation. It has always worked with problems like yours, and in a couple of weeks we'll have progress that might amaze both of us."

AVERSION THERAPY

Just as with systematic desensitization, we find a storm of controversy over the utility of aversion therapy as seen in the light of conditioning theory (McConaghy, 1972; Hallam, Rachman, and Falkowski, 1971). Once again, we are far less concerned about the theoretical niceties involved than we are to evaluate the effectiveness of a treatment that is already currently in use in many areas. Whereas systematic desensitization appears to be fairly innocuous in terms of side effects, negative side effects have been documented in the use of the aversion techniques. For this reason, the present writers will demand that these approaches show a rather high standard of effectiveness before we will recommend their use. Rachman and Teasdale (1969) have compiled a listing of the negative side effects. They note that resentment, and sometimes overt aggression on the part of the patient, result from these treatments. Fortunately (for children and adolescent patients, if not for science) very few studies of aversion procedures have been conducted with young people, except in the aversive treatment of enuresis.

Just what are the overall therapeutic results of aversive therapies, then? In our estimation they are quite disappointing. Some case histories have shown dramatic effects. For instance, Alexander *et al.* (1971) eliminated a severe psychosomatic cough in a 15-year-old boy, even though the cough had survived eight hospital emergency-room visits and 25 hospital admissions. This was accomplished through the administration of an electric shock each time the boy coughed during a treatment session. This produced such intense hostility in the boy, however, that the therapists chose to change the procedure to a "shaping" process, whereby the boy could avoid a shock by restraining his cough for initially short but progressively lengthened periods of time. In another case study that speaks for the use of the aversive condition, Wolpe (1964) reports the successful treatment of drug addiction in a physician.

In more adequately controlled studies with larger groups of patients, the effectiveness of such treatment has not been clearly demonstrated. Mixed results have generally been reported when various forms of aversion therapy were attempted with alcoholism (Quinn and Henbest, 1967; Wallerstein, 1957; Beaubrun, 1967), smoking (Berecy, 1972), and sexual deviations (Ramsay and Van Velgen, 1968; McGuire et al., 1965; Feldman and MacCullock, 1965).

In weighing the efficacy of the aversive treatment programs we must also be aware that rather a large number of additional studies, mostly more recent, have either failed to find positive results or have uncovered other findings that call for a strong revision of the theoretical underpinnings of the aversive techniques. Some of the studies (for example, Hallam and Rachman, 1972; Beaubrun, 1967) report that improvement occurred in a smaller percentage of the cases studied than we would expect from a truly beneficial "therapy."

The results of some studies of aversion therapy have been reminiscent of those that uncovered the placebo effects in systematic desensitization. Solyom et al. (1971) found that both aversion therapy and desensitization were no more effective than a pseudoconditioning "therapy" in the treatment of hospitalized phobics. In studies of aversion therapy with smokers (Keutzer, 1968; Ober, 1968; Carlin and Armstrong, 1968), alcoholics (Madill *et al.,* 1966), phobics (Solyom *et al.,* 1971), and homosexuals (McConaghy, Proctor, and Barr, 1972), several conditions that were theoretically irrelevant to the treatment were applied, and they resulted in improvement equivalent to that seen in the aversion groups. Weingartner (1972) also attributed change in hallucinating schizophrenics to placebo effects.

Because of these probable placebo effects, the mixed experimental results with aversion techniques, and the problem of negative side effects, we do not encourage the use of these treatment methods at present. As with other techniques whose effects on younger persons have not been thoroughly evaluated, we would recommend that particular caution be used with child and adolescent patients. We would prefer to wait for further experimental results before we evaluate the appropriate place these procedures might ultimately have in a psychiatric treatment program (that is, with which patients they should be used, and what specific techniques should be applied).

COVERT SENSITIZATION

While covert sensitization is gaining a growing number of adherents, and has reached a position nearly equal to that of systematic desensitization in the favor of behavior therapists, it presents a significant problem in terms of its underlying theory. All classical conditioning methods that rely on a visualization process take the procedures out of the area of direct observation and allow for other interpretations of the underlying process. Once again, we note these theoretical problems simply to warn the novice that he should not accept a closed and final belief in this technique too early. The question of the effectiveness of covert sensitization remains open; and the research and conclusions here parallel those on systematic desensitization to a significant degree.

To note briefly examples of the usefulness of the covert sensitization approach, it has shown some degree of effectiveness with sexual disorders (Cautela, 1967; Davison, 1968; Barlow, Leitenberg, and Agras, 1969; Segal and Sims, 1972), alcoholic behavior (Anant, 1967), smoking (Berecz, 1972), and overeating (Stuart, 1967; Janda and Riam, 1972; Sachs and Ingram, 1972). This evidence, then, would lead us to conclude that for certain specific behavior problems, this may be the treatment of choice. However, all the shortcomings of systematic desensitization seem to apply equally to covert sensitization. The treatment requires that the patient be able, or willing, to work at the techniques of relaxation and to engage in direct cognitive fantasy. The research on systematic desensitization indicated that only those persons who had no pervasive emotional disturbance could benefit from the procedure. Research on covert sensitization has generally been concerned *only* with the relatively healthy individual; and there seems to be no reason to believe that the neurotic or psychotic individual would fare better in this treatment than in the other. Also, there is the same question of its usefulness with the behaviorally disordered child or adolescent. Only further research can help us here.

Finally, we again find that the placebo operates here. Ashem and Donner (1968) and Sachs and Ingram (1972) found that improvement occurred in groups treated by techniques that were similar in most respects to covert sensitization, but "violate learning parameters" (Sachs and Ingram, 1972). Yet the degree of improvement in these groups was comparable to that found with the actual "treatment" procedures. While the placebo effect has not yet been strongly demonstrated here, we expect to see more convincing evidence with the advent of more extensive research into the action of placebo factors in this technique. It would be interesting to see whether the strong pseudotherapy used by Efran and Marcia (1967), Marcia, Rubin, and Efran (1969), and Fix (1970) would be as effective in comparison with covert sensitization as it was in comparison with systematic desensitization. Until these types of studies are run, we recommend that the practitioner of covert sensitization mobilize whatever placebo factors are available, in order to gain the most from the treatment.

FLOODING

Because implosive therapy is analogous to "shutting the person in" with his phobias, it is an intensely uncomfortable technique for the patient. The patient's motivation for change must therefore be higher for this treatment than for most other therapies. This factor alone to a great degree excludes the potential applications of the flooding approach. Most patients are quite ambivalent about their symptoms, and when they do make the commitment to relinquish them, they desire to do so as painlessly as possible.[4] This is particularly true of younger patients. Very few adolescents, for instance, have high motivation for personal behavioral change, even in the best of circumstances; and those who do want to make such a change do not want to undergo emotional pain in order to achieve it. As Marks (1972) pointed out, a program of flooding, if begun without the patient's full knowledge and commitment to the

[4]When they compared the effects of systematic desensitization and flooding in phobic patients, Marks, Boulougouris, and Marset (1971) did not find this to be true. The authors did not study the question in a systematic way, but they found flooding to be "surprisingly acceptable to most patients," and three patients preferred flooding to systematic desensitization. We will continue to hold our reservations until controlled studies on the issue prove us to be in error.

treatment procedures, can actually produce negative results, more so than other forms of therapy. Let us consider, for example, the patient who finds the procedures too disturbing and discontinues treatment. He thus escapes the discomfort involved, and persists in the same avoidance behavior that he has shown before therapy. This, then, does not reduce his tendency to avoid—it may even enhance this tendency. This is a hazard that other forms of treatment theoretically do not entail.

A more rare, but very serious risk, is the possibility that physical disorders will be precipitated by the stress of the treatment. Marks (1972) flatly recommends that "patients with cardiac, respiratory, or other physical disorders that might be aggravated by acute anxiety should not be treated by flooding" (p. 136).

Implosive therapy has been less objectively studied than systematic desensitization, possibly because many therapists react adversely to the demands this technique makes upon their ingenuity, and also to the necessity in this procedure of inflicting a degree of discomfort upon the patient. Where the two approaches have been compared (Willis and Edwards, 1969; Barrett, 1969; DeMoor, 1970; Calef and MacLean, 1970; Marks, Boulougouris, and Marset, 1971), the results are mixed; which technique proves superior to the other depends apparently on what types of patients are studied, and on the target symptoms.

Although we have presented some of the reasons why we feel the technique would be difficult with many, if not most, hospitalized patients, we know of only one study that has evaluated implosive therapy with this group (Marks, Boulougouris, and Marset, 1971). They found flooding to be significantly more effective than systematic desensitization in reducing phobias. As expected, desensitization was found to promote only minor change in these disordered individuals. Flooding, on the other hand, induced changes that could be measured by psychiatrists' ratings, the patients' subjective reports, and physiological indices (heart rate and skin conductance). Strange to say, while flooding reduced the physiological responses to discussions of the phobias, systematic desensitization actually produced an *elevation* of the physiological signs of anxiety.

It is also more difficult to find studies that evaluate the effects of suggestion, or placebo, in the mechanisms of implosive therapy than was the case with systematic desensitization. Murray and Jacobson (1971) contended that placebo effects are indeed active. They interpret the available evidence as suggesting that the effective component of the flooding technique is that it helps the patient to change his beliefs about his ability to handle his fears.

These authors have no clear experimental proof that this hypothesis is true of implosive therapy, however. Probably the biggest boost to these authors' arguments is the theoretical problems that plague all the classical conditioning therapies. We have spoken of some of these in connection with systematic desensitization and covert sensitization; the same criticisms hold true for implosive therapy. As London (1972) points out, each of these approaches can be seen better as a structure created in analogy to a scientific procedure than as a precisely derived system, rooted firmly in laboratory-proven learning principles. One of the foremost theoretical problems at the outset is that these systems jump from the demonstration of conditioning processes in animals to the as yet unproven operation of these principles in humans, through processes of the imagination. In evaluating systematic desensitization and covert sensitization, we have seen that the placebo effect is probably the most potent effect generated by these procedures. Implosive therapy, which has much in common with these approaches (particularly the basic commitment to the visualization-conditioning process), will probably share the same fate under the scrutiny of research. As with the other two approaches, we do not recommend the use of flooding procedures with the vast majority of psychiatric inpatients, at least until future research specifically spells out its proper application to these patients and the specific precautions to be taken by the practitioner. Here we share the conclusions of two reviewers of the research on flooding, Frankel (1972) and Ayer (1972). Both authors express the conviction that the theoretical foundation of this approach is far from secure, the controlled assessment of its effects inadequate, and the investigation of all potential side effects incomplete.

Conclusion

We have presented the major classical conditioning therapies, and have evaluated their potential use with psychiatric inpatients. On balance, our evaluations of these techniques have been somewhat negative, due to lack of evidence for their usefulness with relatively disturbed patient populations, the evidence of their potential negative side effects, and the relatively poor theoretical underpinnings of these procedures. There is a positive side, however. We have noted that some case-study data indicate that there may be particular, individual cases in which some of these approaches can be useful. In addition, whether or not the theoretical basis of these approaches is satisfactory, they do stem from an orientation that emphasizes research, as opposed to dogma. This carries with it the promise that revision of the techniques, as well as of theory, will grow out of future progressive studies of the various processes involved. Moreover, we have found that the therapeutic effectiveness of these procedures can be enhanced through persistent capitalization upon the dramatic placebo effects. Perhaps the "wave of the future" is to combine whatever are found to be effective components in the various strategies of classical conditioning and other approaches. The work of Leitenberg and Callahan (1973) indicates that an eclectic approach such as this could be useful. They developed a procedure that they call simple "reinforced practice"; it is a blend of the following components, which the authors contend have been individually demonstrated to provide therapeutic results: "graduated and repeated practice . . . reinforcement for gains . . . feedback of measurable progress . . . and instructions designed to arouse expectations of gradual success" (p. 19). Although it is possibly a theoretical polyglot, the technique does seem to reduce both clinical neurotic phobias and other less severe fears. If this finding holds up under further scrutiny, it will provide reinforced practice with a higher level of effectiveness than any of the theoretically "purer" approaches. Theory then will be advanced to explain the findings and will provide the basis for even more powerful clinical techniques in the future.

SUMMARY

The procedures of the classical conditioning techniques represent an extremely loose application of the fundamental knowledge on classical conditioning to a broad band of clinical approaches. Pavlov's production (1941) of what he termed "experimental neurosis" through conditioning techniques has led to Wolpe's ultimate contention (1958) that all neuroses and various isolated symptoms can be eliminated simply by reversing the conditioning procedure; that is, by treating patients via counterconditioning. Contrary to the past claims made for classical conditioning techniques, however, current research suggests more modest expectations. Our assessment of the research brings us to three major conclusions: 1) The classical conditioning techniques have not been shown to be effective in combating neurotic or psychotic disorders, although they are helpful for changing specific unwanted emotional or behavioral reactions in otherwise stable personalities; 2) The benefits derived from classical conditioning procedures may not be due to counterconditioning at all, but may stem mainly from the patient's belief in the procedures (the placebo effect); 3) The flooding technique, also called implosive therapy, may produce negative side effects in some people. The most recent reports indicate that new techniques are being developed that use the best features of both operant and classical conditioning and also make positive use of the patient's expectations of success.

Part III

MODELING AS THERAPY

Chapter 8

THE BASIC METHODS OF MODELING

. . . children do not do what adults tell *them to do, but rather what they* see *other adults* do.[1]

MODELING AND OPERANT CONDITIONING

In the previous chapters we have not directly considered the possible effects of providing a behavioral example (that is, a "model") for the patient who might gain from the emulation of a new behavior pattern. When the therapist chooses not to provide such an example, he is assuming either that he can instill new modes of behavior into the patient through shaping procedures, or that something inherent in the talking process of psychotherapy will release the desired behavior pattern from bondage. The former

[1]Gladys Reichard. Social Life. In *General anthropology.* F. Boas (ed.), Boston: Heath, 1938, pp. 409–486 (471).

assumption rests on the belief that the operant techniques in themselves provide the most efficient mode of effecting overt behavioral change in the psychiatric patient. The latter assumption is based on the premise that positive behaviors, no matter how complex or how long dormant and unused by the patient, are in some way natural and inherent, and only need the trigger of "insight" or "catharsis" to emerge full-blown. When we do provide an example of desired behavior for the patient, the procedure is called modeling.

The principles of modeling and the therapeutic techniques that use behavioral modeling are fully embedded within the framework of learning theory. Modeling simply adds a dimension to the learning principles we have presented earlier. Without modeling, we will find it very difficult to achieve the behavioral goals that we set with our patients. When modeling is added to our behavioral approaches, the achievement of these goals may be quite strongly enhanced. Just as Mowrer (1960), early in the clinical development of operant conditioning, chided its practitioners that they could not teach a parrot to talk through their shaping procedures, so the clinician who does not incorporate measured modeling procedures into his treatment program may in many cases fail to achieve the behavioral goals he sets with his patients.

Let us consider the analogy of the parrot for the dramatic example it can give us of the facilitative effects of modeling upon learning. Think for a moment how a therapist who is rigidly committed to operant conditioning might attempt to teach a parrot to say, "Good morning." He would first deprive the bird of food, then he would wait for some sound to come for the bird. When the bird made such a sound, the trainer would quickly reward it with a grain of seed; then he would wait carefully for the animal to make a sound slightly more similar to the sound of a human voice. Again the bird would be rewarded. This shaping routine would continue until the bird emitted a sound resembling "Guh," then "Good"; and after weeks of tedious and laborious sessions, the *trainer* might finally be rewarded with the bird's culminative achievement of the phrase, "Good morning!"

Of course, such a scene is absurd. Not even the most dogmatic operant practitioner would be blinded to the simple procedural advantage of providing the animal with a model to emulate. He provides the model simply by repeating often and distinctly, in the bird's presence, the words "Good morning." Eventually this spontaneously produces the entire response. To date, we know of no operational rejoinder to Mowrer's challenge; that is, to our knowledge no one has yet taught a bird to speak any words at all through strictly operant procedures.

Similar in some ways to the example of the bird is the situation that virtually every father faces who attempts to find the most efficient method of teaching his child to play a sport. Imagine for a moment that a hypothetical parent wanted to use "scientific" operant procedures to teach his child batting skills. He could, if he chose, first reward the youth for picking up the bat, then successively reward him for ever closer approximations toward the proper grip, stance, and swing. Or he could use the much easier route of providing a model, at the same time giving directive instructions. "I hold the bat at the narrow end with both hands. I swing the bat like this, so it is very important that I put my left hand lower than my right. See what happens to me if I put my right hand below my left? Then my swing is awkward and I can't swing as hard." He takes the youth to a local ball game, which provides him with more models and so gives him a fuller concept of the various actions within the complex set of behaviors that comprise a sport. Of course, his attention must be guided to many of the finer points of play-execution. He is likely to note the most salient and easily reproduced behaviors first, such as the confident, cocky stride of the short-stop returning to the dugout, the lazy leaning upon his bat of the first baseman as he awaits his turn at the plate, and the manager's serious countenance and manner of expectoration following a critical play.

Modeling can be thought of as a means of shaping many discrete behaviors simultaneously. Some of these may be in the person's repetoire of behaviors, and others may be in some way innate. But modeling can help him to combine them in a complex form, such as swinging a bat or manifesting a cocky stride.

Of course, these examples of shaping a bird's speech behavior or a child's athletic activity seem far removed from the clinical setting. Yet, as we noted in presenting the operant approaches to therapy, such examples illustrate very neatly the manner in which operant procecures have been used in early attempts to modify the social behaviors of human beings. Today there are many well-directed behavioral treatment programs which still rely almost exclusively on the operant methods to promote behavioral change. The efficacy of these programs could be enhanced severalfold if correct modeling procedures were incorporated within them.

We can also use these examples to clarify the relationship between modeling and operant conditioning. The most important point is that modeling techniques do not supplant, but rather supplement the procedures of a behavioral treatment program. Both the bird and the child can learn the expected behaviors far more rapidly through exposure to an appropriate model and an appropriate reward system than through simple shaping procedures alone. The very powerful operant techniques can still be employed, supplemented by the modeling presentation. The bird and the boy can both be rewarded whenever they make the responses that gain closer approximation to successful achievement of the desired skills. By rewarding successive approximations in this way, we are still using shaping procedures. We have simply added a dimension that significantly enhances their effects.

HOW TO USE MODELING

While it is easy to recognize the utility of modeling in examples like these, what the student or beginning practitioner really needs is a *technique* that can be applied over a wide range of cases. In the examples of modeling that we have presented, the most important factors underlying the successful techniques are manifest. If we were to put them into the form of rules, we would have the following:

PROVIDE A MODEL.   Provide the patient with a clear, unambiguous demonstration of the behavior that he is expected to display. This can be accomplished through a live demonstration by the therapist himself or by an assistant, or through videotapes, audiotapes, or films.

PROVIDE DIRECTION.   While the model demonstrates a therapeutically important behavior, he may simultaneously be providing the patient with a number of therapeutically irrelevant cues, such as hairstyle, manner of walking, cultural dialect, and so on. The therapist should direct the patient's attention to those aspects of the model's behavior that are to be the present focus of the patient's strivings.

SHAPE BEHAVIOR.   By "shaping" we mean that the therapist should encourage small step-by-step progress toward the goal behavior rather than expecting the patient to adopt the total goal behavior immediately. A boy will not become a power-hitter overnight, no matter how great the skill of his model. Also, a fearful, shy adolescent will not immediately flash a warm grin, present a solid handshake, and maintain steady eye contact during an interview with an unfamiliar adult. These skills will have to be gradually practiced. Ideally, the model should not only display the goal behavior, but should himself demonstate the shaping, or hierarchical progression, by exhibiting the various steps along the way toward the target.

REWARD.   The therapist should reward the patient for the successful performance of each step toward the behavioral goal. As is the case with all behavioral methods, any type of reward can be used depending on what can be agreed upon by the therapist and patient. Simple social rewards (praise, information about the patient's progress) may be the most effective. In addition, the model's behavior should result at each point in consequences clearly rewarding to himself (the model).

These rules are gross generalizations of the findings of the research conducted on modeling conditions. They also represent an extrapolation of the major points made in several publications by Albert Bandura, the foremost researcher and primary developer of the modeling approach to behavior modification (see especially Bandura, 1971). Bandura and his colleagues have systematically evaluated a number of factors that influence the potential impact of modeling upon an observer's behavior, and have evolved techniques that incorporate the above principles.

Although modeling aids (such as films and videotapes) can be helpful, they are not entirely necessary to the promotion of behavioral change. In a study by Sarason and Ganzer (1969), therapists and assistants worked with delinquent boys in all sorts of stressful situations. These workers actually demonstrated by their own actions the specific behaviors that the boys should use to cope best with these situations. Among the problems presented were dealing with an authority figure, handling job expectations, and countering peer pressure toward deviant behavior. The therapists repeatedly rehearsed with the boys the skills that they had witnessed. Compared to control groups, the treated boys showed greater adaptability and more successful mastery of such situations.

An Example: A Case Study

Bill was a quiet and retiring adolescent who had participated only rarely in sports, but had no physical impairments. In the course of treatment, it became obvious that this was a factor in his self-concept and in his relations with others.

He agreed to attempt to become more involved in constructive physical interaction with his peers, but he just did not know how to do this. We started by providing a therapist who modeled effective participation in athletics; and our program to teach Bill volleyball began. Each day, the therapist and Bill played volleyball with the adolescent patients, and Bill was given direction by being shown how to play. He quickly learned appropriate technique in volleyball. His behavior was shaped and verbally rewarded by the therapist.

The fascinating part of this process was to watch Bill imitating complex behaviors. He was moving in an assertive way, with many of his therapist's mannerisms; he inflected his verbal exclamations in the same way as his therapist. He was copying complex, assertive athletic behaviors. This pattern has been maintained; Bill receives rewards from his peer group regularly for his newly learned skills. He has individualized his expressions and has progressed in his physical skills, so he is not becoming a copy of his therapist. But we feel that without an effective model, it would have taken much longer to help Bill to develop skills in *both* areas; how to play volleyball and how to act when playing volleyball.

SUMMARY

The modeling techniques are fully compatible with both the operant and classical conditioning approaches. If the therapist who is applying these techniques is also able to supply a model of the goal behavior for the patient, the time it takes the patient to reach the behavioral goals may be reduced.

Four rules underlie the proper application of any modeling approach: provide a model for the patient, provide clear direction toward the goal behavior, use operant methods to shape behavior, and reward the patient's improvements. These steps were illustrated through a case study.

Chapter 9

RESEARCH ON THE MODELING METHODS

In human societies, the provision of models not only serves to accelerate the learning process but also, in cases where errors are dangerous or costly, becomes an essential means of transmitting behavior patterns. One would not, for example, permit an adolescent to learn to drive a car by means of trial-and-error procedures, nor would one entrust a firearm to an armed services recruit without a demonstration of how it should be handled.[1]

HISTORY

Bandura (1969) traces the history of the study of "observational learning" to the turn of the century:

The earliest formulations date back to Morgan (1896), Tarde (1903), and McDougall (1908), regarding modeling

[1]Albert Bandura and Richard H. Walters. *Social learning and personality development.* New York: Holt, Rinehart and Winston, 1964, p. 52.

as an innate propensity. These instinctual interpretations dissuaded empirical investigations of the conditions under which modeling occurs; and because of the vehement reactions against the instinct doctrine, until recently even the phenomena subsumed under the concept tended to be either repudiated or widely ignored in theoretical explanations of the learning processes. [pp. 120–121]

It was the work mainly of Bandura himself, with his colleague R. H. Walters, and the publication in 1963 of their book *Social learning and personality development,* that ignited the resurgence of interest in the phenomena of observational learning. In that volume the authors skillfully arranged an impressive number of studies that they and other researchers had been quietly publishing in the social science journals during the previous decade. The book's major focus was upon the original acquisition and maintenance of various general behavior patterns, such as aggression, dependency, and sexual behavior. The potential application to clinical work was immediately obvious.

The authors presented wide-ranging evidence, which repeatedly demonstrated that exposure to a model is a powerful positive influence toward the patient's future demonstration of the observed behavior. In doing so, Bandura and Walters clearly showed that modeling is a force to be contended with in the development of human behavior. Even in the absence of clearly developed clinical modeling techniques, it was obvious that these findings could potentially contribute additional influences to behavioral change, beyond those already available.

MODELING AND AGGRESSIVE BEHAVIOR

Nowhere is violence in the cause of good more consistently and more enthusiastically touted than in movies and on TV. [2]

[2]Leonard Berkowitz. Impulse, aggression and the gun. *Psychology Today,* 1968, *2,* (October): 20.

The work presented in the volume by Bandura and Walters, supplemented by strong confirmatory evidence from the laboratory of Leonard Berkowitz at the University of Wisconsin, caught the notice of President Johnson's Advisory Commission on the Causes of Violence. The inquiries of this commission marked one of the first occasions that scientific researchers in the social sciences had received both priority hearing and wide publicity on issues of national legislative importance. One of the subjects of major interest to that commission was the effect of televised violence on the propensities of citizens themselves, and particularly children, to engage in violent, aggressive behavior. At least one of the studies mentioned by Bandura and Walters is now a classic in the field (Bandura, Ross, and Ross, 1963).

In this project, Bandura, Ross, and Ross (1963) compared the effects of various forms of modeling upon the aggressive behavior of three- to five-year-old children. Children in the experiment first observed one of the following models: an adult, in a playroom with the children, who merely sat quietly (a nonaggressive live model); an adult who attacked a large inflated clown and treated it with great violence (an aggressive live model); an adult on film who violently attacked the inflated clown (an aggressive film model); and a film cartoon character who used the same violent actions as the real models (an aggressive cartoon model). The children were then individually given mild frustration by being shown very appealing toys but not being allowed to have contact with them. Each child was then left alone in the playroom with the less attractive toys. The activities of all the children were filmed through a one-way mirror, and the aggressive behaviors were counted.

The pictures that accompany the text of the Bandura, Ross, and Ross study vividly depict how remarkably similar the actions of the children were to those of the models that they had observed. A more precise indication of the effects of the modeling came from the enumeration of the average number of aggressive behaviors shown by each group of frustrated children who had been exposed to one of the various models:

	Average number of aggressive acts per child[1]
Aggressive cartoon model	99
Aggressive film model	92
Aggressive live model	83
No model	54
Nonaggressive live model	41

These results indicated that exposure to aggressive models can influence the aggressive behavior of children. In addition, they suggested that the provision of a nonaggressive model possibly can actually reduce the "natural" (that is, emerging without a model) frequency of aggressive acts by children.

Liebert and Baron (1972) strongly confirmed these findings, and added an extra dimension of persuasiveness. These authors evaluated the effects of viewing televised violence or nonviolence upon the behaviors of children in an actual free-play setting. The aggressive program elicited a significantly greater amount of aggressive play among young viewers than the nonaggressive program.

Even though the study by Bandura, Ross, and Ross (1963) and subsequent studies on the same issues have been clearly and dramatically relevant to the always serious problem of aggression in our society, no one has expected them to stand alone in suggesting policy positions on social

[1]A child could produce as many as 240 aggressive responses during the observation period. Each child was rated every 5 sec. for 20 min. (240 rating units). Any aggressive behavior within the 5 sec. interval was scored as an "aggressive response." (From Bandura, 1962.)

issues such as the control of content of television programs. Nor is there any widespread claim that the results of a few such studies will provide fundamental proof that the observation of models is one of the factors that have important effects upon human behavior. Rather, it is the progressive accumulation of many studies that adds weight to the conclusions of each. Alberta Siegel (1970) has made this same point:

> One reason that Bandura's work is so widely respected by other psychologists is that conclusions from it do not rest on a single study. Rather he has conducted a series of investigations over the years, using different children and different films. Each study adds to the strength of the conclusions we can draw. [p. 218]

As a sidelight on the issue of televised violence, Berkowitz (1968a, 1968b) has expanded Bandura's findings. His work has shown dramatically that video programming of violence may not only be potentially dangerous to our culture, but the style in which the media usually portray violence may be the most dangerous factor of all. Through rather complex experimental procedures, Berkowitz has demonstrated that *justified* violence is more likely to induce aggressive behavior in the viewer than is nonrationalized violence or no violence at all.

Without going into detail, the basic method of the Berkowitz studies has been first to arouse anger in the subject toward an experimental stooge. This is usually accomplished through ridicule, or other such methods. The experimental subject next views one of two films: a bloody fight (a scene from *Champion*), or a nonviolent but exciting track battle between two of the earliest four-minute-mile runners. Half of the subjects who view the fight scene receive a plot summary that indicates that the loser "had it coming," while the other subjects find out that the brutal beating was clearly not deserved. Finally, each subject is given the chance to administer an "electric shock" to the stooge that has antagonized him. The subjects who have viewed the violent scene consistently administer stronger shocks than other persons. Those exposed to the justified violence deal out the worst shocks of all. These are so severe that it is fortunate for the stooge that the "shock" is also counterfeit, and delivers no actual damage.

This basic experimental design has since been used by a number of researchers, who have all supported the basic findings of Berkowitz, and have added important refinements. For example, Waldman and Baron (1971) showed that angry subjects who viewed a nonaggressive model gave shorter shocks than subjects who viewed no model at all. Baron (1971) produced similar results, but he found that if the subject viewed both an aggressive and a nonaggressive model in an anger-provoking situation, the latter model always had a restraining effect on the delivery of the shock; but this model was most effective when he was observed before rather than after the aggressive model. In a study by Meyer (1971), the justification of violence influenced the shock level even more than did the modeling itself; this indicated (in agreement with Berkowitz) that not all of the complex effects of modeling have yet been fully analyzed and established in solid principles. One point that is quite consistent and clear throughout all these and other similar studies is that the effects of observing a model upon the subsequent aggressive or unaggressive behavior of a young person are greater than the effects of being frustrated (Savitsky et al., 1971; Kuhn et al., 1967) or being angered. Finally, a study by Cohen (1971) indicates that with children, peers may be the most effective models in determining the level of aggression that will be displayed. In terms of clinical practice, this may suggest that an effective treatment program for aggressive young people would incorporate a number of solidly nonaggressive young persons. Alternatively, the program could make the viewing of videotapes of such children a regular component of its scheduled activities.

The implications of the Berkowitz studies is that the manner in which we have most commonly presented violence through our mass media may be the most dangerous form of presentation that we could choose. Not only is the violence we view often presented as justified, but the winner of the violent confrontations usually receives several rewards after his victory. This ties in very neatly with the findings that the prestige of the model (Bandura, 1969b) and the consequences to the model of his behavior (Baer, Peterson, and Sherman, 1967; Bandura, 1971) affect the probability that the viewer will engage in similar actions. The classical television hero is, almost by definition, a person of high status. His success in violent encounters invariably brings him gratifying results, if not outright approbation and respect. Thus the time-honored guideline for violence on the media—that it is acceptable if the violence of the "good" side defeats the violence of the "bad" side (in other words, if it is justified violence)—may result in the most socially damaging context possible for the depiction of violence. A far better rule for a society that desires to encourage a nonviolent standard in the conduct of its citizens might be to depict the users of violence as unattractive, incompetent, and stupid people who never profit from their aggressive acts.

These studies have made landmark contributions to psychology, because they were among the first to derive evidence of actual behavioral effects from witnessing the social behavior of others. Before the development of these experimental designs, a large proportion of the work had been designed to elaborate theoretical explanations of aggressive behavior. An even larger number of studies had focused upon the delineation and measurement of "attitudes" (usually as defined by paper-and-pencil responses). In the type of study initiated by Bandura, on the other hand, actual, overt aggressive or nonaggressive *acts* were related to the stimuli to which the individual had been exposed.

The studies we have mentioned thus far, by both the Bandura and the Berkowitz groups, have served as foundations for further documentation and specification of the effects of the modeling influences of television on the aggressive behavior of children and adolescents. Yet our purpose here is not to seek to influence the media, even though as citizens we are clearly interested in the issues that surround the contents of the media. It is more pertinent to the goals of this book simply to illustrate the types of study that have served as foundations for many of our clinical applications of modeling techniques.

THE CLINICAL STUDIES

The clinical applications of these findings came rapidly. Hill, Liebert, and Mott (1968) produced a film for presentation to pre-school boys who were immoderately afraid of dogs. The viewers of this film saw a young boy overcoming his fears of dogs by himself watching an older boy play with one. The fearful boy slowly joined in the play activity. After they had seen the film, the experimental subjects were given an opportunity to approach a live dog. Eight out of nine boys willingly did this, while fearful boys who had seen no film refused.

This elementary study was not meant, of course, to establish for all time a technique for the treatment of clinical syndromes, even if the syndrome in question were manifested by a fear of dogs. The major original contribution of this study was to document further the potential impact of television content upon children's behavior. In addition, the study accomplished two other goals of note. First, it demonstrated that television programming can be used to foster adaptive, as well as negative, behaviors in children.

Second, it presented a potential method for the systematic use of modeling principles in the treatment of a quasi-clinical emotional difficulty. A more directly clinical application followed shortly, when Herskovitz, Liebert, and Adelson (1971) produced a film that showed a boy overcoming his fear of dentists. This film was first presented to children whose mothers stated they were afraid of the dentist, then to a group of hospitalized retarded and disturbed children; the children's fearful behavior was much reduced in real-life dental encounters.

Now that we have given some background for our interest in the effects of modeling in behavioral adaption, let us take a look at some of the therapeutic applications that have been developed to date, as reviewed by Bandura (1971). The practitioners of the modeling systems have produced clinical techniques that have at least one feature very strongly in their favor: the reports of their therapeutic effects have been consistently documented, and their results carefully compared with those of control groups.

FEAR-REDUCTION STUDIES IN NON-CLINICAL POPULATIONS

Studies designed to evaluate the effectiveness of a treatment procedure in alleviating simple fears are at once the most satisfying and the most frustrating investigations available. Their strengths lie in several factors, one of which is their sheer number; they are churned out *en masse* by doctoral candidates in clinical psychology university departments around the country. The results of these studies are usually as clear and unambiguous as are ever likely to appear in therapy studies; how closely the subject is able to approach the feared object is a clear and simple measure of the treatment's effectiveness. Because of the simplicity of these studies and their uncluttered designs, they have been the vehicles chosen to probe the workings of virtually all of the newer behavioral techniques. Studies of simple, nonclinical fears now comprise the backbone of current evaluations of the classical conditioning therapies. Therefore the effectiveness of one fear-reduction technique (for instance, systematic desensitization) can be plainly compared with that of other methods (implosion, placebo). Such comparisons are of inestimable value to the clinician, as well as to the health and progress of this area of behavioral science.

The shortcomings of these studies, however, are also significant. They traditionally deal with single, easily measured fears, for example of cats, rats, snakes, or spiders—not the type of thing that usually brings people to clinical attention. While a few studies (for example, Gelder and Marks, 1966; Agras, Leitenberg, and Barlow, in press) have examined full clinical phobias (agoraphobia, fear of leaving the house), the milder, monosymptomatic fears have received the overwhelming bulk of investigation. Also the subjects for these studies by and large have been not clinical cases, but normally functioning college students. Therefore, even the clear demonstration that a treatment technique is of significant value in reducing the fear of snakes in college girls does not necessarily show it to be effective in reducing *all* fears, or even in reducing the fear of snakes in psychiatric patients.

These studies have, therefore, been criticized as superficial and irrelevant to the treatment of broadly anxious patients with full-blown clinical syndromes. Holding these criticisms in mind, we will reiterate our reasons for viewing the studies on the treatment of simple fears as the most vital and helpful research currently available for those choosing between the various therapeutic strategies. These studies have repeatedly evaluated both the relative effectiveness of a number of therapeutic techniques and their efficiency in terms of time and manpower.

The first of a series of these explorations on a modeling treatment was conducted by Bandura, Grusec, and

Menlove (1967) on children's fears of dogs. Some of these fearful children observed a peer model interacting with a dog in a graduated manner. Others simply observed a dog from a distance during their "treatment" sessions, and still others engaged in activities unrelated to dogs. The modeling procedure was clearly the superior of the three techniques in enabling the children to have contact with dogs in a "real-life" setting. Bandura and Menlove (1968) extended this research to determine whether providing more than one model for a behavior would be even more successful than the single-model procedure. They found that while both groups of fearful children—those who observed only a single model interacting with a dog, and those who saw several models—relinquished their avoidant behavior immediately after treatment, the single-model children were more likely to show some regression than the multiple-model children. Still, even the children who showed regression did not revert to nearly their pretreatment level of avoidance.

Probably the best study that we have found of the effects of modeling techniques in fear reduction is that conducted by Bandura, Blanchard, and Ritter (1969). It is discussed at length in Bandura (1971). The importance of this study stems from the thorough planning that went into it; as a result, an impressive amount of information was harvested from the outcome data. In this work, the authors compared the effectiveness of a guided-participation modeling approach with that of systematic desensitization. The goal was the reduction of the fear of snakes in adults and adolescents. The subjects were females whose fears of snakes were ostensibly severe enough to interfere with some aspects of their daily functioning. The effects of a modeling technique without guided participation were also studied. (In the latter, the patients themselves controlled the presentation of a film that depicted a model in increasingly intense contacts with snakes.) That the guided-participation treatment was no simple intellectual exercise can be appreciated from Bandura's description (1971):

> The therapist himself performed the fearless behavior at each step and gradually led subjects into touching, stroking, and then holding the snake's body with gloved and bare hands while the experimenter held the snake securely by head and tail. If a subject was unable to touch the snake following ample demonstration, she was asked to place her hand on the experimenter's and to move her hand down gradually until it touched the snake's body. After subjects no longer felt any apprehension about touching the snake under these secure conditions, anxieties about contact with the snake's head area and entwining tail were extinguished. The therapist again performed the tasks fearlessly, and then he and the subject performed the responses jointly; as subjects became less fearful, the experimenter gradually reduced his participation and control over the snake, until eventually subjects were able to hold the snake in their laps without assistance, to let the snake loose in the room and retrieve it, and to let it crawl freely over their bodies. Progress through the graded approach tasks was paced according to the subjects' apprehensiveness. When they reported being able to perform one activity with little or no fear, they were eased into a more difficult interaction. [p. 680]

While both the film-viewing ("symbolic modeling") and the systematic desensitization procedures reduced snake-avoidant behavior significantly, as compared to that of an untreated control group, the guided-participation technique brought about behavioral change significantly beyond even the achievements of these otherwise successful treatments. In fact, the authors reported successful "elimination" of snake fears in 92 per cent of the live cases treated by modeling with guided participation.

It should be noted that if this study had been conducted simply as a test of systematic desensitization or of simple "exposure to a model," the results in each case would have categorized the treatment as "successful." The significant superiority of the guided-participation method over two otherwise successful treatments constitutes a remarkable demonstration of the power of such procedures.

In addition to assessing the subjects' post-therapeutic behavior toward snakes, Bandura and his colleagues also measured the strengths of several other fears that the subjects held, even though these had not received direct treatment. Both modeling procedures were showed to be clearly superior over systematic desensitization in reducing these "extraneous" fears. The desensitized individuals showed some reduction of extraneous fears. They tended to respond with a somewhat lower fear-rating to a variety of animals they had previously feared. The symbolic modeling group showed this reduction and a scattered lowering of fears in other areas as well. Those who engaged in the guided participation virtually unanimously reported lowering of fears in all areas, including reactions to interpersonal threats. Bandura (1971) explains how he feels this occurred: "Having successfully overcome a phobia that had plagued them for most of their lives, subjects reported increased confidence that they could cope effectively with other fear-provoking events" (p. 684).

SUMMARY

We have presented a number of nonclinical and clinical studies that demonstrate the effectiveness of modeling in modifying behavior. The evidence indicates that modeling is a learning technique that effectively reduces the level of anxiety or inhibition in an individual. There is some evidence that it can be used to inhibit behaviors but it appears to be weaker as an inhibitor than as a disinhibitor. In the next chapter we will review details of the modeling process.

Chapter 10

CRITICAL ASSESSMENT OF THE MODELING METHODS

In many institutions, when a youth does something wrong, such as calling the psychiatric aide an obscene name, the aide himself has a tantrum and shouts, "You can't call me that!" The aide engages in the very behavior he should be teaching the youth to avoid. Many parents, teachers and spouses do the same thing.[1]

BASIC CONCLUSIONS

After reviewing the research available on modeling to date, we have come to the following conclusions: (1) The theory that modeling is one factor that influences human behavior has been fully substantiated; (2) techniques of

[1]Elery L. Phillips, Elaine A. Phillips, Dean L. Fixsen, and Montrose M. Wolf. Behavior shaping works for delinquents. *Psychology Today*, 1973, 7 (June): 75–79 (79).

behavioral change that apply modeling principles in a systematic fashion have been demonstrated to be effective additions to psychiatric treatment; (3) when any conditioning approach to behavior modification is used with a patient, the effectiveness of this treatment can be significantly enhanced through the systematic incorporation of modeling procedures; (4) the influence of modeling factors upon behavioral change in patients has been more extensively studied, and more thoroughly and unambiguously proved, than any of the more widely known classical conditioning therapies.

COMPARISON WITH VISUALIZATION PROCEDURES

Advocates of systematic desensitization, or other conditioning procedures based upon visualization, could argue that while modeling techniques may ultimately be more beneficial to the patient, the necessary materials are too difficult to acquire and maintain. To continue this contention, it could be argued that the great advantage of those techniques in which the person imagines a personally difficult situation is that the entire treatment is conducted *in his head.* Extraneous materials need not be elaborately constructed to present the person with the precise situation that causes him difficulty. Further, the specific circumstances can, through fantasy, be individualized for each person. Once the individual determines exactly which things bring on his disordered behavior, he can best establish in his own imagination the conditions that most closely approximate the critical situations.

This argument might be countered on several levels, but we think that two considerations in particular should not be overlooked. The first must be formulated in light of the evidence on the effectiveness of systematic desensitization, implosive therapy, covert sensitization, and any of the other imaginal therapies. These treatments have thus far not been found effective with persons who display more than monosymptomatic disorders. Looking back to our review of the research on the therapeutic outcome of these approaches, we repeat our conclusion: the imaginal therapies are useful in reducing unreasonable fears or other behavioral anomalies in relatively healthy individuals; but for persons with more pervasive behavioral or emotional disorders, these techniques have thus far failed to establish their clinical usefulness.

On the other hand, as we have noted earlier, modeling procedures have been tested on a broad spectrum of subjects, ranging from healthy college students and vocational counselees to severely disturbed psychotic patients. As Cowden and Ford (1962) and Meyer and Crisp (1966) indicate, it often appears that many hospitalized patients either cannot or will not visualize the scenes required for the imaginal treatments (and it is often nearly impossible for the therapist to determine whether the patient is really visualizing, or is visualizing adequately); hence it seems to us that simple, demonstrable, repeatable behaviors, openly modeled and practiced, would be the most appropriate prescription from the standpoint of both therapist and patient.

The second point concerns the nature of the symptoms, or disordered behaviors, that the patient presents. For research purposes, fairly innocuous fears of snakes, spiders, dogs, or other environmental stimuli are the "symptoms" most often explored. In such cases, one could argue that it might be easier to have the patient visualize his uniquely feared object than to maintain on hand a supply of snakes, spiders, rats, cats, and dogs for therapeutic purposes. But these are not the types of disorders that are usually treated clinically. It is very rare that a person seeks out a mental health professional to help him with a simple fear of an animal or some other specific object. People usually come, or are brought, to treatment because they have difficulties with other people. There may be minimal social interaction, assaultive behaviors, timid or nervous idiosyncrasies, school failure that is not due to lack of intellectual capacity, suicidal threats or gestures, marital and family conflicts, or other manifestations of social dysfunction. Positive social skills are quite open to training through modeling. No special equipment is needed; people are almost ubiquitous.

SOME LIMITATIONS

Although the concept of modeling would theoretically seem to be almost without limit, in terms of the persons whom it can help and the behaviors it can influence, recent research is indicating that this influence has some boundaries. Reviewing the literature on the "moral development" of children, Hoffman (1970) pointed out that, while modeling had been shown to "disinhibit" all sorts of behaviors successfully (that is, to influence people to demonstrate behaviors that they have not shown in the past), it has not been shown to influence people to "inhibit," or restrain, negative behaviors. Clinically this would mean that modeling influences could help individuals to approach things that they fear, to speak more openly and more forcefully, or to adopt more confident mannerisms, but could not help them to cut down on swearing, smoking, or handwashing. Modeling was seen to be ineffective whenever reduction of a habit, or resistance to temptation was the goal.

Rosenkoetter (1973) felt that the only fair way to give this an adequate test would be to provide a situation that offered such high levels of temptation that subjects who viewed neither a yielding nor a resisting model would show a relatively high level of spontaneous yielding. In this way the influence of models could be compared: would yielding models influence subjects more strongly to yield than resisting models influenced them to resist? Rosenkoetter designed the following situation to test this: children were told to listen to the sound track of a cartoon, and to record those points at which there were "flaws" in the film. The cartoons were projected out of the visual range of the subjects, who were told not to leave their seats during the film's running time. Models were of course provided for most of the children. Some models resisted the temptation to leave their seats; others yielded to the temptation. It was found that exposure to the deviant models did, in fact, greatly increase the amount that children "normally" (that is, without viewing a model) broke the rules. Resistant models, on the other hand, reduced the level of deviancy somewhat, but they did not affect behavior as much as the deviant models. These results partially support Hoffman's (1970) conclusion. It appears that modeling, at least as currently employed, is most powerful in releasing inhibited behavior. At this point, it does not seem to be as effective in reducing or restraining behavior that the individual already shows. If we look back to the findings of Bandura, Ross, and Ross (1963) on the effects of modeling on children's expression of aggression, we can note the remarkable similarity to Rosenkoetter's results. Aggressive models influenced aggressive behavior to a greater extent than did the nonaggressive models, even though the latter models did show a moderate dampening influence upon the children's aggressive behavior.

We can accept these findings as a restriction upon global claims for the utility of modeling. However, they probably do not mean that we cannot gainfully incorporate modeling into the treatment of an individual who desires to reduce negative behavior. Modeling may yet be quite helpful in providing the patient with *alternative* responses, in those situations where his undesired behavior is most likely to occur. As with the operant conditioning procedures, then, the clinician's aim may sometimes be not so much to help the patient to restrict his behavior as to help him to find and practice alternative behaviors to replace the nondesired activities.

A second restriction upon claims for the effectiveness of therapeutic modeling stems from the lack of research on the effects of these methods in mentally retarded groups. Altman, Talkington, and Cleland (1972) have shown that retarded patients tend to show a low level of spontaneous response to modeling influences. Baer, Peterson, and Sherman (1967) show that modeling can be useful with these patients if it is combined with a well-planned operant program, and with effective rewards. With retarded patients, then, modeling systems may need to be more strongly embedded in an operant reward system than is necessary with other types of patients.

INFORMAL USES OF MODELING

There are a few simple rules that can be kept in mind to make modeling an unofficial (as well as official) part of the therapeutic milieu. Just as we feel that positive psychotherapy can pervade the atmosphere of the treatment milieu and can take place during any verbal interaction with the patient, we also feel that appropriate modeling is essential in the behavioral patterns of the caretaking personnel. In hiring staff to work with psychiatric hospital inpatients, most administrators naturally make some attempt to select those who can provide positive examples for emulation by the patients. We also feel that each part of the treatment program will benefit from careful scrutiny of the staff's social behavior as it will be observed by patients. This can help the staff to establish policies of behavior that will provide models of the type of social functioning that they hope to encourage in the patients. It seems to us that people who are working in a therapeutic program must *demonstrate* that their life styles are successful, rewarding, and interpersonally satisfying. Life styles that are effective for the persons living them can provide attractive daily models for the hospitalized patient whose life style has not satisfied his needs efficiently.

It is useful to ask a number of questions concerning the behaviors we expect the patients to learn, and to ask ourselves how our behaviors correspond to those we mean to teach. Do we, for example, expect the patient to learn to be open, honest, and self-exploring in order to gain the most from psychotherapy? If so, do we expect the same from ourselves, or are we defensive and abstruse? In psychotherapy do we reciprocate with the patient in discussing our feelings, our emotional responses, and the effects of our behavior on others? Or do we let the patient know that he is the one to be treated, while we sit back and analyze or criticize? If under the latter conditions the patient finds therapy a difficult task, do we help by "opening ourselves up," or do we let the patient know that he is "not cooperating," and that this is probably due to his residual hostility or weakness?

MODELING AND PSYCHOTHERAPY

Direct research on the usefulness of modeling procedures in combination with effective psychotherapy skills is sparse to nonexistent. The need for well-designed studies in this area is great; yet it should not be difficult to design the appropriate investigations. Strangely enough, the study that comes closest to examining the effects of modeling in combination with psychotherapeutic processes was not done in a clinical setting at all. Instead, Savicki (1972) used an experimental setting to study the degree to which a person's self-disclosure would be influenced by observing a peer disclosing his own inner life. When the peer, who was a trained confederate of the experimenter, disclosed at only a low level, the subject predictably disclosed little about himself. At all levels of self-disclosure by the confederate, the subject showed similar levels of disclosure. This certainly is not a surprising finding, but if the results are verified in therapeutic settings, they could provide the clinical practitioner with a new mode of operation. He may need to become trained in setting the patient at ease by initiating self-disclosure. In group sessions he could do the same, or he could have confederates or long-term patients set examples of self-disclosure for the newer members. Possibly even pretherapy tape recordings that the patient could hear while waiting for the therapist could provide a "warm-up" for therapy.

The learning of empathy by trainees in counseling has also been shown to be enhanced by modeling. A study by Payne, Weiss, and Kapp (1972) did not bear on its potential for training patients in empathy skills, but the results once again show modeling to be useful in the teaching of therapy skills. In this situation, the levels of empathic communication shown by students were affected both by listening to a lecture about the importance of empathy in counseling and by listening to models of empathic skills. Not unexpectedly, those students who were exposed to both the lecture and the modeling rated highest of all in the communication of empathy. Those students who simply conducted an interview, and were then supervised in a nondirective manner, gained nothing from the experience in terms of their ability to express empathy. The suggestion presents itself that perhaps, as in Carkhuff's vision of "training as treatment" (1971), the patients might benefit from being treated as *students* of effective communication and interpersonal relationships.

Many of the arguments according to which the therapist should function as a model of effective interpersonal functioning have been presented by other writers. Regarding group therapy, Garetz and Fix (1972) have stressed a number of these same points:

> Perhaps therapists who avoid full emotional participation in groups should ask themselves if they are expecting more of their patients than they are asking of themselves. Should they expect more? The answer seems to be that if a group leader expects emotional honesty from the other group members, he should be the first to demonstrate it in his own functioning.
>
> The rapidly growing literature on modeling also supports the concept that the patient benefits when his therapist is honest about his feelings. That is because people learn most rapidly by observing a model, whether they are being trained as a baseball player, cook, or psychotherapist, or whether a patient is being taught to deal more effectively with life situations. Psychotherapists often overlook one of their most important functions—to show the patient "how it's done." Many focus on the patient's inability to express or handle certain emotions, or his inaccurate labeling or denial of them, when they might better demonstrate honest self-exploration and reflective appraisal of their own emotional life.
>
> The therapist can become a model actively and openly taking part in the total life of the group. That will encourage the members to risk similar behavior and will give them an opportunity to decide how useful such behavior would be in their own lives. [p. 250]

Possibly the basic concept here is stated in the authors' criticism of therapists who "expect more of their patients" than they do of themselves. We urge those involved in treatment programs not to demand behavior from their patients that they are not willing to demonstrate themselves. Do we expect a patient to stop fighting? Then we must demonstrate effective methods of handling our own angry feelings without hurting another human being. We must show that we can use negotiation skills to handle all sorts of interpersonal conflicts, whether these occur with a patient, with our supervisors, or with other staff members. In addition, *we must control ourselves from responding in a harmful or punitive way to a patient's physical aggression.* If he needs to be controlled in order to protect himself or another person, then such control must be administered with a minimum of force. Physical control should be given in a calm manner, accompanied by reassurances that we do not intend to harm or humiliate the patient.

Do we expect the patient to attend classes, meetings, and other activities? The staff members who are involved in each of these events must be punctual and consistent in their attendance.

Do we expect the patient to interact with others in a pleasant, cooperative manner? Then one of the guidelines for our behavior should be to treat him and others in a respectful, courteous, cordial fashion. We will not *order* him to rise in the morning, to "get to industrial therapy," or to clean his room. We will rather inform him of the time in the morning, assure him that we will help him to be at work on time, and inform him of our reaction to the dirt in his room and the actions that will be taken if it remains, such as withholding passes or special privileges until the room is clean.

Do we expect appropriate sexual conduct from our patients? In our relations with members of the opposite sex, then, we must show behavior that is warm, friendly, and open but not suggestive or seductive. We must demonstrate communication patterns with members of the opposite sex that give precisely the messages that we want to convey regarding sexuality; that and our manner of dress should convey an accurate statement of the way we want others to respond to us sexually. Style of communication and dress may speak most eloquently to those patients who often provoke sexual responses that they do not ostensibly desire from others.

MODELING BY PARENTS

The possibility that therapeutic modeling can be useful in some of the areas just mentioned is suggested by studies which indicate that the models provided by his parents have already strongly influenced the individual's behavior patterns. In some studies, parental behavior has been shown to have more influence on their children's actions than the disciplinary techniques by which the parents attempt to guide their offspring. The parental model has a much stronger effect than other sources of influence in the case of aggressive behavior (reviewed in Bandura and Walters, 1964), cynical and selfish philosophies of life (O'Kelly and Solar, 1971), and even the misuse of drugs (Smart and Fejer, 1972). Indeed, Fazio (1972) found greater evidence that semiclinical insect phobias were vicariously learned in the family than that they were developed through a traumatic conditioning process. Bandura and Walters (1964) have commented on the list of studies which have shown that higher aggressiveness is found in · children whose parents use physical punishment of aggression, while lower aggression is found in children of parents who use nonviolent means of control.

> A parent who attempts to modify his child's behavior by inflicting severe physical punishments is providing an aggressive model from whom the child may learn aggressive means of responding in interpersonal situations. Although, because of fear of retaliation, the child may not counteraggress in the parent's presence, he may nevertheless model his behavior after that of his parent when he himself wishes to cope with or control the behavior of others. [p. 194]

The embodiment of this orientation to everyday modeling appears in a popular adage, which we have given prominent display on our office wall.[2] It reads:

[2]Copyright John Phillip Co., 1963.

Children Learn What They Live

If a child lives with criticism,
  He learns to condemn.
If a child lives with hostility,
  He learns to fight.
If a child lives with ridicule,
  He learns to be shy.
If a child lives with shame,
  He learns to feel guilty.
If a child lives with tolerance,
  He learns to be patient.
If a child lives with encouragement,
  He learns confidence.
If a child lives with praise,
  He learns to appreciate.
If a child lives with fairness,
  He learns justice.
If a child lives with security,
  He learns to have faith.
If a child lives with approval,
  He learns to like himself.
If a child lives with acceptance and friendship,
  He learns to find love in the world.

                              Dorothy Law Nolte

THE UNDERUSE OF MODELING

It has been a puzzle to us that the modeling procedures have not received the wide interest and application
that have accrued to many other forms of treatment. The
research and theoretical underpinings of the modeling
techniques seem to us more secure than those of any of the
purely classical conditioning approaches; yet clinical applications seem to be confined to a rather small (although
widely dispersed) group of practitioners. We are aware of
no survey on this, but we would estimate that the number
of psychiatrists and clinical psychologists who use operant
or classical conditioning procedures without systematic in-

corporation of modeling factors exceeds the number of their model-using colleagues by a ratio of 10:1 or more. A rough scan of the research literature lends some support to this estimate: it contains a disproportionately high number of articles on token economy systems and other conditioning topics, as compared to the number of articles on modeling. Recently, though, the latter topic does seem to be receiving an increasing amount of attention, particularly as it relates to children and adolescents.

There are probably several reasons why the modeling procedures have not been as enthusiastically implemented as the "pure" operant or classical techniques. One of the major reasons may be that the modeling activities demand more work from the therapist and more immediate involvement with, and attention to, specific patient behaviors. Modeling treatment strategies are redundant, sometimes tedious, and often unfulfilling for a professional clinician. The use of modeling strategies can often seem more like routine, repetitive labor than productive, stimulating intellectual exercise.

Another reason for the slow adoption of these techniques may stem from the mode of dissemination of the research from which they have developed. Bandura and his colleagues have presented their findings in a controlled, scientific manner. They have worked carefully, checking many hypotheses, and have built, piece by piece, a clinical approach out of a rather esoteric corner of research inquiry. They have been cautious in their claims and critical of generalizations that move ahead of the data. They have not engaged in polemics or the high-impact salesmanship of theory or techniques. Therefore, the findings of these investigators have not become as visible as other orientations, and many practitioners remain quite unaware of the clinical applicability of much of the research on modeling.

Still another reason why clinical practitioners have been slow to incorporate these techniques may be the self-consciousness of the professional himself. In most forms of modeling therapy at the present time, the therapist is called upon to demonstrate the behavior that he strives to encourage. For many therapists, this type of direct involvement, this degree of attention to his own (rather than the patient's) behavior, may evoke a degree of discomfort. Some therapists are more at ease when analyzing, diagnosing, and directing behavior than they are when displaying it. These therapists would be understandably slow to move into the behavior-modeling field.

A final possible reason for the slowness of incorporation of modeling procedures into psychiatric treatment programs may involve professional reactions to behavioral modes of treatment in general. Many professionals have shown considerable reluctance over the last years to move away from an exclusive talk orientation in therapy. In addition, the frequent use of unexciting procedures in behavior-modification approaches, and the emphasis on precision and documentation of patient change, have all been strongest in the case of modeling. Further, while some of the foremost advocates of certain of the conditioning techniques have either been psychiatrists themselves or have utilized psychiatric journals for the dissemination of their thoughts and research, the modeling approaches have been developed almost entirely by social, experimental, and clinical psychologists. Therefore, the modeling techniques may not have received the push and support that the other procedures have gained from psychiatry, the pinnacle profession of the "mental health team." We hope that the presentation in these chapters will encourage practitioners to make greater use of modeling procedures in patient therapy.

SUMMARY EVALUATION

The last three chapters have contained a short survey of the studies of modeling as a therapeutic procedure. They have also carried descriptions of some of the still unresolved issues in the field, as well as our own evaluative observations. Bandura's (1971) excellent review has served as the basis for a major portion of the research described. Here and there we have added a point of our own for consideration, and we have referred to a few studies that were published too late for inclusion in Bandura's (1971) article.

In our opinion, the modeling techniques have clearly demonstrated their usefulness as effective therapeutic techniques. They have been shown to be more effective in inducing behavioral change than the simple classical conditioning methods. Given the lack of documentation of specific behavioral changes that result from traditional psychotherapeutic activities, the behavioral results attained by means of the modeling procedures show that they are probably superior to the traditional approaches as well.

Two particular advantages of modeling aid us in the interpretations we can make from the data. Because of these advantages, we can make rather specific recommendations for the application of modeling principles to the treatment of psychiatric patients. The first of these advantages has been the clear demonstration that treatment effects are not placebo-dependent. Researchers have failed to uncover evidence that a placebo effect contributes to the target behavior of any modeling therapy program. This stands in contrast to the classical conditioning approaches, which, if not themselves pure placebos, are at least haunted by the spectre of the placebo (it has often shown as much therapeutic impact as the "more scientific" treatment).

The second advantage is that the research has evaluated the modeling procedures with a wide range of patients. We mentioned before that it has been very difficult to determine whether the classical conditioning techniques can be appropriately applied to the child or adolescent patient, since so few of the studies on those techniques used younger persons as subjects. Even more critical has been the lack of solid evidence that the classical conditioning techniques are effective with persons who suffer from more than simple, single behavioral anomalies. Here the researchers in modeling have been typically thorough. They have demonstrated the utility of their methods not only with college girls who fear snakes, but with patients of various clinical descriptions. Further, the modeling processes are widely applicable to the treatment of patients at the lower socioeconomic levels. This is potentially of far-reaching importance, since these patients, as Goldstein (1973) points out, not only comprise the majority of cases served by public psychiatric agencies, but they are also the patients who fail to derive significant benefit from the existing psychological techniques.

How can modeling be incorporated into a psychiatric treatment program? What is the role or place of modeling in such a system? In Chapter 7 we outlined the principles that should be followed in setting up a specific modeling treatment program aimed at individual problem behaviors. We now advocate that such programs be established whenever possible within, or in addition to, the usual treatment system.

Part IV

ECLECTIC THERAPY AND POSTSCRIPT

Chapter 11

COMBINING THE PSYCHOLOGICAL
THERAPIES

*It is unfortunately true that a token system by itself doesn't teach
the most important social skills. . . . Many clinical colleagues
have told us all along that the "relationship" is an essential
component of any therapy. We are now convinced that they are
right . . . we have been able to show new teaching-parents . . .
how to interact effectively.* [1]

THE ECLECTIC USE OF THE PSYCHOLOGICAL THERAPIES

The major treatment methods have been presented
separately, as if they could be administered independently.
Any particular theoretical orientation or specific treatment

[1]Elery L. Phillips, Elaine A. Phillips, Dean L. Fixsen, and Montrose M.
Wolf. Behavior shaping works for delinquents. *Psychology Today,* 1973,
7, (June): 75–79.

technique *by itself,* however, will probably not induce a higher or more effective level of change than would be found without therapeutic intervention. We believe that an effective program must combine those therapeutic ingredients that have the best scientific evidence of their validity at this time, regardless of their theoretical orientations. A blending of those approaches that really work into one program can, we hope, lead to the effective and efficient treatment of human emotional and behavioral disorders, unencumbered by the dogmatic formations derived from a bias in favor of one or another theoretical doctrine.

The more a person applies and combines the four components of psychological treatment in a psychiatric setting (psychotherapy, operant conditioning, classical conditioning, and modeling), the more he will come to see how, rather than clashing or being contradictory, they are all amazingly consistent with one another. It is also soon found that each approach is often dependent upon the successful operation of the others for its own success. We are convinced, for example, that none of the behavioral modification techniques can be effective if communication to the patient is negative and destructive (poor psychotherapy). We view psychotherapy as the backbone of any psychological treatment program. If positive psychotherapy is administered in all contacts with the patient, the other treatment techniques acquire increased potential for evoking constructive change in the patient.

At the same time, well-constructed behavior modification systems must be operated effectively to keep conflict between staff and patient at a minimum, so that constructive therapeutic communication can be maintained at a maximum level.

Modeling of goal behaviors can enhance the effectiveness of the psychotherapeutic and behavior modification systems. Classical conditioning procedures, when indicated (and when administered with a clearly communicated ex-

pectancy for success), will enhance the success of psychotherapy in attaining specific target behaviors.

PSYCHOTHERAPY IN BEHAVIOR MODIFICATION

We view psychotherapy (defined as facilitative interpersonal communication) as the basis for all effective psychological therapy. Behavior modification or other technique systems of treatment may also be effective, as has
been indicated by a considerable body of research. Yet we
believe that such technique approaches are only effective
when bolstered by a substrate of effective communication.
Behavior modification without facilitative interpersonal
communication is merely behavior control, and to date we
have no evidence that behavior control technologies
change the subject's behavior outside the controlling environment.

The facilitative communication skills that were reviewed in Chapter 3 probably enhance the effectiveness of
the operant behavioral techniques because of their high
potency as *social reinforcers.* Social reinforcement seems to
be a major component of the verbal therapies (Krasner,
1962), and while the material reinforcements seem to get
the bulk of the glory in behavior modification programs,
the social foundations of these programs are probably the
actual therapeutic agents. Kuypers, Becker, and O'Leary
(1968) came unexpectedly to this conclusion when they
attempted to discover the reason for the failure of a token
classroom system that had earlier been reported remarkably successful by O'Leary and Becker (1967). They found
that the teachers in the successful program had been
trained in the use of contingent social reinforcement, while
the teachers in the unsuccessful program had not. Thus,
even though the token payoffs were theoretically set up for
a maximal influence on behavior in both programs, these

tangible reinforcers were apparently *superceded* in importance by the underlying social components.

Let us illustrate the underlying power of psychotherapy with a hypothetical example: a therapy program that on the surface appears strictly behavioral in nature, but when analyzed further is perhaps better described as a "programmed psychotherapy approach." Our hypothetical example is a single operant conditioning program as it might be put into practice by different nurses. The nurse in Program I is low in psychotherapeutic skills, while the nurse in Program II functions at a high psychotherapeutic level. In the following illustrations, both programs have the same reinforcement schedules. On the surface, then, they are the same operant treatment program; but we expect that they will produce dramatically contrasting results. The patient is a middle-aged male inpatient. The program is designed to help him to interact positively with others as a first step toward better interpersonal relations outside the institution. He is to receive two tokens each time he makes a socially positive response to one of the staff members, and he is to lose two tokens each time he makes a socially negative response.

The nurse in Program I deals with the patient's negative response in the following manner:

Nurse: Good morning, Mr. Jones.
Patient: Go to hell.
Nurse: Oh! You are insulting again, Mr. Jones. How many times do we have to tell you that you must learn to be polite? You just don't want to learn, I guess. I am taking your two tokens and I will report you to your doctor. Now, don't you wish you had treated me more nicely?

Here is the nurse in Program I in action again; this time the patient shows more positive responses.

Nurse:	Good morning, Mr. Jones.
Patient:	Good morning, Mrs. Smith.
Nurse:	Well now! Aren't we pleasant this morning! Now *that's* the way to speak to me. Very good, Mr. Jones. Do you know what that's earned for you? Two tokens. Very good.

With such a destructive communication substrate as this, we see only a slim chance that Program I could ever lead to positive behavioral change outside the institution, even though it is solidly based on good token economy principles.

Here is the nurse in Program II, with the same patient and the same token values:

Nurse:	Good morning, Mr. Jones.
Patient:	Go to hell.
Nurse:	Oh, I see you are not in a good mood this morning. I'll mark down minus two tokens and I'll see you when you are feeling better.

Finally, here is the nurse in Program II when the patient receives his positive tokens:

Nurse:	Good morning, Mr. Jones.
Patient:	Good morning, Mrs. Brown.
Nurse:	Hey, good to see you feeling chipper this morning! Here are your two tokens. I have to finish my rounds with the medications, but I'll see you later.

Of the two programs, our bet is that the second will have the best chance of promoting positive behavioral change outside the hospital. Yet so far, the divisions between the behavioral and the psychotherapy camps have tended to restrict the research on the facilitating effects of interpersonal communications skills in behavioral treatment programs.

We have been able to find only three studies on this issue; they all support our contention that positive communications skills can produce better outcomes in behavioral programs. Vitalo (1970) showed, in a verbal conditioning task, that successful "verbal conditioning" (that is, getting the subjects to say what the experimenter wanted them to say by "verbally reinforcing" them for the desired words) was best elicited by persons who scored high on Carkhuff's measures of empathy, respect, and so on. Persons low in these skills were able to induce no more learning in their subjects than was shown by an unconditioned control group.

Cairns (1972) showed that the therapist's level of warmth, genuineness, and empathy was related to the outcome of systematic desensitization. That is, patients of therapists who were high in these skills showed a high rate of improvement, while patients of low-functioning therapists showed minimal change. In the only other controlled study relevant to this issue, Ribes-Inesta *et al.* (1973) found that token reinforcers were effective for *some* of the children they studied. Yet they were not always useful in changing behavior, and social reinforcers were found to be as effective as the tokens in many instances. Cautiously (because of the small size of their study), the authors derived some tentative, but very important, theoretical propositions:

> The study shows with some restrictions that . . . the reinforcing effects of tokens are mediated by concurrently provided social reinforcement . . . although until now it has been thought that tokens become conditioned reinforcers by means of their exchange for primary reinforcers, our study seems to point to a different view at least in some cases. Tokens seem to provide a formal manner of specifying and scheduling the reinforcing agents' behavior. That is, social reinforcement is provided by those who deliver tokens in a restricted and contingent way because tokens set an objective frame for reinforcing the behavior of others . . . the

results of this study point to some weakness in the traditional explanation of token effects in human applied settings, and suggest the necessity of doing a more systematic and thorough evaluation of the role of social reinforcement in the implementation of tokens as conditioned reinforcers. [pp. 127–128]

We agree that this is an area of great importance for future research. It is important not only for theoretical purposes, but particularly for the potential value of achieving an ultimate compatible union of the behavioral and the psychotherapeutic approaches to the psychological treatment of psychiatric patients. The programmed skills of operant conditioning, classical conditioning, and modeling will probably always be seen as important and effective techniques for the high-functioning therapist. Our contention is that when the significant questions have been studied, these techniques will not in themselves be found to be effective therapeutic agents with human beings. When combined with the high-functioning communications skills of facilitative psychotherapists, however, we expect that these techniques will demonstrate the high effectiveness that has been claimed for them in the past. The union of effective psychotherapy with behavior modification techniques will attain the persistent and generalized behavioral change that has not hitherto been achieved by operant intervention.

These considerations suggest that persons working with patients will enhance their reinforcing power by communicating with their patients at high levels of psychotherapeutic functioning. In addition, the more effective workers will serve as living models for the type of behaviors that they attempt to induce in their patients. These behaviors may include nonviolent arbitration of interpersonal conflicts, and gentle but persistent attention to the expressed needs and feelings of other human beings.

BEHAVIOR MODIFICATION IN PSYCHOTHERAPY

Being warm and accepting of the individual in no way impairs the helping person's ability to push for behavioral change in the patient with whom he is working. Most research in psychotherapy and behavior modification now indicates that establishing a relationship is only one step toward the production of measurable improvement in the patient (Lazarus, 1971). The remainder depends on helping the patient to recognize the areas of needed change, and providing him with opportunities for safe practice of the new responses. "Confrontation" (Carkhuff and Berenson, 1967) may provide part of the interpersonal insight experienced in psychotherapy. The learning of new responses can come through a combination of shaping, modeling, "instrumental practice," and "success experiences."

MODELING IN PSYCHOTHERAPY

Often, when he is teaching a new skill to someone, the instructor is called upon to function as a model, or example, of "how it's done." In his work the psychotherapist must function as a model of effective interpersonal functioning.

The therapist often attempts to help his patient to become more socially perceptive, objective, and introspective. He may also try to teach the patient to resolve interpersonal differences through arbitration and tolerant compromise. He encourages the patient to adopt these reactions to interpersonal conflict, rather than to responding with withdrawal, character assassination, property damage, or self-harm. In teaching all these responses, the therapist may need to take the first step by demonstrating these qualities himself (Garetz and Fix, 1972).

There is nothing new about encouraging parents, psychiatric staff, or other care workers to set an example. To-day, however, we have the benefits of some excellent research on the effects of setting examples (modeling) on the patient's behavior. We can now be more precise in defining our standards of personal conduct, and we can estimate the benefit that our actions, as observed by the patients, can bring to them.

MODELING IN BEHAVIOR MODIFICATION

In helping the patient to adopt a new set of social behavior patterns, the mere application of conditioning techniques does not exhaust the intervention skills at the disposal of an adequate therapist. A great deal more can be given to *any* treatment program based on conditioning, whether operant or classical, by adding effective models of the target behaviors.

As a therapeutic technique, modeling fits quite snugly into the behavior modification approaches. The most convincing early studies that demonstrated the importance of observed behavior in affecting future behavior of the observer stemmed directly from the basic inquiries into human learning. The father of the literature on modeling, Albert Bandura, has shown that the rules of modeling are the same as those of operant conditioning (Bandura, 1971). The well-planned use of modeling can make unique contributions to a psychiatric treatment program.

CURRENT APPLICATION OF THE PSYCHOLOGICAL THERAPIES

The research on the four treatment modalities reviewed in this volume will suggest what we feel is the basic reason for the poor showing of psychiatric intervention up to this point. It is our conclusion that the psychiatric treatment of hospitalized patients in general has not been applied in an effective fashion. When psychotherapists are hired by institutions or are given professional accreditation on the basis of their academic credentials, rather than of their proven practical effectiveness, we believe that psychotherapy is not being administered in the most positive manner. When theoretical factions exist that prevent one form of therapy from being harmoniously combined with a complementary procedure, we are suspicious that the most effective treatment is not being given. When behavioral programs are implemented without adequate knowledge of research on psychotherapeutic outcome, or vice versa, we assume that improvements in treatment could be made. When procedures that have given high evidence of effectiveness, such as modeling, are relatively little used, while programs that have been shown useful for only a narrow range of individuals, such as systematic desensitization, gain much wider publicity, we question the current approaches to treatment. The failure of Anthony *et al.* (1972) to show that psychiatric hospitalization produced measurable benefits does not to us indicate that psychiatric treatment is intrinsically ineffective. We prefer to suppose (at least until the necessary research provides a different answer) that such results merely reflect the current failure to apply the available effective psychological approaches to the psychiatric patient. That Anthony *et al.* found that two programs did show significant patient improvement, ostensibly through the application of these largely unused approaches, lends support to this assumption.

The evidence suggests three probable conclusions on the effective application of psychological treatment in modern psychiatric facilities. First, truly beneficial psychotherapy may scarcely exist in today's psychiatric institutions. Where it does occur, it is probably given informally, sporadically, and in a nonprogrammed fashion. Second, many of the behavioral interventions, when used, may often be misapplied. Third, too much emphasis seems currently to be placed on the *technical* delivery of both psychotherapy and the behavioral approaches. This often leads to an exclusive reliance on one form of treatment, where a compatible union of approaches might be more effective. We believe that ineffective treatment, which is often based on false premises, is given mainly because the majority of those who administer psychological therapy have not been made aware of the great bulk of the available research on the basic treatment modalities. Thus, in this volume we have hoped to acquaint the clinician with the results of the research in his and related fields which can lead to a sharpening of his skills and a measurable benefit to his patients.

RECAPITULATION

When the psychological components of psychiatric treatment are combined in the way we have suggested here, theoretical disputes, such as conflicts between behaviorism and humanism, fall by the wayside. No such conflicts need exist; some scientific evidence justifies the incorporation of both orientations into successful treatment. Virtually everyone agrees that people do behave. We have examined the evidence which shows that for a large number of behavioral deficiencies, behavior-oriented techniques can be quite helpful to the patient desirous of change. At the same time we have looked at the evidence which shows that, for reasons not yet fully explained theoretically, patients tend to show improvement in a number of ways when they receive warm, respectful, and honest communication from therapists. We have even suggested (or contended) that facilitative communication may be the factor that determines the effectiveness of the behavioral treatment techniques.

We hope that the evaluation of the various treatment modalities presented in this volume will strike an appeal for an end to conflict between the advocates of the various specific treatment techniques. Transactional analysis will not take over the world, any more than will Rogerian theory or systematic desensitization. None of these approaches has been shown to have the solution to all clinical problems. Today we do not yet have this solution. We do have a self-correcting method to identify all the psychologically beneficial and harmful forces in the lives of people. Dogma is not self-correcting; it is self-perpetuating. Scientific investigation is a self-correcting process. Our efforts to bring together the various orientations toward psychological therapy may be one of the signs that the science of psychology, and the professions of counseling and psychotherapy, are reaching a full, useful maturity.

We have already labeled our approach "eclecticism." Yet it is a selective eclecticism: its basic pattern is to take from each of the current psychological therapies those factors that have been scientifically proved to produce therapeutic change in the patient. Our eclecticism does not simply combine techniques that "sound good" or have gained popular support; it is based on our best judgment of the evidence that we have at hand. In this volume we have not presented or advocated any system of treatment in full and final form, permanent and unchangeable. As evidence accumulates, some of our conclusions will change, perhaps radically. Others will show more subtle evolution into more simple and more precise forms, leading ultimately toward the most effective delivery of psychological therapy possible. There is a great need for increased evaluative research and theoretical development. We believe that a progressive revolution in the mental health fields is under way. This revolution has the capacity to change the mental health professions markedly, and ultimately to change society as well. Our culture may ultimately become the first to possess valid psychological treatment that actually offers more than placebos for emotional and behavioral difficulties.

Chapter 12

POSTSCRIPT: LESSONS FROM THE PAST

Science is the best method that man has invented for obtaining agreement about man's knowledge of the universe. Its aim is to surmount the foibles of superstition and wishful thinking by a method aimed at objectivity, that is, a method for discovering facts and relationships in the world of inanimate and animate objects that can be known, communicated, and verified by others. . . . Controversies in science have a productive role in sharpening distinctions and in requiring proof from adversaries instead of assumptions. They commonly lead to exaggerations on both sides, for science is a human enterprise, carried on by human beings, with all their limitations. [1]

Quantitative research on psychoanalytic therapy is a stepchild of the psychoanalytic profession. Rare is the therapist who knows of even two quantitative studies in the area, and still

[1]Ernest R. Hilgard. The domain of hypnosis. *American Psychologist,* 1973, *28:* 972–993.

rarer (if any exist at all) is the therapist whose practice has changed as a result.[2]

In Retrospect: Theory as Guideline for Clinical Practice

For approximately the first 50 years of this century, psychiatry and clinical psychology failed to produce significant improvement in psychotherapy. This seems to have been mainly because the advocates of the Freudian orientation had placed blinders on these professions. Those who adopted the total psychoanalytic position made what we consider to be one very serious mistake: they expected that total solutions to the highly complex problems of emotional disturbance would ultimately spring full-blown from the brain of one individual. This Messiah would need only his experience as a person, a physician, and a counselor to ordain the crucial answers to the questions of emotional disturbance and psychological therapy.

Freud supplied a system which bolstered a belief that has existed in man for many centuries: that one human being can ease another human being's distress, irrationality, and emotional suffering simply by talking to him. However, the followers of the psychoanalytic system were not inclined to test the actual effectiveness of the treatment they were applying.

Careful evaluative studies should have been made of the efficacy of psychoanalysis (and later of the sister therapies to this approach); instead, there was essentially blind faith in the procedures that psychiatrists and other therapists practiced. There are probably a myriad of reasons why

[2]Lester Luborsky and Donald K. Spence. Quantitative research on psychoanalytic therapy. In *Handbook of psychotherapy and behavior change.* A. E. Bergin and S. L. Garfield (Eds.). New York: John Wiley & Sons, 1971: 408.

this faith tended to persist without scientific verification. Five occur to us as most probably contributing to this endurance.

The Logical Soundness of Freud's Theory

Psychoanalytic theory won wide support in many sections because it offered an explanation for previously quite inexplicable phenomena of human behavior. It held answers for age-old questions of how people could engage in acts of which they had no awareness, how their minds could play "tricks" on them, how they could have strong fears without knowing why, and how their bodies could come to respond no longer to their conscious desires, even in the absence of any medical basis for paralysis, blindness, or other apparently physical disorders.

Psychoanalytic theory also provided plausible explanations of the common experiences of all mankind, such as slips of the tongue, troubling dreams, strong emotional reactions to minor events, and many others. In fact, the person well versed in psychoanalytic theory could find in this theory explanations for any and all human behavior, from physical assault to prayerful meditation. A theory of the human mind that possessed the breadth and scope of psychoanalysis had never before been devised. To a medical profession that was daily faced with the baffling enigmas of human behavior, and owning none of today's chemical and physical means of intervention, an explanatory theory with such powerful therapeutic implications must have seemed a godsend.

To grasp at an explanatory theory in order to give shape to the unknown is not unusual, particularly when people are faced with the need to deal actively with problems outside our realm of current knowledge. As Rosenhan (1973) has pointed out, "Whenever the ratio of what is known to what needs to be known approaches zero, we tend to invent 'knowledge' and assume that we understand more than we actually do. We seem unable to acknowledge that we simply don't know" (p. 257).

Case Histories

Freud applied his technique to a wide range of cases, and reported rather dramatic results. Many of the cases were presented in great detail, and with such vividness that once the student has read them, the impressions tend never to leave him. As with case studies today, the authors (in this case Freud) usually contend that improvement occurred because of the treatment applied, that it would not have occurred with other techniques, and that it was due to the underlying processes hypothesized by the writer. Of course, none of these conclusions can be proved by the case-study method. The influence of other factors must systematically be ruled out to warrant the conclusion that *one* procedure is responsible for a given outcome. Also, the problem of spontaneous remission is never dealt with in case studies. Some persons who receive treatment might improve or recover *without* treatment, the improvement being related to *no* known cause. Today, while case histories are still considered useful, they are not acceptable as proof of the therapist's assumptions. They are seen only as tools, which provide leads with which to test some of the underlying propositions of a general theory.

Personal Experience

Everybody has experienced some of the mental phenomena toward which Freud directed his attention. In addition, every person in any of the mental health professions sooner or later comes upon the very types of patient that Freud described with such clarity. Finally, as the studies of Eysenck (1952) and others were to reveal, many of the patients treated through psychoanalysis do in fact show improvement over time. Since therapists, almost by definition, do not have close observational experience of persons who need treatment but do not receive it, they remain unaware of the improvements that may possibly take place without psychotherapy. All these factors (and probably many others) function to channel the practitioner's vision, and thus constantly reinforce his belief in the validity and utility of the psychoanalytic doctrine.

Personal experience, as a guide to conclusions on the effectiveness of any psychotherapeutic approach, is at best a very shaky tool. Garfield, Prager, and Bergin (1971) show how the "experience" of the therapist (as well as the patient) falls short of scientific tests of validity. These authors asked clients, student-therapists, and their supervisors to evaluate client disturbance before and after a course of psychotherapy sessions. These individuals, who were all involved to some degree in the treatment process, tended to be moderately enthusiastic about the benefits of the course; 85 per cent maintained that there was at least some improvement upon termination. But more objective measures, including personality scales and tape-recorded excerpts of client sessions, failed to uncover any decrease in the patients' levels of disturbance. For some reason, "experience" of this type leads to conclusions that are not verified by the measures currently available to us.

The several papers that deal with illusory correlation (Chapman, 1967) in psychological testing substantiate the contention that in the mental health fields, subjective and erroneous personal experience often influences our opinions to a striking extent. In these studies, subjective but inaccurate impressions in the interpretation of projective test responses were found to be more important than objective evidence in the forming of psychologist's diagnostic decisions (for example, see Chapman and Chapman, 1969). These studies serve as examples of the many faulty conclusions that can stem from primary reliance on personal experience.

Today, objective evidence is the prescription for progress. Of course there will continue to be theories, and hot and bitter arguments over the interpretation of data, as there are in all sciences. It is almost certain, however, that grand conceptualizations of total human functioning—the theories of personality that we have mentioned—have been premature, given the state of development of the science and of psychotherapeutic practice. The theories of today, and of the long-term future, will probably be less encompassing, more specific, and eminently more open to the testing of their predictions. While theories of the nature of man will continue to narrow in this manner, theories of what man can do—of his capacities, and of our abilities to control him—may still continue to reach far beyond the available research data (as in B. F. Skinner's *Beyond Freedom and Dignity*).

Appeal to Authority

During the 1950s, a prominent style of article in the psychiatric journals typically focused on the development of new applications of Freudian theory, and on the derivation of new "insights" into intrapsychic functioning and the therapeutic processes. Themes were developed and presented with genuflections toward psychoanalysis. Freud's name, a psychoanalytic definition, or a quote from Freud prefaced most of the papers. If a concept were introduced in such a manner, the author's ensuing arguments were supposedly unassailable, since they were therefore ostensibly derived directly from psychoanalytic theory. To dispute such an argument, then, it was almost necessary to grapple with the entire theory of psychoanalysis, or to come into conflict with Freud himself. Freud's statements were presented pontifically, as if they were inalterable truths. In many professional meetings learned disputes were waged, if not necessarily won, in contests of who could display the most profound application of psychoanalytic theory. In this environment, not only would it be nearly heretical to ask for objective data on the questions involved, but it would be nearly pointless as well. It was widely felt that Freud himself had collected enough data of a type that could easily be confirmed by anyone who wished to observe human behavior intensively for himself.

Nonscientifically Trained Practitioners

Perhaps the greatest problem in evaluating the results of psychotherapy in a scientific fashion has been the practitioner's lack of scientific training. It is probably true that psychotherapists and their instructors were attempting as best they could, during the first half of this century, to evaluate the various theories of human personality and behavior that had so rapidly appeared. But the need for treatment of the mentally ill was great, and the lack of knowledge was overwhelming. In such an environment, the presence of comprehensive theories probably kept the practitioners from feeling lost or hopeless. At least these explanations of human behavior encouraged people to do *something* for their patients, rather than simply allowing the patients to vegetate without attention.

The physician, who was the person responsible for the care of most emotionally disturbed patients, was seldom a scientist trained in that field. In addition, the fields of psychiatry and psychology during the later decades had failed to provide the world with an impressive array of notable, or even useful, scientific discoveries. The psychologist *was* a trained scientist, but his scientific findings seemed for a long time to have little relevance to his clinical work. (The development of useful estimates of intelligence stood as the lone exception to this state of affairs.) Mental health professionals of all types therefore felt obliged to master as much theory as possible, and to gain as much experience as they could in their efforts to become effective psychotherapists.

Even if the scientific evaluation of psychotherapy had been widely considered, the problems to be overcome would have seemed insurmountable. One problem in particular was especially vexing: in order to evaluate a treatment, some patients must be given the treatment and some must go without. But how could a physician or other practitioner ethically withhold treatment from an individual seeking it? And even if the ethical problem were overcome, there was still this question: how could any individual patient be objectively compared to another patient, whose life history and entire psychological configuration was completely different, and indeed unique? As we have seen, we only quite recently have inched our way to a point from which we can achieve even partial scientific comprehension of the nature of psychotherapy and the factors that influence a patient's improvement.

These considerations, then, help us to understand why psychoanalysis held such great sway over clinical practitioners for such a long time. They also suggest why the basic questions on the effectiveness of psychotherapy were not consistently raised, and why, when they were raised, few applied the *scientific* approach in attempting to answer these queries.

IN PROSPECT: RESEARCH AS THE GUIDELINE FOR CLINICAL PRACTICE

Instead of hearing how many persons have stopped smoking, we learn how many antismoking clinics have opened.[3]

[3]Amitai Etzioni. The grand shaman. *Psychology Today,* 1972, *6* (November): 91.

In the preceding chapters we have advocated the use of certain psychological approaches in psychiatric treatment, while we have cautioned against certain practices. Our judgments in these recommendations have been based on our analysis of the empirical research available to us at the time of this writing. We have avoided appealing to "clinical experience" in assessing therapeutic effectiveness. Time and again, such "experience" has proven faulty or totally erroneous as a guide for clinical activity. This point has been made in a more humorous fashion by Klerman (1973), with his tongue-in-cheek definition of "clinical judgment" as "the name we give to the mistakes we make over and over again without realizing it."

In the psychotherapy professions, on the other hand, there is great resistance against analyzing the effectiveness of treatment. Many therapies are promoted and then widely used, although their only justification is that they stem "logically" from theoretical formulations, or that the formulator of the treatment has seen dramatic "cures" in the people he has treated. In most areas of medicine any treatment, to gain legal sanction, must have empirical evidence of its usefulness and safety, but historically this has not been true in psychiatry. Psychoanalysis, transactional analysis, primal therapy, implosive therapy, client-centered therapy, rational-emotive therapy, psychodrama, group psychotherapy, bioenergetics, encounter groups, behavior modification approaches, and many other forms of treatment have been administered to thousands of patients without any attempt on the part of the practitioner to assess objectively the positive or negative implications and effects of his chosen treatment. In other fields of medicine, such an application of untested procedures would be open to criticism, or even to court procedures. The physician must always be able to justify his choice of treatment, and most methods are restricted until they have been proved safe and effective.

One of the purposes of this comparison of medical and psychotherapeutic activities is to point out that our professions may currently be in a potentially dangerous position. The problem of justifying our practices exists because the basic fact endures that objective evidence (as reviewed in Chapter 2) has tended to find the various approaches to psychotherapy *neither effective nor necessarily safe.*

At this juncture, let us consider some of the implications of these findings. It is our opinion that psychiatry and other psychotherapeutic professions must proceed toward the establishment of valid therapies on the basis of scientific evidence. Unless the field of psychiatry moves toward a better appreciation of, and participation in, the scientific method of answering questions about mankind's mental health, little advance will be made. In addition, all the money and work spent for increasing psychiatric care will produce results that fall far short of the hopes and expectations of the society that supports this care. The results could be socially and politically explosive for the professions involved. Public support for the psychotherapy professions could well evaporate. The disillusionment of a public primed to expect effective treatment and to anticipate genuine cures could lead to the imposing of new and unfriendly regulations upon the professions, and to a major drop in employment opportunities for mental health careerists.

The dogma of psychoanalysis diverted a number of potentially productive minds toward the study and mastery of the Freudian concepts, and it also established a very stultifying model of the means of arriving at the "truth" in the social sciences. This model is only now being cast off by the majority of clinical professionals. In this model, treatment modalities were developed by first creating the most interesting and logically consistent theory of human behavior, and intertwining it with observations of clinical patients. Thus the clinician who possessed the clearest insight into the human mind, and who had the greatest capacity for presenting his theory as logically consistent, would be the leader who provided the great "theoretical advance" in the treatment of psychiatric patients. Thus not only the followers of Freud, but later those who rejected the psychoanalytic orientation as well, still approached the problems of emotional disorders in the manner that Freud had utilized so well. The method called for the development of a theory of personality from which corresponding techniques of psychotherapy could be derived. The process, of course, could be reversed: an example was the "client-centered therapy" of Carl Rogers (1951). Here the method was first to develop a treatment, and then to extrapolate a theory of personality. This latter approach, since it is narrower and more specific in its initial stages, is probably a more solid one. This may in part explain why, of all the systems of treatment based on "experience" and logic, Rogers' is the one that comes closest to current scientific verification.

One of the problems with the "broad theoretical" or "great thinker" approaches is that they foster a conclusive attitude, a belief that the work has been done, the answer found, and that little remains to be done other than to implement the approach. The term "conclusive attitude" may be little more than a euphemism for dogmatism, because those who become convinced of the truth of such a theory or approach follow it to the exclusion of much new and conflicting evidence. It often requires lengthy and painful theoretical revisions to incorporate new data.

Even more serious is the damper these orientations put on the impetus for research. Implementation, not research, is the impulse fostered by systems founded on a broad explanatory network. The belief is easily gained that an answer has been found, when in fact it has not. Practitioners and laymen who have not received systematic training in the techniques of scientific evaluation and the standards for scientific proof are prone to accept a system as containing more proven assumptions than may in fact be the case. The subtle effect that stems from this is the stultification of scientific inquiry, a lack of interest and impetus to go through the dry, tedious process of examining and verifying propositions and assumptions, and a loathness to accept negative findings when they occur.

The belief that "the answer" in finding treatments for medical disorders will arrive all at once, and will need little further revision of its basic precepts, seems to be somewhat unique to the field of psychiatry. Most people would certainly be disturbed if they found that those attempting to conquer cancer primarily applied a number of treatments that seemed theoretically reasonable, and then refused to scrutinize the results for evidence of effectiveness. Today laymen and scientists alike recognize the difficulty of finding a cure for cancer, if in fact any single cure is possible. If such a treatment is ultimately found, it will arrive through patient and repeated empirical demonstration, based upon the accumulated efforts of hundreds of dedicated scientists from many allied fields. It will be the result of hundreds of discarded or partially supported hypotheses, thousands of blind-alley investigations, and the analysis of possibly millions of small, conflicting items of data. The answer will *evolve* through careful, objective, step-by-step examination of the myriads of intricate chemical and physical occurrences at the cellular level, in both the healthy and the diseased organism. Each step of the process will be put to empirical test, and the results of all therapies derived from the research will be assessed not only for concrete evidence of their effectiveness, but also for all indications of negative side effects. In the field of mental health, theories of what man *is* (his personality, his drives, and his mental disorders) will be much narrower and more firmly based on experiment in the future. Grand schemes of the psyche, of the mind, or of the purpose of mankind will probably remain more in the domain of clergymen and philosophers than of psychiatrists and psychologists.

Eysenck and Beech (1971) have stated: "It is possible to specify methods of treatment for neurotic disorders, and to test their efficacy, without postulating a theory of neurosis, or even defining precisely what is meant by the term 'neurosis'. . . . Our theory may be erroneous, in part or *in toto*, yet the methods of behavior therapy may work perfectly well; just as our theory may be along the right lines, while the methods of treatment under discussion may fail for a variety of reasons" (p. 548). This represents a radical change of view from many previous therapeutic approaches, which carried the assumption that the total functioning of the human being had to be explained, and mental aberrations carefully defined, in the light of the prevailing theory before a useful therapy could emerge. The statement by Eysenck and Beech expresses the current openness to testing and objective evaluation of both the treatments and the theories upon which they are based.

In the behavioral therapies, London (1972) has promoted what we call an atheoretical approach to treatment. The therapist should use whatever works, and let the researchers determine later why it works and how it can be refined. The danger in this, of course, is the other side of the problem of dogmatism. If "what works" is allowed to be used for long, without controlled analysis of the results and all side effects, we find a system of treatment techniques growing up unsupervised, becoming time-honored but fossilized in its original form, and demanding—and gaining—little formal theoretical support.

In evaluating the validity of any statement in the social or behavioral sciences, then, do not ask, "Whose theory does that come from?" or "What authority stated that?" or "Is this a logical assumption?" Instead, always unerringly and doggedly ask this question: "What evidence is there to support that statement?"

REFERENCES

Agras, W. S., Leitenberg, H., and Barlow, D. H. Social reinforcement in the modification of agoraphobia. *Archiv. Gen. Psychiat.*, 1968, *19:* 423–427.

Alexander, A. B., Chai, H., Creer, T. L., Miklich, D. R., and Renne, C. M. The use of faradic aversive stimulation in the behavioral treatment of psychosomatic cough. R. A. Cardoso (Ed.). Paper read at the Fifth Annual Meeting of the Association for the Advancement of Behavior Modification, Washington, D. C., 1971.

Allen, G. J. Effectiveness of study counseling and desensitization in alleviating test anxiety in college students. *J. Abnormal Psychol.*, 1971, *77:* 282–289.

Anant, S. S. A note on the treatment of alcoholics by a verbal aversion technique. *Canad. Psychol.*, 1967, *8:* 19–22.

Anthony, W. A., Buell, G. J., Sharratt, Sara, and Althoff, M. E. Efficacy of psychiatric rehabilitation. *Psychol. Bull.*, 1972, *78:* 447–456.

Ashem, B., and Donner, L. Covert sensitization with alcoholics: A controlled replication. *Behav. Res. & Therapy*, 1968, *6:* 7–12.

Authier, J. Analysis of therapist's objective verbal behaviors during the initial psychiatric interview. Unpublished dissertation. Portland, Oregon: University of Portland, 1972.

Authier, J., and Fix, A. J. A step-group therapy program using microcounseling skills. *Small group processes* (1976; in press).

Azrin, N. H., *et al.* Behavioral engineering: Postural control by a portable operant apparatus. *J. Applied Behav. Analysis,* 1968, *1:* 99–108.

Bachrach, A. J. Some applications of operant conditioning to behavior therapy. In *The conditioning therapies.* J. Wolpe, A. Salter, and L. J. Reyna (Eds.). New York: Holt, Rinehart and Winston, 1964.

Baer, D. M., Peterson, R. F., and Sherman, J. A. The development of imitation by reinforcing behavioral similarity to a model. *J. Exp. Analysis of Behav.,* 1967, *10:* 405–416.

Bandura, A. *Principles of behavior modification.* New York: Holt, Rinehart and Winston, 1969. (a)

Bandura, A. Psychotherapy based upon modeling principles. In *Handbook of psychotherapy and behavior change.* A. E. Bergin and S. L. Garfield (Eds.). New York: John Wiley & Sons, 1971: 653–708.

Bandura, A. Social-learning theory of identification processes. In *Handbook of socialization theory and research.* D. A. Goslin (Ed.). Chicago: Rand McNally & Co., 1969: 213–262. (b)

Bandura, A. Social learning through imitation. In *Nebraska symposium on motivation.* M. R. Jones (Ed.). Lincoln: Univ. of Nebraska Press, 1962, 211–269.

Bandura, A., Blanchard, E. B., and Ritter, B. The relative efficacy of desensitization and modeling approaches for inducing behavioral, affective and attitudinal changes. *J. Personality & Social Psychol.,* 1969, *13:* 173–199.

Bandura, A., Grusec, J. C., and Menlove, F. L. Vicarious extinction of avoidance behavior. *J. Personality & Social Psychol.,* 1967, *5:* 16–23.

Bandura, A., Ross, D., and Ross, S. A. Imitation of film-mediated aggressive models. *J. Abnormal Psychol.,* 1963, *66:* 3–11.

Bandura, A., and Walters, R. H. *Adolescent aggression: A study of child-training practices and family interrelationships.* New York: The Ronald Press, 1959.

Bandura, A., and Walters, R. H. *Social learning and personality development.* New York: Holt, Rinehart and Winston, 1964.

Barlow, D. H., Leitenberg, H., and Agras, W. S. Experimental control of sexual deviation through manipulation of the noxious scene in covert sensitization. *J. Abnormal Psychol.,* 1969, *74:* 594–601.

Baron, R. A. Reducing the influence of an aggressive model: The restraining effects of discrepant modeling cues. *J. Personality & Social Psychol.,* 1971, *20:* 240–245.

Barrett, C. L. Systematic desensitization versus implosive therapy. *J. Abnormal Psychol.,* 1969, *74:* 587–592.

Barron, F., and Leary, T. Changes in psychoneurotic patients with and without psychotherapy. *J. Consult. Psychol.*, 1955, *19:* 239–245.

Baum, M. Extinction of an avoidance response following response prevention: Some parametric investigations. *Canad. J. Psychol.*, 1969, *23:* 1–10. (a)

Baum, M. Extinction of an avoidance response motivated by intense fear: Social facilitation of the action of response prevention (flooding) in rats. *Behav. Res. & Therapy*, 1969, *7:* 57–62. (b)

Baum, M. Rapid extinction of an avoidance response following a period of response prevention in the avoidance apparatus. *Psychol. Rep.*, 1966, *18:* 58–64.

Bayes, M. A. Behavioral cues of interpersonal warmth. *J. Consult. Clin. Psychol.*, 1972, *39:* 333–339.

Beaubrun, M. H. Treatment of alcoholism in Trinidad and Tobago, 1956–65. *Brit. J. Psychiat.*, 1967, *113:* 643–658.

Berecy, J. Modification of smoking behavior through self-administered punishment of imagined behavior: A new approach to aversion therapy. *J. Consult. & Clin. Psychol.*, 1972, *38:* 244–250.

Berenson, B. G., and Carkhuff, R. R. Sources of gain in counseling and psychotherapy. New York: Holt, Rinehart and Winston, 1967.

Bergin, A. E. The effects of psychotherapy: Negative results revisited. *J. Counseling Psychol.*, 1964, *10:* 244–255.

Bergin, A. E. The evaluation of therapeutic outcomes. In *Handbook of psychotherapy and behavior change*. A. E. Bergin and S. L. Garfield (Eds.). New York: John Wiley & Sons, 1971: 217–270.

Berkowitz, L. (Ed.). *Roots of aggression: A re-examination of the frustration-aggression hypothesis.* New York: Atherton Press Inc., 1968. (a)

Berkowitz, L. Impulse, aggression and the gun. *Psychol. Today*, 1968, *2* (September): 18ff. (b)

Berne, E. *Games people play.* New York: Grove Press, Inc., 1964.

Berne, E. *Transactional analysis in psychotherapy.* New York: Grove Press Inc., 1961.

Berzins, J. I., Barnes, D. F., Cohen, D. I., and Ross, W. F. Reappraisal of the A-B therapist "type" distinction in terms of the personality research form. *J. Consult. Clin. Psychol.*, 1971, *36:* 360–369.

Berzins, J. I., Ross, W. F., and Friedman, W. H. A-B therapist distinction, patient diagnosis, and outcome of brief psychotherapy in a college clinic. *J. Consult. & Clin. Psychol.*, 1972, *38:* 231–237.

Betz, B., and Whitehorn, J. C. The relationship of the therapist to the outcome of therapy in schizophrenia. *Psychiat. Res. Rep.*, 1956, *5:* 89–105.

Bond, I. K. and Hutchinson, H. C. Application of reciprocal inhibition therapy to exhibitionism. *Canad. Med. Assoc. J.*, 1960, *83:* 23–25.

Bowden, C. L., Endicott, J., and Spitzer, R. L. A-B therapist variable and psychotherapeutic outcome. *J. Nervous & Mental Disease*, 1972, *154:* 276–286.

Branham, L. Effectiveness of automated desensitization with normal volunteers and phobic patients. Canad. J. Behav. Sci., 1974, *6:* 234–245.

Breger, L., and McGaugh, J. Critique and reformulation of "learning theory" approaches to psychotherapy and neurosis. *Psychol. Bull.*, 1965, *63:* 338–358.

Broden, M., Hall, R. M., Dunlap. A., and Clark, R. Effects of teacher attention and a token reinforcement system in a junior high school special education class. *Exceptional Children*, 1970, *36:* 341–349.

Brody, H. A. The effect of three modeling procedures on the frequency of emission of self-referent affect statements. *Diss. Abstr.*, 1968, *29:* 767B.

Brown, R. A. Interaction effects of social and tangible reinforcement. *J. Exp. Child Psychol.*, 1971, *12:* 289–303.

Bucher, B., and Fabricatore, J. Use of patient-administered shock to suppress hallucinations. *Behav. Therapy*, 1970, *1:* 383–385.

Buehler, R. E., Patterson, G. R., and Furniss, J. M. The reinforcement of behavior in institutional settings. *Behav. Res. & Therapy*, 1966, *4:* 157–167.

Cairns, K. Desensitization and relationship quality. Unpublished master's thesis. Alberta, Canada: University of Calgary, 1972.

Calef, R. A., and MacLean, G. D. A comparison of reciprocal inhibition and reactive inhibition therapies in the treatment of speech anxiety. *Behav. Therapy*, 1970, *1:* 51–58.

Carkhuff, R. R. *The counselor's contribution to facilitative processes.* Urbana, Illinois: Parkinson, 1967. (a)

Carkhuff, R. R. *Helping and human relations.* Vol. 1. *Selection and training.* New York: Holt, Rinehart and Winston, 1969.

Carkhuff, R. R. A survey of the levels of facilitative functioning of counselors and psychotherapists. Unpublished manuscript. Buffalo: State University of New York at Buffalo, 1967. (b)

Carkhuff, R. R. Training as a preferred mode of treatment. *J. Counseling Psychol.*, 1971, *18:* 123–131.

Carkhuff, R. R., and Berenson, B. G. *Beyond counseling and therapy.* New York: Holt, Rinehart and Winston, 1967.

Carkhuff, R. R., and Griffin, A. H. Selection and training of functional professionals for concentrated employment programs. *J. Clin. Psychol.*, 1971, *27:* 163–165.

Carlin, A. S., and Armstrong, H. E. "Adversive conditioning": Learning or dissonance reduction. *J. Consult. & Clin. Psychol.*, 1968, *32:* 674–678.

Cartwright, D. S. Note on "changes in psychoneurotic patients with and without psychotherapy." *J. Consult. Psychol.*, 1956, *20:* 403–404.

Cartwright, R. D., and Vogel, J. L. A comparison of changes in psychoneurotic patients during matched periods of therapy and no-therapy. *J. Consult. Psychol.*, 1960, *24:* 121–127.

Cautela, J. R. Covert sensitization. *Psychol. Rep.*, 1967, *20:* 459–468.

Cautela, J. R. Treatment of compulsive behavior by covert sensitization. *Psychol. Rec.*, 1966, *16:* 33–41.

Chapman, L. J. Illusory correlation in observational report. *J. Verbal Learning & Verbal Behav.*, 1967, *6:* 151–155.

Chapman, L. J., and Chapman, J. P. Illusory correlation as an obstacle to the use of valid psychodiagnostic signs. *J. Abnormal Psychol.*, 1969, *74:* 271–280.

Chartier, G. M. A-B therapist variable: Real or imagined? *Psychol. Bull.*, 1971, *75:* 22–33.

Clarke, A. M., Montgomery, R. B., and Viney, L. L. The psychology of punishment and its social implications. *Australian Psychol.*, 1971, *6:* 4–18.

Cohen, S. Peers as modeling and normative influences in the development of aggression. *Psychol. Rep.*, 1971, *28:* 995–998.

Collingwood, T. R. Retention and retraining of interpersonal communication skills. *J. Clin. Psychol.*, 1971, *27:* 294–296.

Cooke, G. The efficacy of two desensitization procedures: An analogue study. *Behav. Res. Therapy*, 1966, *4:* 17–24.

Cowden, R. C., and Ford, L. I. Systematic desensitization with phobic schizophrenics. *Amer. J. Psychiat.*, 1962, *119:* 241–245.

Craighead, W. E. The role of muscular relaxation in systematic desensitization. Paper read at the Association for the Advancement of Behavior Therapy. Washington, D.C.: September, 1971.

Crighton, J., and Jehn, D. Treatment of examination anxiety by systematic desensitization or psychotherapy in groups. *Behav. Res. & Therapy*, 1969, *7:* 245–248.

Crowder, J. E., and Thornton, D. W. Effects of systematic desensitization, programmed fantasy, and bibliotherapy on reduction of fear. Paper presented to the Midwestern Psychological Association. Chicago: May, 1969.

Danish, S. J. Factors influencing changes in empathy following a group experience. *J. Counseling Psychol.*, 1971, *18:* 262–267.

Davison, G. C. Elimination of a sadistic fantasy by a client-controlled counterconditioning technique: A case study. *J. Abnormal Psychol.*, 1968, *73:* 84–90.

Davison, G. C. Systematic desensitization as a counterconditioning process. *J. Abnormal Psychol.*, 1968, *73:* 91–99.

DeCharms, R., Levy, J., and Wertheimer, M. A note on attempted evaluation of psychotherapy. *J. Clin. Psychol.*, 1954, *10:* 233–235.

DeMoor, W. Systematic desensitization versus prolonged high intensity stimulation (flooding). *J. Behav. Therapy & Exp. Psychiat.*, 1970, *1:* 45–52.

Dies, R. R., and Hess, A. K. An experimental investigation of cohesiveness in marathon and conventional group psychotherapy. *J. Abnormal Psychol.*, 1971, *77:* 258–262.

Dollard, J., and Miller, N. *Personality and psychotherapy: An analysis in terms of learning, thinking and culture.* New York: McGraw-Hill, 1950.

Efran, J. S., and Marcia, J. E. Treatment of fears by expectancy manipulation: An exploratory investigation. Proceedings of the 75th Annual Convention of the American Psychological Association. Washington, D.C.: American Psychological Association, 1967, *2:* 239–240.

Ellis, A. Rational psychotherapy. *J. Gen. Psychol.*, 1958, *59:* 35–49.

Evans, D. P. An exploratory study into the treatment of exhibitionism by means of emotive imagery and aversive conditioning. *Canad. Psychol.*, 1967, *8:* 1962.

Eysenck, H. J. The effects of psychotherapy: An evaluation. *J. Consult. Psychol.*, 1952, *16:* 319–324.

Eysenck, H. J., and Beech, H. R. Counterconditioning and related methods. In *Handbook of psychotherapy.* A. E. Bergin and S. L. Garfield (eds.). New York: John Wiley & Sons, 1971: 543–611.

Fazio, A. F. Implosive therapy with semiclinical phobias. *J. Abnormal Psychol.*, 1972, *80:* 183–188.

Feldman, M. P., and MacCulloch, M. J. The application of anticipatory avoidance learning to the treatment of homosexuality. I. Theory, technique, and preliminary results. *Behav. Res. & Therapy*, 1963, *1:* 85–89.

Fiedler, F. E. A comparison of therapeutic relationships is psychoanalytic, nondirective, and Adlerian therapy. *J. Consult. Psychol.*, 1950, *14:* 436–445. (b)

Fiedler, F. E. The concept of the ideal therapeutic relationship. *J. Consult. Psychol.*, 1950, *14:* 239–245. (a)

Fiedler, F. E. Factor analyses of psychoanalytic, nondirective, and Adlerian therapeutic relationships. *J. Consult. Psychol.*, 1951, *15:* 32–38.

Fix, A. J. Treatment of a case of rage reactions by systematic desensitization. Unpublished manuscript. Omaha: University of Nebraska College of Medicine, 1970. (a)

Fix, A. J. The use of the relationship between skin conductance and subjective fear in predicting outcome in systematic desensitization and an expectancy-based therapy. Unpublished doctorial dissertation. Buffalo: State University of New York at Buffalo, 1970. (b)

Fix, A. J., and Haffke, E. A. Relationship between psychotherapy skills and level of training in a psychiatric residency program. *Social Science & Medicine,* 1976 (in press).

Fix, A. J., and Niewoehner, G. J. Facilitative communication levels of parents of normal and disturbed children and adolescents. Unpublished research project. Omaha: Nebraska Psychiatric Institute, 1972.

Freeling, N., and Shemberg, K. The alleviation of test anxiety by systematic desensitization. *Behav. Res. & Therapy,* 1970, *8:* 293–300.

Friel, T. W., Berenson, B. G., and Mitchell, K. M. Factor analysis of therapeutic conditions for high and low functioning therapists. *J. Clin. Psychol.,* 1971, *27:* 291–293.

Fuller, P. R. Operant conditioning of a vegetative human organism. *Amer. J. Psychol.,* 1949, *62:* 537–590.

Garcia, J. The IQ conspiracy. *Psychol. Today,* 1972, *6* (September): 40ff.

Garetz, C., and Fix, A. J. Difficult problems in therapy-group leaderships. *Hosp. & Commun. Psychiat.,* 1972, *23:* 248–250.

Garfield, S. L., and Bergin, A. E. Therapeutic conditions and outcome. *J. Abnorm. Psychol.,* 1971, *77:* 108–114.

Garfield, S. L., Prager, R. A., and Bergin, A. E. Evaluation of outcome in psychotherapy. *J. Consult. & Clin. Psychol.,* 1971. *37:* 307–313.

Geer, J. H., and Katkin, E. S. Treatment of insomnia using a variant of systematic desensitization. *J. Abnormal Psychol.,* 1966, *71:* 161–164.

Geer, J. H., and Silverman, I. Treatment of a recurrent nightmare by behavior modification procedures: A case study. *J. Abnormal Psychol.,* 1967, *72:* 188–190.

Gelder, M. G., and Marks, I. M. Severe agoraphobia: A controlled retrospective trial of behavior therapy. *Brit. J. Psychiat.,* 1966, *112:* 309–320.

Gelfand, D. M., Gelfand, S., and Dobson, W. R. Unprogrammed reinforcement of patients' behavior in a mental hospital. *Behav. Res. & Therapy,* 1967, *5:* 201–207.

Ginott, H. The psychotherapist as parent. *Intellectual Digest,* 1972 (July), *2:* 44–45.

Goldstein, A. P. *Structured learning therapy: Toward a psychotherapy for the poor.* New York: Academic Press Inc., 1973.

Goldstein, A. P., Martens, J., Hubben, J., van Belle, H. A., Schaaf, W., Wiersma, H., and Goedhart, A. The use of modeling to increase independent behavior. *Behav. Res. & Therapy,* 1973, *11:* 31–42.

Haase, R. F., and Tepper, D. T. Nonverbal components of empathic communication. *J. Counseling Psychol.*, 1972, *19:* 417–424.

Hallam, R. S., and Rachman, S. Some effects of aversion therapy on patients with sexual disorders. *Behav. Res. & Therapy*, 1972, *10:* 171–180.

Hallam, R. S., Rachman, S., and Falkowski, W. Subjective, attitudinal and physiological effects of electrical aversion therapy. *Behav. Res. & Therapy*, 1972, *10:* 1–14.

Harper, R. A. *Psychoanalysis and psychotherapy: 36 systems.* New York: Prentice-Hall Inc., 1959.

Hauserman, N., Zweback, S., and Plotkin, A. Use of concrete reinforcement to facilitate verbal initiations in adolescent group therapy. *J. Consult. & Clin. Psychol.*, 1972, *38:* 90–96.

Herman, S. H., and Tramontana, J. Instructions and group versus individual reinforcement in modifying disruptive group behavior. *J. Appl. Behav. Analysis*, 1971, *4:* 113–119.

Herrnstein, R. IQ. In *The Atlantic Monthly*, September 1971. Boston: The Atlantic Monthly Co.

Herskovitz, A., Liebert, R. M., and Adelson, R. A motion picture substitute for experience in a health delivery environment. *J. Biol. Photographic Assoc.*, 1971, *39,* 193–195. Described in Liebert, R. M., and Poulos, R. W. TV for kiddies. Truth, goodness, beauty—and a little bit of brainwash. *Psychol. Today*, 1972, *6* (November): 123ff.

Hill, J. H., Liebert, R. M., and Mott, D. E. Vicarious extinction of avoidance behavior through films: An initial test. *Psychol. Rep.*, 1968, *22:* 192.

Hill, W. F. Sources of evaluative reinforcement. *Psychol. Bull.*, 1968, *69:* 132–146.

Hoffman, M. L. Moral development. In *Carmichael's manual of child psychology.* H. Mussen (Ed.). Vol. 2. New York: John Wiley & Sons, 1970.

Holder, B. T. A follow-up study of the activity—passivity and facilitative-nonfacilitative dimensions of continuing and terminated graduate trainees. Cited in Carkhuff, R. R. *Helping and Human Relations.* New York: Holt, Rinehart and Winston, 1969.

Hollingshead, A. B., and Redlich, F. C. *Social class and mental illness.* New York: John Wiley & Sons, 1958.

Hsu, J. Electroconditioning therapy of alcoholics: A preliminary report. *Quart. J. Studies on Alcohol*, 1965, *26:* 449–459.

Hunt, H. F., and Dyrud, J. E. Commentary: Perspective in behavior therapy. In *Research in Psychotherapy.* J. M. Shlien (Ed.). Vol. III. Washington, D.C.: American Psychological Association, 1968: 140–152.

Ivey, A., Normington, C., Miller, C., Morrill, W., and Haase, R. Microcounseling and attending behavior: An approach to practicum counselor training. *J. Counseling Psychol.*, 1968, 15(II): 1–12.

Jacobson, E. *Progressive relaxation.* Chicago: University of Chicago Press, 1939.

Janda, L. H., and Riam, D. C. Covert sensitization in the treatment of obesity. *J. Abnormal Psychol.,* 1972, *80:* 37–42.

Keutzer, C. S. Behavior modification of smoking: The experimental investigation of diverse techniques. *Behav. Res. & Therapy,* 1968, *6:* 137–157.

Klerman, G. L. Statement made in a workshop on psychopharmacology. Omaha: Nebraska Psychiatric Institute, January 17, 1973.

Kraft, T., and Al-Issa, I. Alcoholism treated by desensitization: A case report. *Behav. Res. & Therapy,* 1967, *5:* 69–70. (a)

Kraft, T., and Al-Issa, I. Behavior therapy and the treatment of frigidity. *Amer. J. Psychotherapy,* 1967, *21:* 116–120. (b)

Krasner, L. The therapist as a social reinforcement machine. In *Research in psychotherapy.* Vol. II. Washington, D.C.: American Psychological Association, 1962: 61–94.

Kuhn, D. Z., Madsen, C. H., and Becker, W. C. Effects of exposure to an aggressive model and frustration on children's aggressive behavior. *Child Develop.,* 1967, *38:* 739–745.

Kurtz, R. R., and Grummon, D. L. Different approaches to the measurement of therapist empathy and their relationship to therapy outcome. *J. Consult. & Clin. Psychol.,* 1972, *39:* 106–115.

Kuypers, D. S., Becker, W. C., and O'Leary, K. D. How to make a token system fail. *Exceptional Children,* 1968, *35:* 101–109.

Lang, P. J., and Lazovik, A. D. The experimental desensitization of a phobia. *J. Abnormal & Soc. Psychol.,* 1963, *66:* 519–525.

Lang, P. J., Lazovik, A. D., and Reynolds, D. J. Desensitization, suggestibility, and pseudotherapy. *J. Abnormal Psychol.* 1965, *70:* 395–402.

Lapuc, P. S., and Harmatz, M. G. Verbal conditioning and therapeutic change. *J. Consult. & Clin. Psychol.,* 1970, *35:* 70–78.

Lazarus, A. A. The results of behavior therapy in 126 cases of severe neurosis. *Behav. Res. & Therapy,* 1963, *1:* 69–80.

Lazarus, A. A. Towards the understanding and effective treatment of alcoholism. *S. African Med. Assoc. J.,* 1965, *39:* 736.

Lazarus, A. A. Where do behavior therapists take their troubles? *Psychol. Rep.,* 1971, *28:* 349–350.

Lazovik, A. D., and Lang, P. J. A laboratory demonstration of systematic desensitization psychotherapy. *J. Psychol. Studies,* 1960, *11:* 238–247.

Leitenberg, H., Agras, S., Butz, R., and Wincze, J. Relationship between heart rate and behavioral change during the treatment of phobias. *J. Abnormal Psychol.,* 1971, *78:* 59–68.

Leitenberg, H., and Callahan, E. J. Reinforced practice and reduction of different kinds of fears in adults and children. *Behav. Res. & Therapy*, 1973, *11:* 19–30.

Levin, S. M., Hirsch, I. S., Shugar, G., and Kapche, R. Treatment of homosexuality and heterosexual anxiety with avoidance conditioning and systematic desensitization: Data and case report. *Psychotherapy: Theory, Research and Practice*, 1968, *5:* 160–168.

Levitt, E. E. Research on psychotherapy with children. In *Handbook of psychotherapy and behavior change*. A. E. Bergin and S. L. Garfield (Eds.). New York: John Wiley & Sons, 1971: 474–494.

Levitt, E. E. The results of psychotherapy with children: An evaluation. *J. Consult. Psychol.*, 1957, *21:* 189–196.

Lichtenstein, E., Harris, D., Birchler, G. R., Wahl, J. M., and Schmahl, D. P. Comparison of rapid smoking, warm, smoky air, and attention placebo in the modification of smoking behavior. *J. Consult. & Clin. Psychol.*, 1973, *40:* 92–97.

Liddell, H. S. The challenge of Pavlovian conditioning and experimental neuroses in animals. In *The conditioning therapies*. J. Wolpe, A. Salter, and L. J. Reyna (Eds.). New York: Holt, Rinehart and Winston, 1964: 127–147.

Lieberman, M. A., Yalom, I. D., and Miles, M. B. *Encounter groups: First facts*. New York: Basic Books, 1973. Excerpted in *Psychol. Today*, 1973 (March), *6:* 69–76.

Liebert, R. M., and Baron, R. A. Some immediate effects of televised violence on children's behavior. *Develop. Psychol.*, 1972, *6:* 469–475.

Lindsley, O. R. Characteristics of the behavior of chronic psychotics as revealed by free-operant conditioning method. *Diseases of the Nervous System*, 1960, *21* (Suppl.): 66–78.

Lindsley, O. R. Operant conditioning methods applied to research in chronic schizophrenia. *Psychiat. Res. Rep.*, 1956, *5:* 118–153.

Lindsley, O. R., and Skinner, B. F. A method for the experimental analysis of the behavior of psychotic patients. *Amer. Psychol.*, 1954, *9:* 419–420.

Locke, E. Is "behavior therapy" behavioristic? (An analysis of Wolpe's psychotherapeutic method). *Psychol. Bull.*, 1971, *76:* 318–327.

London, P. The end of ideology in behavior modification. *Amer. Psychol.*, *27:* 913–920.

Lovaas, O. I. *Reinforcement Therapy* (16 mm. sound film). Philadelphia: Smith, Kline and French Laboratories, 1966.

Lowenbach, H., and Gantt, W. H. Conditioned vestibular reactions. *J. Neurophysiol.*, 1940, *3:* 43–48.

Luborsky, L. A note on Eysenck's article, "The effects of psychotherapy: An evaluation." *Brit. J. Psychol.*, 1954, *45:* 129–131.

Luborsky, L., Chandler, M., Auerbach, A. H., Cohen, J., and Bachrach, H. M. Factors influencing the outcome of psychotherapy: A review of quantitative research. *Psychol. Bull.*, 1971, *75:* 145–185.

Luborsky, L., and Spence, D. P. Quantitative research on psychoanalytic therapy. In *Handbook of psychotherapy and behavior change.* A. E. Bergin and S. L. Garfield (Eds.). New York: John Wiley & Sons, 1971: 408–438.

Madill, M. F., Campbell, D., Laverty, S. G., Sanderson, K. E., and Vanderwater, S. L. Aversion treatment of alcoholics by succinyl-choline-induced apneic paralysis. *Quart. J. Studies of Alcohol,* 1966, *27:* 483–509.

Madsen, C. H., Jr., and Ullmann, L. P. Innovations in the desensitization of frigidity. *Behav. Res. & Therapy,* 1967, *5:* 151–169.

Marcia, J. E., Rubin, B. M., and Efran, J. S. Systematic desensitization: Expectancy change or counterconditioning? *J. Abnormal Psychol.,* 1969, *74:* 382–387.

Marks, I. Perspective on Flooding. *Seminars in Psychiat.,* 1972, *4:* 129–138.

Marks, I., Boulougouris, J., and Marset, P. Flooding versus desensitization in the treatment of phobic patients: A crossover study. *Brit. J. Psychiat.,* 1971, *119:* 353–375.

Marks, I. M., and Gelder, M. G. Controlled trials in behavior therapy. In *The role of learning in psychotherapy.* R. Porter (Ed.). London: Churchill, 1968: 68–80.

Marks, I. M., and Gelder, M. G. Transvestism and fetishism: Clinical and psychological changes during faradic aversion. *Brit. J. Psychiat.,* 1967, *113:* 711–729.

Marlatt, G. A., Jacobsen, E. A., Johnson, D. L., and Morrice, D. J. Effect of exposure to a model receiving evaluative feedback upon consequent behavior in an interview. *J. Clin. & Consult. Psychol.,* 1970, *34:* 104–112.

McClelland, D. C. Testing for competence rather than for intelligence. *Amer. Psychol.,* 1973, *28:* 1–13.

McConaghy, N. Aversion therapy. *Seminars in Psychiat.,* 1972, *4:* 139–144.

McConaghy, N. Subjective and penile plethysmograph responses following aversion-relief and apomorphine aversion therapy for homosexual impulses. *Brit. J. Psychiat.,* 1969, *115:* 723.

McConaghy, N., Proctor, D., and Barr, R. Subjective and penile plethysmography responses to aversion therapy for homosexuality: A partial replication. *Arch. Sexual Behav.,* 1972, *2:* 65–78.

McDougall, W. *An introduction to social psychology.* London: Methuen, 1908.

McGuire, R. J., Carlisle, J. M., and Young, B. G. Sexual deviations as conditioned behavior: An hypothesis. *Behav. Res. Therapy*, 1965, *2:* 185–190.

McIntyre, R. *For love of children.* Del Mar, California: CRM Books, 1971.

McNair, D. M., Callahan, D. M., and Lorr, M. Therapist "type" and patient response to psychotherapy. *J. Consult. Psychol.,* 1962, *26:* 425–429.

Meichenbaum, D. H. Cognitive modification of test anxious college students. *J. Consult. & Clin. Psychol.,* 1972, *39:* 370–380.

Meichenbaum, D. H., Bowers, K. S., and Ross, R. R. Modification of classroom behavior of institutionalized female adolescent offenders. *Behav. Res. & Therapy*, 1968, *6:* 343–353.

Meichenbaum, D. H., Gilmore, J. B., and Fedoravicius, A. Group insight versus group desensitization in treating speech anxiety. *J. Consult. & Clin. Psychol.,* 1971, *36:* 410–421.

Melamed, B., and Lang, P. J. Study of the automated desensitization of fear. Paper presented at the Midwestern Psychological Association Convention. Chicago: May, 1967.

Meltzoff, J., and Kornreich, M. *Research in psychotherapy.* New York: Atherton Press, 1970.

Mercer, J. R. IQ: The lethal label. *Psychol. Today*, 1972, *6:* (September): 44ff.

Meyer, T. P. Effects of viewing justified and unjustified real film violence on aggressive behavior. *J. Pers. Soc. Psychol.,* 1972, *23:* 21–29.

Meyer, V., and Crisp, A. H. Some principles in behavior therapy. *Brit. J. Psychiat.,* 1966, *112:* 367–381.

Miller, N. E. Experiments relevant to learning theory and psychopathology. In *Psychopathology Today.* W. S. Sahakian (Ed.). Itaska, Illinois: F. E. Peacock, 1970: 148–166.

Miller, N. E. Learning of visceral and glandular responses. *Science,* 1969, *163:* 434–445.

Miller, N. E. Studies of fear as an acquirable drive. I. Fear as motivation and fear reduction as reinforcement in the learning of new responses. *J. Exp. Psychol.,* 1951, *38:* 89–101.

Miller, S. B. The contribution of therapeutic instructions to systematic desensitization. *Behav. Res. & Therapy*, 1972, *10:* 159–169.

Mitchell, K. M., and Hall, L. A. Frequency and type of confrontation over time within the first therapy interview. *J. Consult. & Clin. Psychol.,* 1971, *37:* 437–442.

Mitchell, K. R., and Ng, K. T. Effects of group counseling and behavior therapy on the academic achievement of test-anxious students. *J. Counseling Psychol.,* 1972, *19:* 491–497.

Moore, N. Behavior therapy in bronchial asthma: A controlled study. *J. Psychosomatic Res.*, 1965, *9:* 257–276.

Moos, R. H., and MacIntosh, S. Multivariate study of the patient-therapist system: A replication and extension. *J. Consult. & Clin. Psychol.*, 1970, *35:* 298–307.

Morgan, C. L. *Habit and instinct.* London: E. Arnold, 1896.

Mowrer, O. H. Apparatus for the study and treatment of eneuresis. *Amer. J. Psychol.*, 1938, *51:* 163.

Mowrer, O. H. *Learning theory and the symbolic processes.* New York: John Wiley & Sons, 1960.

Mullen, F. G. Treatment of dysmenorrhea by professional and student behavior therapists. Paper delivered at the Fifth Annual Meeting of the Association for Advancement of Behavior Therapy. Washington, D.C.: September 1971.

Mullen, J., and Abeles, N. Relationship of liking, empathy, and therapist's experience to outcome of therapy. *J. Consult. Psychol.*, 1971, *18:* 39–43.

Murray, E. J., and Jacobson, L. I. The nature of learning in traditional and behavioral psychotherapy. In *Handbook of psychotherapy and behavior change.* A. E. Bergin and S. L. Garfield (Eds.). New York: John Wiley & Sons, 1971: 709–747.

National Commission on the Causes and Prevention of Violence. *Violence and the media.* Washington, D. C.: U. S. Government Printing Office, 1969.

Ober, D. C. Modification of smoking behavior. *J. Consult. Clin. Psychol.*, 1968, *32:* 543–549.

O'Connor, R. D. Modification of social withdrawal through symbolic modeling. *J. Appl. Behav. Analysis*, 1969, *2:* 15–22.

O'Kelly, V., and Solar, D. Machiavellianism in parents and children. *Psychol. Rep.*, 1971, *29:* 265–266.

O'Leary, K. D., and Becker, W. C. Behavior modification of an adjustment class: A token reinforcement program. *Exceptional Children*, 1967, *33:* 637–642.

O'Leary, K. D., Becker, W. C., Evans, M. B., and Saudargas, R. A. A token reinforcement program in a public school: A replication and systematic analysis. *J. Appl. Behav. Analysis*, 1969, *2:* 3–13.

O'Leary, K. D., Paulos, R. W., and Devine, V. T. Tangible reinforcers: Bonuses or bribes? *J. Consult. & Clin. Psychol.*, 1972, *38:* 1–8.

Olesker, W., and Balter, L. Sex and empathy. *J. Counseling Psychol.*, 1972, *19:* 559–562.

Orne, M. On the social psychology of the psychological experiment. With particular reference to demand characteristics and their implications. *Amer. Psychol.*, 1962, *17:* 776–783.

Parrino, J. J. Effect of pretherapy information on learning in psychotherapy. *J. Abnormal Psychol.*, 1971, *77:* 17–24.

Patterson, G. R., and Gullion, M. E. *Living with children: New methods for parents and teachers.* Champaign, Illinois: Research Press, 1968.

Paul, G. L. *Insight vs. desensitization in psychotherapy: An experiment in anxiety reduction.* Stanford, California: Stanford University Press, 1966.

Pavlov, I. P. *Conditioned reflexes.* (G. V. Anrep, Trans. London: Oxford University Press, 1927. Reprinted by Dover Publications, New York, 1960.

Pavlov, I. P. *Conditioned reflexes and psychiatry.* New York: International Publishers, 1941.

Payne, P. A., Weiss, S. D., and Kapp, R. A. Didactic, experiential, and modeling factors in the learning of empathy. *J. Counseling Psychol.*, 1972, *19:* 425–429.

Perkins, C. W. The effect of muscle relaxation and suggested therapeutic benefit on the reduction of anxiety. Unpublished doctoral dissertation, 1966. Chicago: University of Illinois.

Peters, H. N., and Jenkins, R. L. Improvement of chronic schizophrenic patients with guided problem solving, motivated by hunger. *Psychiat. Quart. Suppl.*, 1954, *28:* 84–101.

Pierce, R. Counselor respect. In *The counselor's contribution to facilitative processes.* R. R. Carkhuff (Ed.). Urbana, Illinois: Parkinson 1967: Ch. 10.

Quinn, J. T., and Henbest, R. Partial failure of generalization in alcoholics following aversion therapy. *Quart. J. Studies on Alcohol,* 1967, *28:* 70–75.

Rachman, S. Studies in desensitization. I. The separate effects of relaxation and desensitization. *Behav. Res. & Therapy,* 1965, *3:* 245–252.

Rachman, S. J. Pain-elicited aggression and behavior therapy. *Psychol. Rec.,* 1965, *15:* 465–467.

Rachman, S. J., and Teasdale, J. Aversion therapy: An appraisal. In *Behavior Therapy: Appraisal and Status.* New York: McGraw-Hill, 1969.

Ramsay, R. W., and van Velzen, V. Behavior therapy for sexual perversions. *Behav. Res. & Therapy,* 1968, *6:* 233.

Rappaport, H. Modification of avoidance behavior: Expectancy, autonomic reactivity, and verbal report. *J. Consult. & Clin. Psychol.,* 1972, *39:* 404–414.

Razin, A. M. A-B variable in psychotherapy: A critical review. *Psychol. Bull.,* 1971, *75:* 1–21.

Ribes-Inesta, E., Duran, L., Evans, B., Felix, G., Rivera, G., and Sanchez, S. An experimental evaluation of tokens as conditioned reinforcers in retarded children. *Behav. Res. & Therapy,* 1973, *11:* 125–128.

Robinson, C., and Suinn, R. Group desensitization of a phobia in massed sessions. *Behav. Res. & Therapy,* 1969, *7:* 319.

Rogers, C. R. *Client-centered therapy.* Boston: Houghton Mifflin, 1951.

Rosenhan, D. L. On being sane in insane places. *Science,* 1973, *179:* 250–258.

Rosenkoetter, L. I. Resistance to temptation: Inhibitory and disinhibitory effects of models. *Develop. Psychol.,* 1973, *8:* 80–84.

Rosenthal, R. Covert communication in the psychological experiment. *Psychol. Bull.,* 1967, *67:* 356–367.

Rosenzweig, S. A transvaluation of psychotherapy: A reply to Hans Eysenck. *J. Abnormal & Soc. Psychol.,* 1954, *49:* 298–304.

Royer, F. L., Flynn, W. F., and Oscada, D. S. Case history: Aversion therapy for fire setting by the deteriorated schizophrenic. *Behav. Therapy,* 1971, *2:* 229–232.

Sachs, L. B., and Ingram, G. L. Covert sensitization as a treatment for weight control. *Psychol. Rep.,* 1972, *30:* 971–974.

Sager, C. J., and Kaplan, H. S. (Eds.). *Progress in group and family therapy.* New York: Brunner/Mazel, 1972.

Sahakian, W. S. (Ed.) *Psychopathology today.* Itasco, Illinois: F. E. Peacock, 1970.

Sallows, G. Operant behavior modification with conduct problem adolescents: A review of the recent literature. Unpublished manuscript. Eugene: University of Oregon, 1971.

Sanford, N. Clinical methods: Psychotherapy. *Ann. Rev. Psychol.* 1953, *5:* 317–342.

Sarason, I. G., and Ganzer, V. J. Social influence techniques in clinical and community psychology. In *Current topics in clinical and community psychology.* C. D. Spielberger (Ed.). New York: Academic Press, 1969, pp. 1–66.

Savicki, V. Outcomes of nonreciprocal self-disclosure strategies. *J. Pers. & Soc. Psychol.,* 1972, *23:* 271–276.

Savitsky, J. C., Rogers, R. W., Izard, C. E., and Leibert, R. M., Role of frustration and anger in the imitation of filmed aggression against a human victim. *Psychol. Rep.,* 1971, *29:* 807–810.

Schnurer, A. T., Rublin, R. R., and Roy, A. Systematic desensitization of anorexia nervosa seen as a weight phobia. *J. Behav. Therapy & Exp. Psychiat.,* 1973, *4:* 149–153.

Seeman, J. An investigation of client reactions to vocational counseling. *J. Consult. Psychol.,* 1949, *13:* 95–104.

Segal, B. A-B distinction in therapeutic interaction. *J. Consult. & Clin. Psychol.,* 1970, *34:* 442–446.

Segal, B., and Sims, J. Covert sensitization with a homosexual: A controlled replication. *J. Consult. & Clin. Psychol.,* 1972, *39:* 259–263.

Seidman, E. A & B subject-therapists' responses to videotaped schizoid and intropunitive-neurotic prototypes. *J. Consult. & Clin. Psychol.*, 1971, *37:* 201–208.

Sherman, A. R. Real-life exposure as a primary therapeutic factor in the desensitization treatment of fear. *J. Abnormal Psychol.*, 1972, *79:* 19–28.

Siegel, A. E. Violence in the mass media. *Violence and the struggle for existence.* D. N. Daniels, M. F. Gitula, and F. M. Ochberg (Eds.). Boston: Little, Brown & Co., 1970: 193–240.

Skinner, B. F. *Beyond freedom and dignity.* New York: Alfred A. Knopf Inc., 1971.

Skinner, B. F. *The behavior of organisms.* New York: Appleton-Century, 1938.

Smant, R. G., and Fejer, D. Drug use among adolescents and their parents: Closing the generation gap in mood modification. *J. Abnormal Psychol.*, 1972, *79:* 153–160.

Solomon, R. L., and Wynne, L. C. Traumatic avoidance learning. *Psychol. Monographs*, 1953, *67:* 44.

Solyom, L., Heseltine, G., McGlure, D. J., Ledwidge, B., and Kenney, F. A controlled study of the aversion relief treatment of phobias. *Canad. Psychiat. Assoc. J.,* 1971, *16:* 355–363.

Solyom, L., Shugar, R., Bryntwick, S., and Solyom, C. *Amer. J. Psychiat.* 1973, *130:* 423–427.

Spence, J. T. Verbal and nonverbal rewards and punishments in the discrimination learning of children of varying socioeconomic status. *Develop. Psychol.*, 1972, *6:* 381–384.

Srole, L., Langner, T. S., Michael, S. T., Opler, M. K., and Reunie, T. A. *Mental health in the metropolis: The midtown Manhattan study.* Vol. I. New York: McGraw-Hill, 1962.

Stampfl, T. G., and Levis, D. J. Essentials of implosive therapy: A learning-theory-based psychodynamic behavioral therapy. *J. Abnormal Psychol.*, 1967, *72:* 496–503.

Stuart, R. B. Behavioral contracting within the families of delinquents. *J. Behav. Therapy & Exp. Psychiat.*, 1971, *2:* 1–11.

Stuart, R. B. Behavioral control of overeating. *Behav. Res. & Therapy*, 1967, *5:* 357–365.

Sue, D. The role of relaxation in systematic desensitization. *Behav. Res. & Therapy*, 1972, *10:* 153–158.

Suinn, R. M. The desensitization of test anxiety by group and individual treatment. *Behav. Res. & Therapy*, 1968, *6:* 385–387.

Suinn, R., and Brittain, J. The termination of an L. S. D. "freak-out" through the use of relaxation. *J. Clin. Psychol.*, 1970, *26:* 127.

Psychol., 1970, *34:* 302–307.

Suinn, R., and Richardson, F. Behavior therapy of an unusual case of highway hypnosis. *Behav. Therapy & Exp. Psychiat.*, 1970, *1:* 175–176.

Tarde, G. *The laws of imitation.* New York: Holt, 1903.

Teuber, H. L., and Powers, E. Evaluating therapy in a delinquency prevention program. *Proc. Assoc. Res. in Nervous & Mental Diseases*, 1953, *31:* 138–147.

Tharp, R. G., and Wetzel, R. J. *Behavior modification in the natural environment.* New York: Academic Press, Inc., 1969.

Truax, C. B., and Carkhuff, R. R. Significant developments in psychotherapy research. In: *Progress in Clinical Psychology*, L. E. Abt and B. F. Reiss (Eds.). New York: Grune and Stratton, 1964: 124–155.

Truax, C. B. Workshop on interpersonal relations skills. Omaha: Nebraska Psychiatric Institute, April, 1973.

Truax, C. B., and Carkhuff, R. R. *Toward effective counseling and psychotherapy.* Chicago: Aldine Publishing Co., 1967.

Truax, C. B., and Mitchell, K. M. Research on certain therapist interpersonal skills in relation to process and outcome. In *Handbook of psychotherapy and behavior change*. A. E. Bergin and S. L. Garfield (Eds.). New York: John Wiley & Sons, 1971: 299–344.

Truax, C. B., and Wittmer, J. The effects of therapist focus on anxiety source and the interaction with therapist level of accurate empathy. *J. Clin. Psychol.*, 1971, *27:* 297–299. (a)

Truax, C. B., and Wittmer, J. Patient non-personal references during psychotherapy and therapeutic outcome. *J. Clin. Psychol.*, 1971, *27:* 300–302. (b)

Truax, C. B., Wittmer, J., and Wargo, D. G. Effects of the therapeutic conditions of accurate empathy, non-possessive warmth, and genuineness on hospitalized mental patients during group therapy. *J. Clin. Psychol.*, 1971, *27:* 137–142.

Ulrich, R. E., Hutchinson, R., and Agrin, N. Pain-elicited aggression. *Psychol. Rec.*, 1965, *15:* 111–126.

Viscott, D. S. *The making of a psychiatrist.* New York: Arbor House, 1972.

Vitalo, R. The effects of facilitative interpersonal functioning in a conditioning paradigm. *J. Counseling Psychol.*, 1970, *17:* 141–144.

Vitalo, R. L. Teaching improved interpersonal functioning as a preferred mode of treatment. *J. Clin. Psychol.*, 1971, *27:* 166–171.

Vogler, R. E., Lunde, S. E., Johnson, G. R., and Martin, P. L. Electrical aversion conditioning with chronic alcoholics. *J. Consult. & Clin. Psychol.*, 1970, *34:* 302–307.

Vogler, R. E., Lunde, S. E., and Martin, P. L. Electrical aversion conditioning with chronic alcoholics: Follow-up and suggestions for research. *J. Consult. & Clin. Psychol.*, 1971, *36:* 450.

Vogler, R. E., Masters, W. M., and Morrill, G. S. Extinction of cooperative behavior as a function of acquisition by shaping or instruction. *J. Genet. Psychol.*, 1971, *119:* 233–240.

Wachowiak, D. G. Model-reinforcement counseling with college males. *J. Counseling Psychol.*, 1972, *19:* 387–392.

Wahl, G., Johnson, S. M., Johansson, S., and Martin, S. An operant analysis of child-family interaction. Paper delivered at the Fifth Annual Meeting of the Association for the Advancement of Behavior Therapy. Washington, D.C.: 1971.

Waldman, D. M., and Baron, R. A. Aggression as a function of exposure and similarity to a nonaggressive model. *Psychonomic Sci.*, 1971, *23:* 381–383.

Walker, H. M., and Buckley, N. K. Programming generalization and maintenance of treatment effects across time and across settings. *J. Appl. Behav. Analysis*, 1972, *5:* 209–224.

Wallerstein, R. S., Chotlos, J. W., Winship, G. M., Hammersley, D. W., and Friend, M. B. *Hospital treatment of alcoholism: A comparative experimental study.* New York: Basic Books, 1957.

Walton, D., and Mather, M. D. The application of learning principles to the treatment of obsessive-compulsive states in the acute and chronic phases of illness. In *Experiments in Behavioral Therapy.* H. J. Eysenck (Ed.). New York: Pergamon Press, 1964: 117–151.

Warren, V. L., and Cairns, R. B. Social reinforcement satiation: An outcome of frequency or ambiguity? *J. Exp. Child Psychol.*, 1972, *13:* 249–260.

Weingaertner, A. H. Self-administered aversive stimulation with hallucinating hospitalized schizophrenics. *J. Consult. & Clin. Psychol.*, 1971, *36:* 422–429.

White, R. W. *The abnormal personality.* New York: The Ronald Press, 1964.

Whitehorn, J. C., and Betz, B. A comparison of psychotherapeutic relationships between physicians and schizophrenic patients when insulin is combined with psychotherapy and when insulin is used alone. *Amer. J. Psychiat.*, 1957, *113:* 901–910.

Whitehorn, J. C., and Betz, B. Further studies of the doctor as a crucial variable in the outcome of treatment of schizophrenic patients. *Amer. J. Psychiat.*, 1960, *117:* 215–223.

Whitehorn, J. C., and Betz, B. A study of psychotherapeutic relationships between physicians and schizophrenic patients. *Amer. J. Psychiat.*, 1954, *3:* 321–331.

Willis, R. W., and Edwards, J. A. A study of the comparative effectiveness of systematic densensitization and implosive therapy. *Behav. Res. & Therapy*, 1969, *7:* 387–395.

Wilder, S. N. The effect of verbal modeling and verbal reinforcement on the frequency of self-referred affect statements. *Dissertation Abstr.*, 1968, *28:* 4304–4305.

Wolpe, J. An approach to the problem of neurosis based on the conditioned response. M. D. thesis, University of Witwatersrand, 1948. Referred to in Wolpe, J. The comparative clinical status of conditioning therapies and psychoanalysis. In *The conditioning therapies.* J. Wolpe, A. Salter, and L. J. Reyna (Eds.). New York: Holt, Rinehart and Winston, 1964.

Wolpe, J. The comparative clinical status of conditioning therapies and psychoanalysis. In *The conditioning therapies.* J. Wolpe, A. Salter, and L. J. Reyna (Eds.). New York: Holt, Rinehart and Winston, 1964.

Wolpe, J. Conditioned inhibition of craving in drug addiction: A pilot experiment. *Behav. Res. & Therapy*, 1964, *1:* 305–312.

Wolpe, J. *Psychotherapy by reciprocal inhibition.* Stanford, California: Stanford University Press, 1958.

Wolpe, J. The systematic desensitization treatment of neurosis. *J. Nervous & Mental Diseases*, 1961, *132:* 189–203.

Zeisset, R. M. Desensitization and relaxation in the modification of psychiatric patients' interview behavior. *J. Abnormal Psychol.*, 1968, *73:* 18–24.

NAME INDEX

SUBJECT INDEX